To Hann

A fello

Wit

Jill.

Trollope and the Church of England

Winchester Cathedral, by Bruce Rhind

Trollope and the Church of England

Jill Felicity Durey
Senior Lecturer in English and Writing
Edith Cowan University
Perth, Western Australia

© Jill Felicity Durey 2002

All rights reserved. No reproduction, copy or transmission of this publication may be made without written permission.

No paragraph of this publication may be reproduced, copied or transmitted save with written permission or in accordance with the provisions of the Copyright, Designs and Patents Act 1988, or under the terms of any licence permitting limited copying issued by the Copyright Licensing Agency, 90 Tottenham Court Road, London W1T 4LP.

Any person who does any unauthorised act in relation to this publication may be liable to criminal prosecution and civil claims for damages.

The author has asserted her right to be identified as the author of this work in accordance with the Copyright, Designs and Patents Act 1988.

First published 2002 by
PALGRAVE MACMILLAN
Houndmills, Basingstoke, Hampshire RG21 6XS and
175 Fifth Avenue, New York, N.Y. 10010
Companies and representatives throughout the world

PALGRAVE MACMILLAN is the global academic imprint of the Palgrave Macmillan division of St. Martin's Press, LLC and of Palgrave Macmillan Ltd. Macmillan® is a registered trademark in the United States, United Kingdom and other countries. Palgrave is a registered trademark in the European Union and other countries.

ISBN 0-333-98790-X

This book is printed on paper suitable for recycling and made from fully managed and sustained forest sources.

A catalogue record for this book is available from the British Library.

Library of Congress Cataloging-in-Publication Data
Durey, Jill Felicity.
   Trollope and the Church of England / Jill Felicity Durey.
     p. cm.
   Includes bibliographical references (p.) and index.
   ISBN 0-333-98790-X
   1. Trollope, Anthony, 1815–1882 – Characters – Clergy.
2. Christianity and literature – England – History – 19th century.
3. Christian fiction, English – History and criticism. 4. Trollope, Anthony, 1815–1882 – Religion. 5. Church of England – In literature.
6. Religion in literature. 7. Church in literatue. 8. Clergy in literature. I. Title.

PR5688.C53 D87 2002
823'.8 – dc21   2002066323

10 9 8 7 6 5 4 3 2 1
11 10 09 08 07 06 05 04 03 02

Printed and bound in Great Britain by
Antony Rowe Ltd, Chippenham and Eastbourne

For Michael, my husband, lover and dearest friend

Contents

Abbreviations	ix
Acknowledgements	xi
Preface	xiii
The Trollope Family's Ecclesiastical Connections	xiv
Introduction	1

1 Divisions in the Church: Trollope's Decline into Pessimism — 11
- The high church — 13
- The low church — 20
- The broad church — 28
- Trollope's pessimism and schism — 32

2 Patronage versus Philanthropy — 42
- Patronage, birthright and merit — 43
- Motivation and origin of philanthropy — 46
- The varieties of ecclesiastical patronage — 52
- The varieties of philanthropy — 59
- The abuses of patronage — 67
- The abuses of philanthropy — 73
- The consequences of patronage and philanthropy — 77

3 Gentlemen Clergymen — 83
- The gentleman and birthright — 85
- The questioning of inherited integrity — 87
- The questioning of inherited prosperity and inherited integrity — 89
- The questioning of birthright and education — 91
- Birthright distinctions and clerical calling — 92
- Birthright, education and poverty — 96
- Birthright and indolence — 99
- Birthright and laissez-faire — 101
- Birthright and decadence — 102

4 Women and the Church	107
Wives	111
Mothers	116
Daughters	118
Single women	120
5 The Church, Politics and Social Reform	130
Trollope's political and ecclesiastical connections	134
The intermixing of politics and religion	136
The education of the young	142
The sundering of marital ties	144
The disposal of the dead	149
The threat of Roman Catholicism	153
The example of the disestablishment of the Irish Church	161
The threat of disestablishment of the Church of England	165
Conclusion	175
Notes	183
Bibliography	207
Index	218

Abbreviations

An Old Man's Love	Old
Ayala's Angel	Ayala's
Barchester Towers	Towers
Castle Richmond	Richmond
Clergymen of the Church of England	Clergymen
Cousin Henry	Henry
Doctor Thorne	Thorne
Dr Wortle's School	Wortle
Framley Parsonage	Framley
He Knew He Was Right	Right
Is He Popenjoy?	Popenjoy?
John Caldigate	Caldigate
Kept in the Dark	Dark
Lady Anna	Anna
Marion Fay	Fay
Miss Mackenzie	Mackenzie
Orley Farm	Orley
Phineas Redux	Redux
Rachel Ray	Ray
Ralph the Heir	Ralph
The American Senator	Senator
The Belton Estate	Belton
The Bertrams	Bertrams
The Claverings	Claverings
The Duke's Children	Duke
The Eustace Diamonds	Eustace
The Fixed Period	Fixed
The Kellys and the O'Kellys	Kellys
The Landleaguers	Landleaguers
The Last Chronicle of Barset	Barset
The Macdermots of Ballycloran	Macdermots
The New Zealander	Zealander
The Small House at Allington	Allington
The Three Clerks	Clerks
The Vicar of Bullhampton	Bullhampton
The Warden	Warden

Acknowledgements

Nine years in gestation may not be a record for any book, even for one of modest length like this one, but it is a sufficiently long period to require the support, help and kindness of many people. I would like to thank all of these people.

My colleagues at ECU have been especially supportive. When a national grant was narrowly missed twice, the Research and Development Office of Edith Cowan University, under the control of Sybe Jongeling and Toni Lampard, did not hesitate to provide me with enough funds to enable me to visit archives and collect essential data. Nor did the support of the office end there. Sybe and Toni have continued their encouragement throughout the process. No book can be written without library facilities and this book could not have progressed without the extra attention which Jenny Marshall and Julia Gross have paid me. Seldom does an academic in a large university expect to receive any notice from its overworked Vice Chancellor. Millicent Poole will never know how much her interest in my project and knowledge of Barchester reignited my enthusiasm. Andrew Taylor and Beate Josephi's thoughtfulness in enabling Victoria Glendinning to visit ECU not only excited me in the midst of my labours but also stimulated undergraduate curiosity about Trollope. Ed Jaggard's practical help with primary resources and study leave helped me cross the boundary between literature of the past and history. Glen Phillips has shared my highs and lows. Robyn Quin has understood my need for alternate periods of seclusion and participation. Harry Phillips's delight in my progress has spurred me on to subsequent stages. Graham McKay, Bill Louden and Susan Holland have provided quiet and enduring encouragement. Alan Bittles has shared my fascination for genealogy, and Alan Black has helped me to nurture the genealogical offshoot from this project – a biography of Trollope's clerical relative, Bishop Thorold.

ECU's students, too, have helped me. Bruce Rhind has kindly donated his line drawing of Winchester Cathedral: facing the title page. Karen King and Mirella Scarvaci have lent me primary texts relating to Margaret Oliphant and Elizabeth Gaskell. Hannah Rogers shares my enthusiasm for Trollope and has given me materials.

Hugh Trollope, whom one day I hope to meet, has generously provided me over the years with invaluable genealogical documents and has donated the photograph of his famous ancestor that appears on the front cover.

Joanna Trollope responded instantly and positively to an early draft of this book. Frank Leeson expertly drew up genealogical charts from my article, 'Church and Family: Anthony Trollope's Ancestors and Relatives', which he subsequently published in the *Genealogists' Magazine* (1997, pp. 442, 444), and helped secure copyright permission for inclusion of these charts.

Father John Thorold and the Rev. Henry Thorold (deceased) have both given me practical help and encouragement. They have also been personally very kind to me.

Barry Smith, Iain McCalman, Michael Roberts, Margaret Harris, Judy Johnston, Hilary Fraser and Suzanne Rickard have all, over the years, given me information, guidance and invaluable advice, along with their encouragement.

Peter Edwards gave me useful suggestions on very early schematic forays into the project. Juliet McMaster kept alive for me Trollope's genius for theme and character. Graham Handley stoically read two early drafts and gave me expert advice on wider reading. John Letts generously gave me Trollopian materials and showed interest in the project.

The staff at Pusey House, Lambeth Palace Library, London University Library, the Bodleian Library and St Deiniol's Library all made me most welcome and enabled me to cram as much reading of archival and rare printed material as possible into short bursts of precious time.

Palgrave Macmillan's reader turned the project into the book that I had envisaged. Becky Mashayekh's patience in responding to my editorial inquiries has greatly facilitated my completion of the book in the midst of a teaching year in which the overload has been the greatest of my career to date. I would also like to thank Anne Rafique for her meticulous copy-editing.

Robert and Francesca have supplied the necessary antidote to academic research by regularly taking time out of their own demanding careers to turn the parent–child relationship into a rare one of lifelong companionship.

Michael's uniqueness I recognized over thirty years ago. How does one transform oneself from a Slavonic linguist into an academic of English literature with an awareness of history, and still remain a living, breathing human being? Trollope beckoned, but Michael showed me the way.

Preface

Although Trollope has fallen in and out of fashion along with many other authors, he has always had an enduring following, attested by the flourishing Trollope Society. A glaring gap in Trollopian scholarship, however, struck me not quite a decade ago. Why had no one written a book on Trollope and his beloved church? Was it because it seemed too difficult a task to square Trollope's *apparently* irreverent attitude to the church with his regular church attendance? Was it just too unfashionable a topic for secular postmodernity? Such a book became an irresistible challenge for me. For Victorian people, Christianity was such a vital force, either as a guiding light or as a monolith to be buried, that their literature cannot be fully appreciated without an understanding of it. For Trollope, Christianity was indivisible from the Church of England. His most popular characters were Anglican clergymen and almost all of his themes could be traced back to the Church. The dismissive shrugging of shoulders among Trollopians at the very mention of the Church – possibly too wary to go against the tide of secularism – forced the bit between my teeth. I trust that both the Church *and* fellow Trollopians will forgive me.

xiv

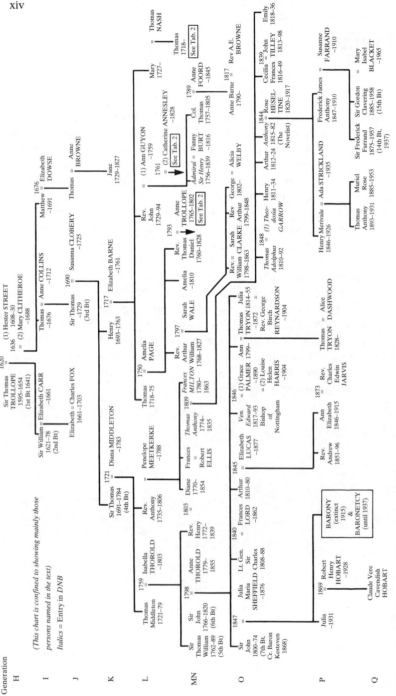

Table 1 The Trollope family's ecclesiastical connections

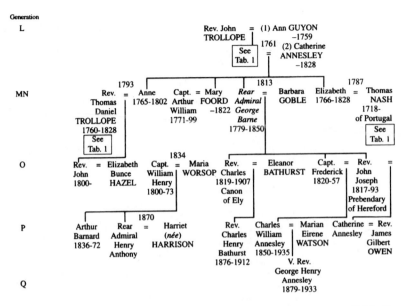

Table 2 The Trollope family's ecclesiastical connections (see notes on Table 1)

Both tables originally drawn up by Frank Leeson, Editor of *Genealogists' Magazine*, to accompany Jill Felicity Durey, 'Church and Family: Anthony Trollope's Ancestros and Relatives", *Genealogists' Magazine*, ISSN 0016-639 (1997), pp. 442, 444.

Introduction

Anthony Trollope wrote 47 novels, 42 short stories, five travel books and many articles, lectures and letters. His voluminous output has attracted scholars from a variety of fields. Literary criticism of his work is arguably among the best that was produced in the twentieth century, and this is primarily *because* of Trollope's large oeuvre. He had so much to say about his world and thus he offers something of interest to almost every kind of reader. He wrote about so many institutions and kinds of human beings that there must be few people who fail to recognise in his work some useful understanding of the human condition. He would certainly have been surprised to find that his industry had stimulated the funding of an institution bearing his name: the Trollope Society. That many members of this Society are prominent in public life would also have astonished and pleased him.

Having been denied, through financial hardship, the university education he desired, he would have been delighted that scholars, not only of literature, but also of history, law, politics and theology, have been influenced by his work. He was a man who, deprived of the higher education and social position he and his family had anticipated, felt inferior to those former schoolfellows who 'would go into Parliament, or become rectors and deans, or squires of parishes, or advocates thundering at the Bar. They would not live with me now . . .'[1]

Despite his disclaimer in his autobiography that he had 'no peculiar intimacy with any clergyman',[2] Trollope had many clerical connections. It has even been bruited that his parents had some idea that Trollope 'might become a clergyman himself', but this was not to be.[3] Besides seven clerical ancestors by birth and seven clerical ancestors by marriage, Trollope had at least nine clerical relatives sharing his surname and 14 other clerical relatives by marriage in his collateral family.[4] Moreover, he actively sought the acquaintance and friendship of clergymen: at least 42 real-life clerics are mentioned in Trollope's correspondence,[5] and all of his teachers at Winchester and Harrow were clergymen. Even in an age when clergymen were more conspicuous than today, this is a great number of clergymen to have in one's life. It is an even greater number for one who professes not to know any. Some of the inspiration for many of Trollope's most famous clerical characters undoubtedly came from relatives, friends and acquaintances. Perhaps his reticence about his qualifications for commenting on the Church was out of consideration for his clerical relatives, who ranged from bishops to curates.

His father planned for him and his two brothers to attend Winchester and then New College, Oxford, but only his eldest brother Tom achieved this.[6] His father had also expected to inherit the vast estate of his childless uncle, the third Adolphus Meetkerke, but this elderly gentleman, within a year of his wife's death, remarried in 1818 and 'produced a son',[7] displacing Thomas Anthony Trollope as heir and dashing his hopes of rapid social advancement and financial security.

Trollope's understatements about his literary worth, expressed in *An Autobiography* (1883), reveal that his humility did not evaporate with success.[8] His posthumous reputation as a writer would have astounded him. Furthermore, as a man with a zest for the society of others, he would have been thrilled to learn that, long after his death, people from all walks of life were still reading and recommending his books.

He would, however, have been disappointed by the absence of a book examining his attitude to the Anglican Church. Scholars have written books about his portrayal of politics, law, history and philosophy, yet no one has written a book on his depiction of the Church of England. There have been some articles and a few books have referred to it in passing or in a single chapter, but no book-length study has been devoted to this subject. Yet Trollope's funniest and most endearing characters were representative in some way of the Church of England. While he loved to entertain and knew that humour was one of the main attractions of his work, he would have regretted that readers in subsequent centuries seemed to ignore the fact that he wrote about an institution which frequently irritated him but never failed to hold his loyalty. The eclipse of the Church of England as a vital institution in most people's lives doubtless explains this omission in Trollopian criticism. Trollope would not have wanted his readers, over a century after his death, to be so distanced from his rhetoric as to believe his disclaimers that he professed no knowledge of ecclesiastical matters. Nor would he have wished them to accept without question his understatements about his commitment to the Church. He would have been horrified that entertainment in his novels was seen as an end in itself. He was proud that 'no girl has risen from the reading of my pages less modest than she was before' and that young men might learn from his work that manliness can be 'found in truth and a high and gentle spirit. Such are the lessons I have striven to teach . . .' But he wanted his 'pulpit' to be 'both salutary and agreeable'. Nonetheless, he emphasized, 'the novelist, if he have a conscience, must preach his sermons with the same purpose as the clergyman'.[9]

The amusing scenes in his work actually had a reflective undertone. Having seen too solemn a treatment of ecclesiastical issues alienate many from religion, he believed that a return to the ancient mode of comedy might be a convincing means of encouraging a review of entrenched attitudes and behaviour. A tolerant man himself, he desired society to be more forbearing and tried to achieve this through his comic fiction. Religion to him was not solemn, as he was dismayed to see was the belief of many of his contemporaries. But it was serious. Like many of his ecclesiastical relatives and friends, he was pained to see people increasingly turn away from religion to secular pursuits. The solemnity associated with religion, he thought, was the cause, and he sympathized with a community weary of religious dissension and propaganda. At the same time, he was disturbed by the unashamed preoccupation with material advantage and believed that he had discovered the solution. Comedy was an age-old device for reminding people of their modest human condition, which might, he hoped, provide the medium to restore some balance between the enjoyment of life's temporalities and appreciation of the spiritual.

Still the most popular of Trollope's fiction, the Barsetshire novels, set in the cathedral town of Barchester, lead us into the temptation of loving the leading ecclesiastical characters for their weaknesses as much as for their strengths. Their human foibles mirroring our own attract our immediate empathy. No one is held in higher esteem by readers than Septimus Harding, the warden of Hiram's Hospital. To win our affection, Trollope introduces the cleric by listing his faults before his virtues. He is not hard-working, but uses his leisure, afforded by his undemanding employer, the Church, to make and compose beautiful music, bringing pleasure to people far and wide. Thrift is not something with which he is familiar. Blessed with a comfortable income, he uses it to indulge himself, his unmarried daughter and anyone with whom he comes into contact, particularly the 12 old bedesmen under his care.[10]

If the Church had increased Mr Harding's workload and tailored his income to his output, would life for the people of Barchester and the residents of Hiram's Hospital have been improved? That is the tacit question asked in *The Warden* (1855), and answered, equally tacitly, in the negative in *Barchester Towers* (1857) and *The Last Chronicle of Barset* (1867). At Mr Harding's funeral, long after he had been forced to relinquish the wardenship of the Hospital amid newspaper charges of malversation, appear his former bedesmen, now reduced in number to five and reduced so much in grief that one of them, John Bunce, dies a fortnight later.[11] The inference to be drawn is that, regardless of the size of workload and income, Mr Harding had been the perfect warden and that reform had aggravated, not improved, life for the bedesmen. Trollope shared his society's cries for reform in the Church of England, but he urged caution. In rectifying ecclesiastical abuses, he knew that society could destroy the Church's very essence.

It is the Church's essence, alongside its problems, that continues to woo readers to the Barsetshire chronicles, for the ironic tension between the two is compelling. Political clamours for reform to put a stop to 'grasping priests of the Church of England' being 'gorged' with 'wealth' belonging rightfully to charities are counterbalanced with Archdeacon Grantly's 'well-turned leg', signifying 'the stability, the decency, the outward beauty and grace of our church establishment', just before he – unsuccessfully – harangues the poor bedesmen into not signing a petition for more money. In their quest for equality, contemporary readers are challenged to weigh utilitarian reform against the timeless splendour of 'that long aisle of Winchester', 'the sweet close of Hereford', and Salisbury's 'unequalled spire', made possible only if it is allowed 'that bishops should sometimes be rich!'[12] Reform is never easy. How *does* one clear out the dirt of the attic while retaining the treasures of the past?

A new broom, wielded by a new generation, tackles these problems head on. Into Barchester come the Evangelical Proudies, bishop and wife, together with the chaplain Mr Slope, ready to stir the old high-and-dry survivors of the former regime into new ways of worship and ministry. The high-and-dries, instead of cleaving to their old relaxed ways, decide to veer to ritualism, and schism, sharp and deep, is born within the Barchester diocese, which '[h]itherto ... had escaped the taint of any extreme rigour of church doctrine'. Headed by the Proudies, 'the lowest possible order of Church of England clergymen' are confronted with 'the very highest', with Dr Grantly as leader. If Dr Proudie 'would abolish all forms and ceremonies', then Dr Grantly would feel 'the sudden necessity of multiplying them'.[13] The echoing by Barchester's cawing ravens, mute swallows and peeling bells of Dr Grantly's rage at Mr Slope's provocative sermon comically implies the extent to which Barchester will be drawn into doctrinal warfare.

But the comedy, as omen, has as deep a bite as the schism into which the cathedral city will be drawn over the following years, for Trollope proceeds to unfold the Machiavellian schemes which both church factions pursue in order to defeat the perceived enemy *within* their beloved church – with tragic results on both sides. Without doubt, Trollope was convinced that it was the infighting within the Church that was its greatest enemy and it is this subject that forms the basis for Chapter 1.

New brooms and new generations nonetheless proceed, despite resistance, to effect change. The vigour of the Evangelicals and Ritualists was so successful in the nineteenth century in increasing congregations and forming new ones that the Church had to recruit far and wide for its clergymen. Its system of remuneration came under close scrutiny. No longer could the younger sons of the aristocracy, whose income had always been supplemented by private means and by patronage, supply sufficient numbers to swell the ministry needed for the expanded flock. Whatever their faction, if clergymen were not found comfortable livings by wealthy patrons and had no private income, their lot was indeed a desperate one and required the same philanthropic measures as other people living in poverty. The Church was embarrassed; its poor clergymen humiliated.

The high-and-dry faction in Barchester had always managed poverty through patronage, without ever advertising the fact. Mr Harding had long been happily indebted to Bishop Grantly, in whose gift had been the wardenship of Hiram's Hospital. In return for gentle duties and liberal income, Mr Harding supplied Bishop Grantly with cosy fireside conversation and equable companionship. The debt on both sides was never perceived as such. Demoted subsequently to the meagre living of St Cuthbert's, Mr Harding, presumably, depends largely on his widowed daughter's finances.

Bishop Proudie's later equivocation over the same wardenship is complicated by his wife's inclination to transform patronage directly into philanthropy by appointing the impecunious Mr Quiverful, whose wife and 14 children, Mrs Proudie believes, make him a more deserving candidate than Mr Harding. The machinations concerning the hospital wardenship are Trollope's way of demonstrating the injustices of church patronage and the follies of philanthropy, neither of which he held in high regard, as Chapter 2 elucidates.

While patronage took a protégé's gentlemanhood for granted, philanthropy assumed the recipient's rank to be lower than the donor's. Therein lay the problem for the Church. The Church's sudden expansion and increase in its clerics had altered its demographic structure. The new generation of clergymen could not necessarily be described as gentlemen; nor could gentlemen clerics always hold benefices enabling them to live like gentlemen. Mr Slope fell into the former category; Mr Crawley, perpetual curate, into the latter. For Mr Harding, Mr Slope's defining moment was his sermon, since 'religion is at any rate not less susceptible of urbane and courteous conduct among men, than any other study which men may take up', and '[c]ourtesy should have kept him silent'. Mr Slope could not possibly be a gentleman, reasoned Mr Harding, because he had forgotten to treat his fellow clergymen with respect, whatever their doctrinal affiliations. But a single glance told Dr Vesey Stanhope that Mr Slope was not a gentleman for he, 'in spite of his long absence [in Italy], knew an English gentleman when he saw him'.[14] For Dr Stanhope, appearance alone marked the gentleman.[15] Mr Crawley's situation was different. His gentlemanly origins were never questioned, but his tiny stipend made him feel inadequate to be the future father-in-law to Dr Grantly's son. To overcome Mr Crawley's 'stiff-necked' pride, the archdeacon's ultimate coup in offering his own income to be 'enough for both' is to remind the curate that they are ' "on the only perfect level on which such men can meet each other. We are both gentlemen" '.[16] Having thus restored the poor curate's self-respect, the archdeacon becomes a kind of patron of his son's marriage, providing philanthropic aid without condescension. To the vexed question of what constituted gentlemanhood and its changing definition Trollope returned again and again, and this is the focus of discussion in Chapter 3.

Gentlemen clergymen were never alone in their quest for self-definition. Their wives and other female relatives, too, discovered in the nineteenth century that their roles were being redefined. The Woman Question that fascinated Victorian society generally filtered into various walks of life and institutions, including that of the Church. The Barchester series of novels adumbrates some of the issues touching women and the Church that Trollope later explored in greater depth.

A bishop in all but name, Mrs Proudie is probably the most famous parody of a prelatess in fiction. Were she simply a bossy woman, she would not be so memorable. It is her assumption of her husband's public role that sets Barchester tongues wagging, torments the bishop and delights the reader. Her intention to take 'the patronage [of the wardenship] out of his hands' made Dr Proudie determined 'to put an end to her interference, and re-assume his powers'. His failure to do so causes much consternation to the fictional characters. A comic horror she may be, but Mrs Proudie was not the only role model of priestess. Mr Harding relates to Mr Arabin the old legend of an 'illustrious' priestess of St Ewold, 'famed through the whole country for curing all manner of diseases', whose well remained part of 'the consecrated ground of the parish church'. The dismissive rejoinder of Mr Arabin, still a bachelor, is firmly squashed by Mrs Grantly, the archdeacon's wife, because 'no parish was in a proper state that had not its priestess as well as its priest', and 'duties are never well done . . . unless they are so divided'. While she may sympathize with Mr Arabin's fear of having his position usurped, Mrs Grantly's expert eye in examining the dean's new parish 'showed that she had not herself been priestess of a parish twenty years for nothing'.[17] Mrs Proudie was not alone in her womanly influence over her clerical husband; Trollope fictionalized many other forceful women who were significant within the sphere of the Church. Chapter 4 investigates his ambivalence on the changing roles played by women in this area.

Far less ambivalent was he on the ever-encroaching steps of politics into the realm of the Church. Though understanding of worldly concerns, since Trollope shared them himself and openly admitted as much throughout *An Autobiography* (1883),[18] he disapproved of clergymen allowing politics to supersede their ministry. A bishop like Dr Proudie, whose first consideration was to 'give to the government, in matters theological, the full benefit of his weight and talents', while parading his political importance to his archdeacon, is swiftly diminished in the reader's eyes. Rendered as an excuse for having no transport for diocesan visiting, Dr Proudie's retention of his horses in London to facilitate his duties on committees for university improvement and the preparation of reports on Sunday Schools is acceded to solemnly by deep bows on the archdeacon's part. More eloquent is Dr Grantly's accompanying silence, for 'he could have bought every individual possession of the whole family of the Proudies, and have restored them as a gift, without much feeling the loss'.[19] In short, Dr Grantly's wife had always had at her disposal her *own* horses. Dr Proudie's political preoccupations are as scorned as is his inability to provide his wife with independent transport. Political duties were part and parcel of the Established Church, especially at a time when reforms were expedient, but Trollope believed that careful boundaries should be drawn between church and state and that both institutions should respect each other's territory, a difficult topic that is the primary point under inspection in Chapter 5.

To describe Trollope's most popular series as a skit on the Church would probably be greeted in the twenty-first century by nods of assent. Yet this would do less than justice to Trollope's dual-handed approach to criticism in general, and especially to the Church of England. Out of the mouth of Mr Arabin, poised before marriage after years of being sequestered in the halls of academe but about to travel the world once the marriage register has been signed, comes a critique of criticism summarizing Trollope's awareness of his art: '"It is so easy to condemn . . . to show up the worst side of everything . . . What could be so easy as this when the critic has to be responsible for nothing? . . . for eulogy charms no listeners as detraction does."' Trollope was keen to keep his listeners' attention through amusing 'detraction', but was careful to retain a murmur of 'eulogy', especially at strategic points in the narrative. *Barchester Towers* (1857) ends with a eulogy, not only to a clergyman, but also to the Church of England, for we leave Mr Harding 'as a good man without guile, believing humbly in the religion which he has striven to teach, and guided by the precepts which he has striven to learn'.[20]

This book provides an examination of Trollope's attitude to the Church, through his presentation of Church characters and references to issues, both social and clerical, which came within the Church's remit. Its intention is, primarily, to unmask Trollope's modest self-assessment, genuine though it was, both of his qualification to judge the Church and of his actual achievement. In addition, it seeks to promote a balance in literary research between Trollope's comic criticism of ecclesiastical policy and practice and his enduring advocacy of a Christian way of life. He was both critic and believer.

My impetus lies in the realization of the impossibility of understanding Trollope's fiction and the society in which he lived without some comprehension of the Anglican Church. As his work illustrates, it was one of the most powerful institutions of his time, even though its jurisdiction and authority were already being undermined. Trollope himself feared that the forces of politics and money were superseding the Church and its values and, as he explains in *An Autobiography*,[21] this had prompted him to write *The Way We Live Now* (1875).[22] The prompt in itself is but one testimony to his belief in the Church.

Some scholars are already questioning the tendency to assert too dogmatically the victory of secularism over religious belief in the nineteenth century. John Keane, a political scientist, has pointed to the contemporary endeavour of non-believers to 'sacralize' secularism following the 'extrusion' of religion from 'law, government, party politics and education' in 'the separation of Church and State'.[23] Literary scholars of novelists other than Trollope are beginning to realize, too, the neglect of this area of research. Irene Collins's book, *Jane Austen and the Clergy*, has redirected critical focus to Jane Austen's origins and actual world, which the novelist herself could not have imagined without the Church.[24] Using her journals as well as her fiction, Peter Hodgson's book, *Theology in the Fiction of George Eliot*, has shattered twentieth-century criticism labelling Eliot a *secular* moralist.[25]

This book attempts to achieve a similar effect with reference to Trollope, although, unlike Collins in her main concerns, it does not scrutinize clerical life as such, and unlike Hodgson, does not investigate Christian doctrine, but offers a preliminary examination of the people and ecclesiastical issues behind Trollope's work. It does not give a close textual analysis of Trollope's fictional world of clerics, nor does it try to give an exhaustive discussion of their historical context. Rather, its aim is to supply an entry-point to illuminate the depth of strong feeling on Church matters exemplified by many of Trollope's characters. The book extends beyond Trollope's most popular novels to lesser known works and to his non-fiction, as well as to other primary and secondary sources, to elucidate his concerns as they are related to the Church and religion. In spite of his criticism or perhaps because of it, for Trollope, the Church was of vital importance. It was the only institution that had the saving grace of compassion, because '[h]ow much kinder is God to us than we are willing to be to ourselves!'[26]

1
Divisions in the Church: Trollope's Decline into Pessimism

Sometimes critical of the Church as an institution, Trollope was not opposed to the divisions themselves which had sprung up within its portals. In *Barchester Towers* (1857) he comments that '[w]e are much too apt to look at schism in our church as an unmitigated evil. Moderate schism, if there may be such a thing, at any rate calls attention to the subject, draws in supporters who would otherwise have been inattentive to the matter, and teaches men to think upon religion'.[1] Provided people were open to another's viewpoint, Trollope thought that multiple perspectives were healthy. For him religion was too important a subject not to be discussed. In fact he enjoyed debate as a process. Almost all of his novels contain some kind of internal dichotomy, sometimes within one character, sometimes among groups of characters. Whether the debate concerns different courses of action or different points of view, Trollope's narratorial voice even-handedly balances each possibility. No character is so thoroughly bad that some inherent good cannot be found and no opinion is so thoroughly wrong that it cannot have some intrinsic merit. The key to Trollope's statement about schism in *Barchester Towers* is the word 'moderate'. As long as views were not held to the total exclusion of others, the Church, Trollope believed, could and should tolerate difference. What alarmed him was the extreme form some people's views took and he deplored the entrenched positions adopted by the main three factions within the Church of England.

This chapter will focus on Trollope's growing alarm at the changing situation in the contemporary Church of England. As dissension and disagreements developed between the church factions, Trollope felt compelled to make some kind of comment or reference, however brief, in his works. He was irritated by clergymen who, whatever their allegiance, allowed their strongly held Christian beliefs to be expressed through unyielding dogma and practices. Several critics have already commented on Trollope's seeming bias towards the high-and-dry faction in his affectionate portrayals of Mr Harding and Dr Grantly, his negative portrayals of the Evangelicals in the guise of Dr Proudie, Mr Maguire, Mr Prong and Mr Slope, as well as in his cursory glance at the broad church. Trollope's portrayal of the Evangelicals, for example, has rightly been judged too simplistic and inaccurate in the finer points of detail.[2] But focusing on Trollope's minor errors runs the risk of missing his main purpose, which was to entertain, for humour can only include a certain amount of detail. Trollope was not consciously recording cultural details for the future, but he did want to draw attention to the weaknesses of all church factions. He thus did not reserve his mocking humour for just one faction. His description of the different schisms is less schematic than critics have allowed.

Trollope, knowing the link between schism and clerical status, emphasized the individual frailties of clerics in order to stress human fallibility. In his writing, the wearing of a mode of dress and the assumption of priestly calling do not prevent the incumbent from pursuing a course of action likely to divide the community. Schism was dangerous, Trollope showed, because it often caused clerical status to be taken too seriously by the incumbents and their institutions. His satirical treatment of infighting among clerical members of all factions actually predicted the gradual decline of the Church of England. His novels betray his growing disillusionment with the Church as an institution, despite his remaining a devout member of it.

Initially I am concerned with Trollope's outline of factional characteristics in his character portrayals, while I later demonstrate that Trollope's increasing pessimism was due to his informed judgement and not, as critics have suggested, to his depression about growing old and losing popularity as a writer.[3] Referring both to Trollope's fiction and non-fiction, I argue that Trollope's more negative portrayals of the Church had tangible foundation and were shared by leading church members. For further evidence of the causes of his growing pessimism I also use secondary and primary historical sources, including documents concerning the Salisbury diocese and the correspondence between the high church Henry Parry Liddon and Walter Kerr Hamilton, Bishop of Salisbury. The Hamilton–Liddon correspondence confirms that Trollope's fears were held secretly by some high church leaders, with many of whom he was acquainted. Open expression of their fear would have been too dangerous and would have invited more disputation.

Trollope, in contrast, was free to comment on all factions and his criticism, throughout his oeuvre, was not reserved for one group.

Trollope's multiple family connections with the Church and close contact with many churchmen of all kinds gave him such easy access to the opinions of the Church's leaders that he was able to distil their views and graft onto them his own. Consequently, Trollope's fears for the Church were not *coincidentally* shared by leading Church leaders. Within his own family, Trollope had leading examples of the Church's schisms and perfect sources for information. His cousin, Edward Trollope, who became Bishop Suffragan of Nottingham in 1877, was a leading member of the high church. His relative by marriage, Anthony Wilson Thorold, who became successively Bishop of Rochester in 1877 and Bishop of Winchester in 1891, was a leading Evangelical.[4] His headmasters at Winchester and Harrow, Charles Longley (1794–1868)[5] and Thomas Arnold (1795–1842), both of whom he admired intensely, were leading members of the broad church.[6] All three factions, Trollope believed, weakened the Church as a whole by defending their ideological positions far too rigorously.

These three factions are often known by the terms ritual (high), spiritual (Evangelical) and *via media* (broad), yet all these designations are to some extent misleading. Despite this, they remain the simplest way in which to begin to look at the Church of England in the nineteenth century and Trollope's depiction of it.

The high church

In the late eighteenth and early nineteenth century, before Trollope began writing, the high church became strongly influenced and shaped by the Hackney Phalanx, a close community formed through family and friendship ties. The Hackney Phalanx's qualities in their supposed formal and spiritual lives led to the term 'high and dry', for which the Church of England became famous. The term came to be synonymous with indolence and fondness for the comforts of life, although their later complacency belies their early vigour, for they initially helped to establish missionary societies overseas. Unfortunately, the intransigence of the Church of England during the 1830s allowed of no real reforms in response to the radical changes that were taking place in England. Its high-and-dry clergymen gave the very strong impression to Victorians seeking reform that the Church was content with the status quo.

The high-and-dry party is epitomized in Trollope's Barchester fiction partly by Mr Harding and partly by Archdeacon Grantly, although neither fully accords with general perceptions of the movement. Mr Harding develops a guilty conscience about his relaxed attitude to duty and prefers to resign as warden of Hiram's Hospital rather than continue in his alleged sinecure: 'he was anxious neither to accuse... nor to defend himself'. In playing his violincello, as he always did when under pressure, he acknowledged 'his easy work' with 'a long wail of sorrow'. Nor is Dr Grantly's energy in keeping with the relaxed indolence ascribed to high churchmen at this time. Always seemingly on the move, he jumps to his father-in-law's defence immediately, summoning the most prominent barrister, Sir Abraham Haphazard, to help save Mr Harding's wardenship,[7] and later, in order to intimidate his low church bishop, quickly stirs his intoning clerical brethren into provocative action, even though 'he could not himself intone'.[8] The high church party's legacies from the eighteenth century were complacency and interest in temporalities. Mr Harding and Dr Grantly, then, are somewhat old-fashioned in their 'vices', although their 'virtues' actually distinguish them from their earlier counterparts. Trollope uses their likeable qualities to engage the reader in the high church's losing struggle to maintain its supremacy in the Barchester diocese. Despite the amiability of both Mr Harding and Dr Grantly, their attempts to thwart the low church hierarchy and the general infighting between factions are made to look ridiculous.

Towards the middle of the nineteenth century the high church party acquired the title Tractarian. The Tractarians in Barchester were Dr Grantly's intoning brethren, the younger generation of high church clerics, rather than either Dr Grantly or Mr Harding of the old high-and-dry school. The term derived from the tracts now being written by the new generation of high churchmen. The high churchmen responsible for the tracts effectively established the Oxford Movement and included John Keble (1792–1866), John Henry Newman (1801–90), Henry Manning (1808–92), Edward Bouverie Pusey (1800–82) and Henry Parry Liddon (1829–90).[9] Trollope knew Manning from Harrow and became increasingly friendly with Newman and Liddon as his fiction became well known. Pusey, a close friend of Liddon, had relatives in Lincolnshire close to Sir John Trollope, with whom Trollope often stayed.[10] Trollope, therefore, had two means by which he would have known Pusey.

The most identifiable Tractarian in the Barchester series is Mr Arabin, who had 'sat for a while at the feet of the great Newman'.[11] Newman, a leading Tractarian, shared his movement's dislike of rationalism, liberalism, Utilitarianism and Erastianism. Tractarians regretted the lack of aesthetics in contemporary social thought and looked back to the early Church and the Middle Ages for inspiration and renewed energy. They also admired the 'Arminian' policies of the unfortunate Archbishop William Laud (1573–1645), who promoted the beauty of holiness and ordered altars to be moved to the east end of churches during the reign of Charles I. Laud stressed the actual and material presence of Christ (Real Presence) in the Eucharist.[12] Laudianism's delicate theological position, poised between popery and moderate Calvinist forms of Protestantism, prefigured that of the Tractarians in Trollope's era. Even the eastern position of the altar was to become an issue later in the nineteenth century.

Similar questions of doctrine and practice distinguishing High Anglicanism from Roman Catholicism, including the issue of celibacy, tormented Newman, and following a period of reflection at Littlemore in 1845,[13] he came to a painful conclusion. His decision to convert to Roman Catholicism terrified the Tractarians, not just because it triggered the exodus Romewards of others, but because it preceded the so-called Papal Aggression and the famous Papal Bull of 1850, which the English Crown and ordinary people alike feared might lead to the revival of Roman Catholicism in England. Newman and others who had followed his example sometimes became 'as isolated in their new spiritual home' as they had been in their old one,[14] but the general disquiet remained.

Trollope, aware of this fear, informs his readers in a flashback in *Barchester Towers* (1857) that Mr Arabin had been 'saved' from taking the path to Rome by Mr Crawley.[15] The novel is actually set in the 1850s yet Mr Arabin's earlier doubts have real-life parallels in the Liddon–Hamilton correspondence from as early as the 1840s until the mid-1860s. Liddon, for example, agonizes over the flight to Rome of leading high church figures, including the brother of Denison, Bishop of Salisbury (1837–54); another brother was on the verge of going, just before Denison's marriage in 1845.[16] Over 20 years later in 1866, Liddon's fear sharpened when four undergraduates took the road to Rome.[17] Yet Liddon clandestinely conversed with Newman two decades after his conversion, adding that 'this is strictly private'.[18] Mr Arabin's earlier flight to Cornwall to prevent a flight to Rome does not, then, in light of the Liddon–Hamilton correspondence, seem fanciful. This form of high churchmanship was in direct contrast to the more relaxed attitude toward worship of older high-and-dry churchmen like the fictional Mr Harding and Dr Grantly, who were reluctant to surrender their privileged way of life acquired through patronage.

The involvement of writers and newspapers in the factional fray is alluded to by Trollope more than once. In *The Three Clerks* (1858) the allusion is made by Charley Tudor, generally thought to have been based loosely on Trollope himself. Charley refers to his own writing in the fictional *Daily Delight* and the joke lies partly in the name of his hero, Sir Anthony. When asked how his story will end, Charley replies that Sir Anthony stops drinking, goes to church, 'becomes a Puseyite . . . and reads the Tracts. At last he goes over to the Pope, walks about in nasty dirty clothes all full of vermin, and gives over his estate to Cardinal Wiseman.'[19] The self-mockery allowed Trollope extra licence to treat such conversions to Rome as melodramatic foolishness. The factions are treated with scorn, but so, too, is the critic. On Charley's own admission, his method of narration is formulaic: '. . . if you touch him [the reader] up with a startling incident or two at the first go off, then give him a chapter of horrors, then another of fun, then a little love or a little slang . . . you may describe as much as you like, and tell everything about everybody's father and mother for just as many pages as you want to fill.'[20] Trollope used this kind of self-deprecation to encourage readers to laugh at his early attempts to write *and* to laugh at the seriousness with which people regarded the faction to which they belonged.

Trollope's fondness for playing this double balancing role can be seen also in his early Irish novels, *The Kellys and the O'Kellys* (1848) and *Castle Richmond* (1860). One of his least attractive characters, Mr O'Joscelyn, an Irish Church clergyman of blinkered fanaticism, accuses Oxford of being 'a Jesuitical seminary, devoted to the secret propagation of Romish falsehood', whose clergy subsequently take into the churches of England 'their bowings, their genuflexions, their crosses and their candles'.[21] No reader, having reached this late page of the novel, could mistake Trollope's double swipe at extremists among high and low churchmen. In *Castle Richmond*, too, Trollope expresses people's fear of Puseyism in the words of a staunch member of the Irish Church, who had a 'horror and hatred of popery' and dreaded the thought that her nephew Herbert Fitzgerald might 'become a Puseyite!' To soften her views and at the same time reduce her credibility, Trollope makes Miss Letty imagine her nephew, who had recently attained a Bachelor of Arts, to 'assume the higher title of a married man of arts' in just 'a very few years'.[22] Her hilarious lack of comprehension prevents her role as critic from being taken seriously.

The Tractarians claimed in their heyday to be the *via media*, but Newman's flight to Rome annulled this claim and the middle way was ceded to the broad church.[23] The *via media* kept slipping down a notch through the ages in order to realign its position between extremes. The first Tractarians indulged their love of aestheticism through poetry and hymns. Trollope announces that the Tractarian Mr Arabin, shortly after becoming a fellow, was 'chosen professor of poetry', and stresses that, although he had narrowly escaped following Newman to Rome, he continued to like 'the ceremonies of the Church of Rome'.[24] Newman, Keble and Williams, three well-known Tractarians, were poets who 'sought to convey the spirit behind the literal word'.[25]

After Newman's conversion to Roman Catholicism in 1845 and the Papal Aggression of 1850, the Tractarian or Oxford Movement waned. Many Tractarians were fearful not only of others opting for Rome, but also of being tempted themselves. In 1846 Liddon confessed that the conversions around him were making him feel weak.[26] Similarly, Trollope relates that Mr Arabin's resistance to the 'safety of Rome' had to overcome 'the selfish freedom from personal danger which the bad soldier attempts to gain who counterfeits illness on the eve of battle'.[27] Trollope's rhetoric is more colourful than Liddon's but the sentiments are the same.

The younger Tractarians, known later as the Ritualists, became fascinated with ritual and ceremony. The older generation was simply too scared of others following Newman to Rome. In fact, Disraeli's dubbing of ritualism as 'Mass in masquerade' in the House of Commons, just prior to the vote, ensured the passing of the Public Worship Regulation Act in 1874,[28] discussed below. Trollope, laughingly, describes the high church Mr Caleb Oriel's leanings towards ritualism in *Doctor Thorne* (1858) and their effect on the neighbourhood. According to Greshamsbury pundits initially, their rector, whose name is shared by Oriel College, Oxford, the very home of the Oxford Movement, 'is not a marrying man, having very exalted ideas on that point connected with his profession'. His early flirtation with 'the scarlet lady' (Roman Catholicism) both attracts and frustrates young ladies seeking matrimony. He delights 'in lecterns and credence-tables, in services in dark hours of winter mornings . . . in high waistcoats and narrow white neckties, in chanted services and intoned prayers, and in all the paraphernalia of Anglican formalities which have given such offence to those of our brethren who live in daily fear of the scarlet lady'. But instead of giving offence in Greshamsbury, Mr Oriel's popularity grows rapidly, his good looks and gentlemanly manners overcoming his other deficiency: his disinclination for marriage. Nothing daunted, the young Miss Gushing tears 'herself from her warm bed' throughout 'one long, tedious winter' to be Mr Oriel's sole congregation member at his early morning services. But so enthusiastic is she for 'fasting on Fridays' and for 'her priest to give her the comfort of confessional absolution' that Mr Oriel begins to be cured of his devotion to ritualism. Having seen his morning services die 'a natural death', his sister selected her friend to be her brother's wife in order to assist 'his parish work' so that 'Mr Oriel found himself engaged to Miss Beatrice Gresham', while Miss Gushing abandoned the high church for the Independent Methodists and married its preacher. Now an engaged man, Mr Oriel's asceticism wanes. Not only does he desist from conducting morning services, but he also provides himself 'with a very excellent curate', and, when his own wedding celebrations are imminent, he pronounces that '"married life is, I'm sure, the happiest in the world"'. Trollope had already predicted that Mr Oriel would never have become a Roman convert for, despite his zeal at early morning orisons, he would never 'change his very sleek black coat for a Capuchin's filthy cassock, nor his pleasant parsonage for some dirty hole in Rome'.[29] The clergyman's almost violent capitulation to a state of being that had formerly not coincided with his 'very exalted ideas' reduces the issue under fierce debate to a question of immature zealotry. Trollope's lightness of touch is deliberate, for passions ran high about conversions to Roman Catholicism. He knew that a joke could help diffuse a tricky situation which, taken too seriously, could inflame political as well as religious passions.

The brilliant young winner of a double first at Oxford, George Bertram, holds nothing but scorn for the works of the Tractarians in *The Bertrams* (1859), written just one year after *Doctor Thorne*. Bertram's gaining of the Newdigate prize in poetry, the intellectual field shared by the Tractarians Keble and Faber, appears to diminish the Tractarians' intellectual abilities. By contrast, the 'plodding' second-class honours man, Arthur Wilkinson, 'proclaimed himself, while yet little more than a boy, to be an admirer of poor Froude and a follower of Newman'.[30] The implication seems to be that Tractarianism is attractive to second-class minds and is therefore not of value.

Yet, in noting in *North America* (1862) that 'Protestant Episcopalians muster strong in all the great cities', Trollope seems to approve of their 'taking the lead of the other religious denominations in New York' and casually reveals that they tend to follow 'high church doctrines'.[31] His matter-of-fact manner bears a distinct tinge of satisfaction, and the high church influence seems to have his approval.

Whereas the older Tractarians had been based primarily at Oxford, the new Ritualists began at Cambridge, and were 'another part of that almost universal turning from the head towards the heart' in their predilection for outward ceremonial.[32] The Tractarians themselves were incensed at the charge of ritualism often levelled against them; they actually 'feared that Ritualist excesses were discrediting the liturgical and rubrical renewal' inspired by them.[33] Ritualism encouraged symbolism, and the lighted tapers, incense, vestments, chanting, intoning, crossings and candles caused Trollope to write amusingly of them in *Miss Mackenzie* (1865), when he speaks of Mr Paul's closet candles, kept 'on an inverted box . . . inside his bedroom – a strong provocation to the strict Evangelical set in Littlebath known as the Stumfoldians'.[34]

Beyond the pages of fiction, ritualism incited Evangelical and broad church litigation in notorious cases like the one in Folkestone concerning the Rev. C. J. Ridsdale, and the other in Rochester involving Arthur Tooth, who was jailed after the Public Worship Regulation Act of 1874 had forbidden the eastward position of the clergyman during the Eucharist and the use of candles unless the light was poor. Feelings ran very high. Among the most famous Ritualists was John Mason Neale (1818–66), an acquaintance of Trollope's.[35] Neale was subjected to riots because of his ritualistic practices and feared for his life.

The Public Worship Regulation Act 1874 had been instigated by Archbishop Tait of the reassigned *via media*, the broad church. Ironically, this very Act, imposed to keep the peace, prolonged the bitterness between high and low church parties. The court cases became so acrimonious that the original disagreement was transformed into a kind of warfare. Tooth claimed that his health had been broken by the lengthy court case, consequent imprisonment and loss of position, although he did not die until 1931, after 'directing an orphanage, a nunnery and a home for drunkards'.[36] Trollope was all too aware of these difficulties. His use of 'closet' in *Miss Mackenzie* (1865) is carefully chosen, for the satire both attenuates and augments the gravity with which the majority of church leaders, of both high and low factions, viewed ritualistic practices, even before the 1874 Act. The Church Commission, founded in the very year in which *Miss Mackenzie* was published, used the Church courts, five years *before* the Public Worship Regulation Act and just prior to the publication of *He Knew He Was Right* (1869), to try Ritualists for what they deemed to be Romanist practices. In this novel Trollope, to demonstrate his impatience with the stubborn positions pursued by the factions, has the radical Hugh Stanbury who, like Charley Tudor, bore resemblances to himself, pointedly inform his aunt Stanbury that his colleague Scruby had 'touched up the Ritualists . . . and then the Low Church bishops' in the fictional *Daily Record*. The acidic journalism is directed at both high and low church factions, leaving neither of them 'a leg to stand upon'.[37] This impartial indictment bears all the hallmarks of Trollope's censuring of both factions for allowing doctrine to override common sense.

Although it is difficult now to appreciate the intense acrimony aroused by ritualistic practices, there were certainly some extreme examples to offend Protestant sensibilities. Purchas, for instance, was a high church cleric. On Whit Sundays he used to suspend a stuffed dove over the altar, and his colleague, Hawker of Morwenstow, used to dress in a claret-coloured suit, blue jersey and pink hat.[38] Had Trollope ascribed these practices to one of his fictional ritualists, modern readers would have accused him of exaggeration.

The low church[39]

While the high church enjoyed ceremony, the low church preferred 'spreading the word', as the term Evangelism implies. Critics have commented that Trollope shows less tolerance towards the Evangelicals than towards other factions, and suggest that his portrayal is unfair.[40] One particular claim, repeated more than once, that Trollope detested the Evangelicals,[41] appears to have speculative grounds, for the writer's noisy behaviour at a dinner is attributed to a probable disagreement with the low church Bishop of Ripon, another guest![42] Certainly Trollope amused his readers often at the expense of the Evangelicals, but, as with the Tractarians, he also tempered his criticism. The teasing to which the Evangelical Mr Snape is subjected in *The Three Clerks* (1858) is labelled 'very cruel', while his 'autobiographical character', Charley Tudor, who might join the 'infernal navvies' in their 'malpractices', could not help his 'kind heart' sympathize 'with the daily miseries of Mr Snape'.[43] It is true that the novelist poked fun at Evangelical solemnity, but his portrayal was not exaggerated; nor did he criticize Evangelicals exclusively. He did not, for instance, as the British *Quarterly Review* noted in 1867, resort to the heavy-handed criticisms associated with the broad church's Liberation Society or to the tracts of the high church in their repudiation of low church practices.[44] Nor did he follow his mother's example in her damning indictment of Evangelicalism in *The Vicar of Wrexhill* (1837), in which an Evangelical vicar, having disgraced himself with a female parishioner, is shown to be banished from the village with every other Evangelical, restoring it to being 'happy and gay'.[45] Frances Trollope was rather too negative. Her son is more subtle, and the picture he gives is more authentic.

Trollope may not have allowed his humour to develop into the kind of satire associated with his mother, but there were several aspects of Evangelicalism that provoked him. He took issue with the Evangelicals mainly over their lack of education deriving from their modest social station, their seriousness, their sermons and their increasing fondness of temporalities. Above all, he abhorred the factional squabbles between the Tractarians and the Evangelicals, and saw their long-running disputes as utterly futile and destructive for the Church as a whole.

Trollope made a point of contrasting the education of Evangelicals with that of the Tractarians. His snobbish attitude that Evangelicals were largely ill-read, ill-educated and uncultured was a popular one and not without some truth, for aristocrats like Charles Simeon had established the Simeon Trust in 1817 to secure livings for worthy Evangelical clergy in order to raise their social status and overcome their lowly education.[46] Trollope draws attention to these educational and social contrasts in *Barchester Towers* (1857), and in *The Last Chronicle of Barset* (1867) the high church Mr Crawley is a Greek scholar, but the Evangelical bishop, Dr Proudie, did not know the difference 'between an iambus and a trochee'.[47] This contrast was reflected in Trollope's own family. Edward Trollope was a high church scholar and wrote ecclesiastical works; Anthony Thorold was no scholar, but was an Evangelical 'devoted and faithful in the work assigned to him'.[48] Yet both were bishops in the Church.

The level of education of the Evangelicals was to some extent linked to their social backgrounds. Trollope, while not criticizing them overtly for their social inferiority, nevertheless could not resist making fun of their social pretensions. For example, Dr Proudie's family connections with the aristocracy, 'an Irish baron by his mother's side' and his wife's connections with 'a Scotch earl' are emphasized,[49] but the additional information that Dr Proudie's aristocratic relations were Irish on one side and 'Scotch' on the other was mischievous, for Trollope's readers would have known that Irish and Scottish titles did not carry the same cachet as English ones.

Trollope was not the only novelist to refer to the Evangelicals' impoverished education. George Eliot's Amos Barton in *Scenes of Clerical Life* (1857) not only knew no Greek or Hebrew, despite having 'gone through the Eleusinian mysteries of a university education', but also had trouble with English grammar and spelling, a fact which did not escape the surprised notice of his parishioners. His fellow clergymen, however, having 'gone through the mysteries themselves' were the 'least surprised'.[50] At least Trollope does not suggest that either Mr Slope or Dr Proudie has trouble with his native language.

He does suggest, however, that the Evangelicals tended to overcompensate for their lack of education, social cachet and sophistication through their concentration on the serious side of life. He teases the Evangelicals in *Rachel Ray* (1863) for their suspicion of leisure pursuits and Sunday activities, apart from Church attendance. Even tea-drinking at the Dorcas meetings could be suspect![51] Just as suspicious for Evangelical consciences were card-playing, hunting and dancing.[52] Trollope's enthusiasm for hunting only partly accounted for his impatience with Evangelical disapproval of this sport for clergymen. He notes in 'About Hunting' (1867) that clergymen 'rarely pay', for they have to act as 'chaplains to the hunt' to avoid episcopal scrutiny of their names 'on the lists'. He is less circumspect in his sequential article (1868) about condemning this prejudice, for 'clergymen require distraction as much as other men' and, if their parochial duties are rural, 'no recreation can be better suited to them' than hunting, since their very presence 'improves the hunting-field'.[53] When the low church Mr Groschut in *Is He Popenjoy?* (1878) attempts to convince the bishop that the Dean of Brotherton's hunting might lead 'to gambling on the turf', the bishop retorts that 'riding after a pack of dogs isn't gambling on the turf', while acknowledging to himself that it was only 'the idea of being beaten' by the Dean that prevented his admonition.[54] The worldly Dean was just too powerful for him. By his late work, *An Old Man's Love* (1884), Trollope felt able to depict with authenticity a young curate, the Rev. Montagu Blake, whose 'lines had fallen in pleasant places', but who cared not one iota for Evangelical scruples in his enjoyment of 'the innocent pleasures of this world', which included dining out, playing cricket, reading a novel, and, 'should he chance, when riding his cob about the parish ... to come across the hounds', a little hunting 'over a field or two'. The reader cannot fail to detect, however, Trollope's complete lack of respect for Montagu Blake, the 'garrulous young parson' and braggart. He may act as cupid to facilitate a reconciliation between his former Oxford friend and the heroine but, as his own fiancée confesses, he 'never seems to think he's a clergyman at all'. To which remark, the 50-year-old hero of the title, having nobly liberated the young heroine from her promise to marry him, ventures that '[i]t will be better for him [Blake] ... and for those about him, that he should remember the fact and never seem to do so'.[55] Trollope, a strong believer in individual liberty and moderation in the pleasures of life, did not condone those who flaunted their advantages to the discomfort of others, particularly if they held the privileged position of a clerical appointment *and* a private income. Disapproving of Evangelical severity, he was equally disapproving of complacent excesses among the clerisy, whatever their creed or faction.

The Evangelicals were generally treated with contempt within the Church until well into the nineteenth century,[56] since they regarded art and secular literature, particularly by the second revival of Evangelicalism in 1858, as a waste of time, which could have been spent reading the Bible or working. Many Nonconformists, too, disapproved of 'light' reading, which was noticed by writers other than Trollope. Mrs Gaskell, for instance, stresses in *Cousin Phillis* (1863–4), written at the same time as *Rachel Ray*, that the Nonconformist minister would not be pleased to know that his daughter Phillis had been given a novel to read, enlightened though he was compared with most real-life 1840s clergymen.[57] Moreover, she pointedly describes the new vicar of Helstone in *North and South* (1855) as a 'teetotaller', presumably an Evangelical, who has seven children, but whose vigorous 'turning things upside down' may have 'very little purpose'.[58]

Impatience with those wishing to curb the pleasures of others is wittily expressed, too, by Gaskell in a series of 'letters' in the *Pall Mall Gazette*, entitled 'A Parson's Holiday' (1865). The letters are purportedly from a Dissenting minister, desirous of escaping from the prying eyes of his congregation. His income of £200 a year and his six children, suddenly enhanced by a small legacy, enable him and his wife to go to Europe, leaving the children with their grandmother. He is mortified when his flutter on the gambling tables at Baden and quiet game of cards at Neuchâtel are discovered by his deacon, Mr Woodhouse, who, with half of the minister's congregation, is enjoying a Cook's tour of Europe. What a pity, wrote the minister, that Mr Cook had begun his business by 'taking teetotalers' to the beauty spots of Britain and Europe; if only he 'had drunk himself to death in early youth!'[59] Community awareness that Gaskell and her husband were Unitarians would have sharpened the humour for readers; her point was that congregations were often stricter adherents to orthodoxy than clerics. Trollope was thus not alone in deploring solemn Christianity.

Evangelicals of the second revival were in fact 'more fanatical, more bigoted and more introverted' than the earlier generation of Evangelicals 'who had followed Wilberforce and Shaftesbury'. The serious side of Evangelicalism is thought to have been partly responsible for England's relative stability during the nineteenth century, while Europe was often in the grip of revolution. Queen Victoria had had an

Evangelical tutor as a child and, despite her broad church *public* espousal as queen, retained Evangelical sympathies. She even postponed a Sunday journey from Crewe to London when a lady of the bed-chamber admonished her for her lack of seriousness.[60] Trollope lampoons the Evangelical Mr Slope's horror of the 'desecration of the Sabbath' in *Barchester Towers* (1857), especially his letters on the bishop's behalf to the Barchester branch railway's manager advising that Sunday trains be discontinued.[61] There is also Mrs Proudie's solemn belief in *Framley Parsonage* (1861) that the islanders of Papua New Guinea 'can never prosper unless they keep the Sabbath holy',[62] as well as her fear in *Doctor Thorne* (1858) that 'danger was to be apprehended from' visits to the city of Rome because of 'idolatry' being 'more rampant than ever' there and the fact that there was 'no such thing at all as Sabbath observances'.[63] Twice in *The Belton Estate* (1865) characters who are not 'card-carrying' Evangelicals display a reluctance to offend against the low church Perivale belief in Sabbatarianism.[64] Clara Amedroz later regrets not having travelled back on the day after her father's funeral, because she had been 'deterred by her dislike of making a Sunday journey'. In jest but also in frustration, Will Belton declares to his invalid sister: 'If I thought that no one would see me, I'd fill a dung-cart or two, even though it is Sunday.'[65] Such was the tyranny of community disapprobation that people with quite mild views on religious practices were afraid to step out of line. Trollope grew impatient with this strict curb on individual behaviour. It is significant that his article, 'The Fourth Commandment' (1866), supports the view of the *low* church Norman Macleod,[66] in opposition to many Scottish Presbyterians, that on Sundays the Commandment requires 'simply rest', not abstinence from activity.[67] Trollope's sincerity about religious issues is paramount in his letter published in the *Pall Mall Gazette*, in which he waxes indignant at the *Saturday Review*'s rebuke for his having stepped beyond fiction to write 'The Fourth Commandment' (1866) in the first place.[68] He was affronted that his occupation should be seen as precluding him from serious comment.

Sermons were a necessary part of the Evangelical emphasis on a sober approach to life. Trollope had a horror of them. His jocular references to long sermons are obviously directed against the Evangelicals. Besides the famous sermon denouncing intoning by the Evangelical Mr Slope in *Barchester Towers* (1857),[69] there are other allusions to the dreariness of Evangelical sermons. Gertrude Woodward in *The Three Clerks* (1858) would rather speak of anything dull, including 'Mr Everscreech's long sermon', than of her supposed lover, Harry Norman.[70] Mr Prong's tedious sermons, composed with 'laudable care' in *Rachel Ray* (1863), were as sincere as they were severe, 'never spar[ing] himself or his congregation much under an hour', unlike his high-and-dry neighbour, Dr Harford, who 'never exceeded twenty minutes, and had often been known to finish his discourse within ten'. Almost as long and plodding in *Rachel Ray* were Mr Comfort's 'half-hour as usual' pulpit condemnations of 'this world in all things', after which, as his name implies, that clerical gentleman is shown to indulge himself in all the comforts of life, for he was, to quote his landowning son-in-law, '"made of money"', having been '"blessed with the most surprising number of unmarried uncles and aunts"'.[71]

In sharp contrast to customary Evangelical solemnity was a growing awareness among members of this party of the delights to be enjoyed from the fruits of social and ecclesiastical success. Trollope makes barbed comments on Evangelical temporalities. He refers in *Framley Parsonage* (1861) to Mr Jones's struggle between God and Mammon, and to the excesses of both high and low church, commenting teasingly on the use of ginger,[72] for stimulants had once been denied by the low church. These comments would have struck a chord with readers. The rise of the Oxford Movement led to the weakening, for a while, of the Evangelicals, particularly since several from prominent families came under its spell. The Oxford Movement began in 1833, with Keble's assize sermon denouncing the government for its 'sacrilegious' conduct in Ireland,[73] and the appearance of the first tracts. It coincided with the end of the earlier Evangelical era. The passing of the slavery bill in the same year was both a tribute to the older Evangelicals, who had fought for it, and a sign of Evangelicalism's 'increasing debility', for 'fewer than half the Evangelical M.P.s' had supported the bill. Evangelicalism before the death in 1833 of William Wilberforce, the father of the Wilberforce brothers, had become relaxed, seeking worldly comfort in good wine and food. Simeon was known to love 'the comforts of life', was 'something of a dandy', was decidedly partial to 'the pleasures of the table', and regarded his horses as 'a matter of pride and intense concern'. Trollope's charge of weakness levelled against the Evangelicals, when confronted with a choice between God and Mammon, was widely held.[74] A renewed vigour after the 1840s among the Evangelicals, now reconciled to being called the low church,[75] came in response to the rise of the Ritualists, who offended the older Tractarians and the younger Evangelicals. The Papal Bull of 1850 also incited Evangelical wrath. Trollope mentions specifically that the mission of *The Brotherton Church*, the extreme Evangelical weekly newspaper in *Is He Popenjoy?* (1878), 'was to put down popery in the diocese' and that it 'distinguished itself by its elaborate opposition to ritual'.[76] Self-denial and sobriety had once again become characteristic of Evangelical belief. Trollope scorned both extremes: asceticism and self-indulgence.

Not that asceticism and self-indulgence were confined to the Evangelicals, for the Tractarians, as noted earlier, had also had phases when their adherents had veered either to one extreme or to the other. This is possibly why Trollope was so infuriated by the fighting between them. Not only did their battles leave the Church as a whole that much weaker, but their ideological disputes seemed so pointless, particularly since several leading figures had been aligned with both factions. Gladstone, high churchman, had been brought up as an Evangelical, and many Tractarians either had an Evangelical upbringing or an Evangelical 'phase'. Included among these were Samuel Wilberforce, Newman, Manning, Liddon and Pusey. Of these, Samuel Wilberforce and Manning became Roman Catholic. Trollope would have been well aware of the Evangelical origins of these high churchmen, for he reveals detailed knowledge of well-known people in the Church in his naming of Dr Grantly's children in *The Warden* (1855). His sons are called 'Charles James, Henry, and Samuel' after the three prominent bishops, Charles James Blomfield (1787–1857), Henry Phillpotts (1778–1860), and Samuel Wilberforce (1805–73). His daughters, Florinda and Grizzel, are named after the Archbishop of York's wife and the Archbishop of Canterbury's sister. These Church leaders and their wives were high church, in keeping with Dr Grantly's convictions.[77] Trollope, therefore, knew sufficient details about the leading men in the Church to be all too conscious of their often shared ideological origins.

The high and low factions shared other similarities. Both reinstated hymn singing, although the Tractarians took their lead from the Evangelicals. Both re-established a rigorous adherence to Christian principles, and both were interested in the spiritual. The difference was that the Tractarians sought the spiritual through liturgy and form by way of the Church as an institution, mainly through the written word, whereas the Evangelical theology was simpler, propagated through the spoken word of persuasive clergymen, hence Trollope's emphasis on lengthy Evangelical sermons. This does not mean that the high church did not have its great orators; Liddon's sermons, for example, attracted huge congregations at St Paul's.

Given these shared interests, the antipathy between low and high church followers seemed to Trollope even more incomprehensible. He was bemused that Protestant nonconformists outside the Established Church were often more acceptable to the low church than other factions *within* the Church, and he qualifies Slope's tolerance of dissent in *Barchester Towers* (1857) by stressing his aversion to the Puseyites.[78] In this, perhaps, lay the early seeds of Trollope's later fears for the decline of the Church. The warring between the high and low church dominates the Barchester series. The change of bishop from the high church Dr Grantly to the Evangelical Dr Proudie parallels the actual change in Winchester from the high church pluralist George Pretyman Tomline, the last of a series of high church bishops, to the Evangelical Charles Richard Sumner, Bishop of Winchester from 1827 to 1869. Sumner's older brother, the Evangelical John Bird Sumner, was Archbishop of Canterbury from 1848 to 1862.

Trollope's perceptive depiction of the furore caused by the change of bishop in Barchester cannot be appreciated without some idea of the actual warring between high and low church in Victorian England. A long period of Evangelical litigious fighting against ritualism began with the Gorham case in 1850, which started a series of court victories in favour of the Evangelicals. George Cornelius Gorham, vicar of St Just, Cornwall, annoyed his bishop, Phillpotts, by advertising in 1846 for a curate who was not a Tractarian. In revenge two years later when Gorham applied for a transfer, Phillpotts examined Gorham on his beliefs concerning baptismal regeneration and declared his doctrine unsound. The Court of Arches supported Phillpotts, but the Privy Council, on Gorham's appeal, overturned the judgement in 1850, to the relief of the Evangelicals. The Court of Arches was the principal and most ancient ecclesiastical court under the jurisdiction of the Archbishop of Canterbury. Thus a secular body had intervened in ecclesiastical affairs in order to avoid a 'mass exodus... of many of the six thousand Evangelical clergy', at the cost, though, of several leading high church leaders, including Manning and Wilberforce, taking the path to Rome.[79]

Trollope deplored the Gorham case and the chain of court cases that followed in its wake. In the earlier version of *The Three Clerks* (1858) he offers another of his double balancing acts of criticism directed at both Tractarians and Evangelicals, as the fictional Harry Norman's 'unmeasurable disgust for Mr Gorham', in his espousal of Tractarianism and in his general conduct, is presented as immature, unreliable and lacking integrity.[80] Trollope had no patience with either the low or high church party over ideological wrangles leading to litigation.

The Evangelicals were victorious in the Gorham case partly because England's leaders were terrified of Roman Catholicism's threat. After the case, aristocratic patronage once again ensured Evangelical success.

Palmerston, intent on keeping the Church of England established, saw to it, with the Evangelical Lord Shaftesbury, that 16 out of the 27 bishops were Evangelical,[81] because the Evangelicals by this time had become politically conservative, having returned to their pious ways. Trollope illustrates this policy in *Barchester Towers* (1857). Dr Proudie's good fortune is due to the change in political ministry taking place just before the old bishop's death. He was chosen, not for his talent, but for his 'toleration' of the extremes of religious belief and practices, and 'if he did not do much active good, he never did any harm'.[82] Thus Trollope illustrates the vagaries of the political climate. He may have had no time for the polarities of Evangelical zeal, but neither did he have any more time for Tractarian zeal. Fervour of any factional complexion leading to the imposition of doctrine and practices on others prompted Trollope's comic condemnation. The Barsetshire series was his sweet revenge.

The broad church

The latitudinarianism of the broad church contrasted starkly with the ideological intransigence of the high and low church parties. Its *extreme* breadth of tolerance attracted Trollope's contempt. It did not draw his allegiance, as has been suggested.[83] The broad church in itself is difficult to define, for it filled the vacuum between high and low church. The Church of England as the established church, of necessity, embraced a wide range of belief; the broad church even seemed to extend to unbelief. Many of its supporters were 'literary figures' who replaced the difficult aspects of Anglican theology with 'mythic or symbolic interpretations of the Bible', yet they had little influence on ordinary Anglicans 'at mid-century and for long afterwards'.[84] This is possibly why Trollope did not allocate much fictional space to the new *via media*.

The term *via media* was initially alluded to by the first Elizabethan Archbishop of Canterbury, Matthew Parker, who advocated a golden mediocrity, his Roman Catholic friends preferring to describe this pejoratively as 'an unfortunate compound of Popery and the Gospel'.[85] The broad church itself grew out of the eighteenth-century latitudinarians and it was this liberalism which the Church took into the twentieth century, and which many now believe threatens its very survival. It enjoyed its period of strength, when the schisms in the Church of England began the prelude to its steady decline in the years from 1868 to 1882, during Tait's tenure as Archbishop of Canterbury. After the

Barchester series was concluded, the strength and power of Tait as Church leader effected compromises between the warring factions and ensured that the link between the Church of England and the state was maintained into the twentieth century. The broad church's liberalism may have taken the Church into the next century but it was this liberalism which the high church leaders, Liddon, Pusey and Hamilton, feared would eventually reduce the hold that the Church had on society. The high church wished for disestablishment in order to govern itself without state interference. Liddon averred that broad church Erastianism, 'in serving the nation instead of Christ . . . will do more to prevent men taking orders, and in the end to break up the Church of England than anything else'.[86]

The most controversial broad churchman was Colenso (1814–83), the Bishop of Natal (1853–83). His work, *The Pentateuch and Book of Joshua Critically Examined* (1862–63), had stunned the Church by arguing that the 'numerous inconsistencies and inaccuracies' in biblical history made the Bible 'unreliable' as history and was therefore 'properly to be used only as a source for "religious ideas"'.[87] The work caused what is now known as the Natal 'schism',[88] as well as rifts among different groups of worshippers in England, far from South Africa's shores.

Trollope's attitude to Colenso and to those influenced by his teaching was not fixed, and his changing views are interesting to document. In the same year as Liddon expressed his fears about Erastianism, Trollope was scathing in *Clergymen of the Church of England* (1866) about the broad church's so-called tolerance, noting that 'the clergyman who subscribes to Colenso' is noted for tolerating his own doubts, rather than being tolerant of the doubts of others, a trait which had previously characterized broad churchmen. As he 'is on terms of personal intimacy' with at least one of the liberal churchmen who wrote the controversial *Essays and Reviews* (1860), the broad churchman refuses to 'declare his opinion' that they 'should be unfrocked'.[89] Furthermore, he adds doubts of his own.[90] Trollope's article, while seemingly defending the right of Colenso and the new breed of clergyman to question biblical exegesis, strongly puts the opposing case by voicing the concerns of 'antediluvian rectors and pietistic vicars', who query 'that want of professional thoroughness, that absence of esprit de corps' exhibited by the new liberal clergyman, as well as his right to 'take four hundred a year out of the Church, when he doesn't believe one of the Articles he has sworn to'. Despite Trollope's epithets describing Colenso's critics and followers as 'antediluvian' and 'pietistic', the article gives the impression that these criticisms are valid. Moreover, Trollope describes the new broad churchman equally unattractively as having 'something of a subrisive smile in which we rather feel than know that there is a touch of irony latent'. His doctrines are 'ill-defined', and yet 'he is, almost always, a true man'. Trollope concludes that the doubts cast by the new theology have 'made it impossible' for people 'to stay' on 'the old shore' of belief.[91] His article sharply defines Colenso's ideas as ground-breaking but disconcerting and troubling. Clearly Trollope felt that he himself should be open to new ideas, but nonetheless was disturbed by them, and was doubtful, as were many others, as to the quality of the scholarship behind these ideas.

Besides his non-fictional discussion, Trollope provided two fictional examples of negative reactions to the disturbing new theology. Both examples are spinsters leading a confined life, and both are patently depicted as having opinions to match the narrow strictures of their confinement, and are therefore not to be taken seriously. Miss Aylmer in *The Belton Estate* (1865), which was published in the year in which Colenso was deposed and excommunicated, believed that Colenso 'came direct from the Evil One'. A great reader of novels, Miss Aylmer was, Trollope pointedly observes, 'as ignorant, meek, and stupid a poor woman as you shall find anywhere in Europe'.[92] By the time that Trollope had published *Clergymen of the Church of England* in the following year, Colenso had been reinstated by the law courts to his position as Bishop of Natal. Officially excommunicated by his metropolitan in 1865, Colenso's appeal to the Privy Council had resulted in the judgement being nullified and his retention of the temporalities of his see until his death in 1883, despite public opinion forcing the Church to consecrate a bishop of Maritzburg to satisfy those in the community strongly disagreeing with Colenso's position.[93] But even in 1867, when *He Knew He Was Right* (1869) was being written, the controversy still raged. For Jemima Stanbury, living within Exeter's cathedral close, 'there had never been . . . a traitor so base, or an apostate so sinful, as Colenso'. Trollope adds with emphasis that 'of the nature of Colenso's teaching she was as ignorant as the towers of the cathedral opposite to her'.[94] Thus, in his fiction Trollope illustrates how entrenched people's attitudes can become on issues receiving much publicity, even though their opinions are founded on virtually no information.

Trollope's own quandary about Colenso's teaching at this time can best be seen in the fact that he commented that he had been invited to a dinner in London in the 1860s by a 'gushing friend' who had boasted that '"[w]e have secured Colenso"',[95] but he did not attend that dinner and did not meet Colenso until his South African tour 12 years later,[96] when he made a point of visiting the controversial bishop. After his visit, he is still circumspect about expressing an opinion in *South Africa* (1878), and says that he would not throw doubt 'upon the miracles or upon Colenso', even though he acknowledged that the bishop of Natal was 'not the man to abandon any position of which he is proud'. On hearing Colenso preach at Pietermaritzburg, he was surprised that the bishop's notoriety had neither emptied nor filled the church, and that 'the most trusting young believer in every letter of the Old Testament would have heard nothing on that occasion to disturb a cherished conviction'.[97] Trollope's observation seems not only to question the attention given to the Bishop of Natal but also shows disdain for Colenso's evanescent zeal.

Trollope's contempt for the broad church arose not only from the Colenso case but also from the broad church leadership as a whole. His main concern was that Tait's *via media* ideas of compromise between factions encouraged him to make concessions on behalf of the low and high church factions rather than on behalf of the broad church. Trollope saw this kind of compromise almost as a brand of imperialism based on egoism. Dr Freeborn's latitudinarianism in 'The Two Heroines of Plumplington' (1882) cultivates his anxiety 'for the mundane happiness of his parishioners'. This places him 'in fault', for 'he had no dislike to Papists or Presbyterians, or dissenters in general, as long as they would arrange themselves under his banner as "Freebornites"'.[98] Trollope never did have any patience with people who tried to disguise egotism as ideology or politics.

The struggle between the high church and broad church over the Athanasian Creed resulted in a lengthy, clumsy addendum in 1870 to the damnatory clauses, in order to preclude offence being taken by broad and low church members. Trollope commented sharply in *Clergymen of the Church of England* that few clergymen would openly acknowledge 'the fulminating clause', condemning those whose faith did not carry full conviction to damnation, despite each clergyman's regular declaration as to its validity.[99]

Even earlier, in *Framley Parsonage* (1861), Trollope had spoken of the weakness of the Church and the Establishment question.[100] Tait himself regarded the continued link between Church and state as one of his greatest achievements, but perhaps his success was due to popular apathy, rather than popular support.[101] The Public Worship Regulation Act of 1874 was one more attempt to placate the community, ever fearful of the resurgence of Roman Catholicism. The Act, though, rebounded on the Church with consequent aggressive litigation between high and low church. Extensive newspaper coverage, blamed throughout Trollope's work for fomenting small issues into large ones, condemned the harsh punishments meted out by the courts. Trollope's comment in *Barchester Towers* (1857) about Sydney Smith's liberalism attracting to him the label of infidel would seem to suggest that the novelist,[102] even in the 1850s, feared that broad church compromise might alienate more people than it would placate, an opinion also held by Liddon.[103]

Trollope's pessimism and schism

Whenever Trollope wrote of clergymen he focused on the characteristics of human nature, rather than on theological polemics; he accepted that public office often belied personal foible. In his fiction he draws *dramatis personae* rather than types, and the redeeming or unredeeming features, uncharacteristic of the faction to which his characters belong, mark them out to be more human than fabricated. Archdeacon Grantly's energetic diligence and Dr Proudie's timidity render the high-and-dry and Evangelical factions more credible for their untypicality.

Trollope's concern for the Church's survival, because of these factions, deepened as the years went by. His perception of the difficulties faced by the Church was not that of a casual observer and was in accord with many of his contemporaries. Although his evaluations are expressed comically, the shading of the comedy grows darker as time goes by. Trollope's works, published between 1855 and 1867, make no mention of any real threat to the Church of England itself, although the works reveal the writer's impatience with the different factions *within* the Church. After 1867 Trollope's novels assume a much darker hue, and the Church's future looks increasingly sombre. If the themes of his later works move more deeply into the blacker caverns of the human soul, it is because he feared the waning ability of the divided Church to lighten these caverns.

The schisms within the Church are mildly rebuked and comically portrayed by Trollope in the first 12 years of his writing. In the next three years he shows these schisms to be capable of changing public perception as to the Church's leaders. In the final 13 years of his work these schisms are shown to cause cracks in the structure of the Church itself. Moreover, as the Liddon–Hamilton correspondence shows, Trollope's increasing pessimism was shared by leading members of the Church; Liddon's fears, for example, were very similar to those covertly disclosed by Trollope in his novels.

It has become customary to see Trollope as an advocate of the high church, but in *The Bertrams* (1859) he has fun at the expense of prominent high church members in George Bertram's 'opposition to the Sewells' and 'to Keble and Faber'.[104] Trollope was in fact friendly with the Sewells.[105] He is also as mocking of Mark Robarts' youthful embrace of the high-and-dry weakness for extravagant living and hunting in *Framley Parsonage* (1861) as he is of Mrs Proudie's Evangelical 'firmness ... Sabbath-day observances'. Nor do these differences between factions belong to isolated individuals, for Trollope vividly illustrates the animosity between families with differing ecclesiastical affiliations: 'It was natural that the Grantlys and Proudies should hate each other ... their views on all church matters were antagonistic'. Yet the proprieties between bishop and clergy had to continue and the two wives had to overcome 'this rancour' in order to remain on 'visiting terms'. The latent bitterness activated social competition. Olivia Proudie's engagement to a widowed preacher with three children in Bethnal Green and Griselda Grantly's engagement to the eldest son of the Marquess of Hartletop provide a comic reversal of status in the younger generation,[106] although Trollope's mischief suggests that the Proudies were always socially inferior to the Grantlys. Trollope's humour masks the sharpness of his opinions, but his impatience with schism remains.

Trollope's fictional Barchester in general, divided through doctrinal division, had parallels in the region depicted. Contemporary correspondence between Hamilton and his Salisbury parishioners corroborate the painful divisions. Relating to doctrine, the correspondence reveals personal antipathies. Mr Atkins of Dorchester believed that the high church Hamilton's charge had been 'contrary to the Scriptural teaching of our Church', and complained to the Archbishop of Canterbury about the latter's insistence on Real Presence in the Eucharist and encouragement of auricular confession.[107] Both complaints raise the issue of Roman Catholic practices sidling into the Anglican Church. Roman Catholics believe that the taking of wine and wafer during Eucharist is the actual taking of the flesh and blood of Jesus Christ. Many Protestants, in contrast, have regarded communion as symbolic, even if they believe Christ to be present, hovering in some way during Eucharist. The high church of England, at this time, believed Christ *actually and materially* to be present during Eucharist. It was the question of Real Presence and the *degree* to which Christ was perceived to be present that worried many within the Church, for Real Presence seemed too close to Roman Catholicism. Auricular confession, too, has always been associated with Roman Catholicism. The fear, then, was that Roman Catholicism had crept by stealth into the Salisbury diocese, and Atkins was really accusing Hamilton of Roman Catholic doctrine and practice. Atkins' letter was signed by 72 clergymen and 76 churchwardens. A different parishioner, Mr Wood, complained in 1865 about another of Hamilton's charges, urging him to make concessions, so that the Wesleyan Methodists will 'come back to us'.[108] Trollope's descriptions may focus on the *spoken* interchanges between people and their daily concerns, but these documents confirm that the schisms were very deeply drawn. Trollope fictionalized the problems in interpersonal relations which doctrinal divisions provoked within the dioceses of England.

Rachel Ray (1863), the Devonshire story of a young man's ambition to marry the girl of the title and to 'shut . . . up the apple orchards of the county' by transforming the local brewery from a poor one into a good one, has long been criticized for its anti-Evangelical bias, which centres on the negative depiction of the Evangelical clergymen, Mr Prong and Mr Comfort, the former, an ill-educated, calculating man, and the latter, a hypocrite. The two Evangelical clergymen in fact act as decoys, for, on closer reading, the high church is not portrayed favourably either. Dr Harford, of the high church, accustomed to his comfortable living for nearly 40 years, suddenly found that he had to share his parish with Mr Prong, for 'the presentation to the new benefice was not conceded to him', and he 'did not love Mr Prong'. His hatred of Mr Prong was not because his income had been reduced but because 'his clerical authority' had been 'mutilated', his country 'had allowed its ancient parochial landmarks to be moved, and its ecclesiastical fastnesses to be invaded'. Energetic and industrious in youth, acting as both magistrate and politician in addition to his parochial duties, Dr Harford had become a tired old man, hating Mr Prong 'with an absolute faith, but without any ground on which such faith should have been formed'.[109] The high church cleric is thus no more attractive than his Evangelical counterparts.

Although much of *Miss Mackenzie* (1865), in its tragi-comic narrative of three unattractive suitors pursuing the heroine for her hand in marriage and an inheritance that turns out not to belong to her, focuses on the Evangelical faction, the high church is not ignored, and the ritualists receive a gentle drubbing. Mr Paul, accused by the wife of the Evangelical Mr Stumfold of being 'the most abject of all the slaves of the scarlet woman', utters the rash rejoinder that 'she was another'. This makes him, in Mrs Stumfold's eyes, a 'ribald ruffian', who 'thinks his priestly rags protect him' sufficiently to be able to insult her. Fortunately, 'Mr Stumfold's sacerdotal clothing, whether ragged or whole, prevented him also from interfering', thus averting open factional warfare. Emitted by St Stumfolda,[110] not known for her sense of humour, the comments attract scorn for both factions. Contrary to common allegation, therefore, Trollope did not exclusively ridicule the low churchman in favour of the high churchman.

He is also mild compared with an anonymous letter (year unknown), addressing Liddon as 'The Ritualist', and calling him a 'numbskull'. Pusey is a 'hateful Jesuit, and a narrow-minded blockhead'. The clergy must obey or be 'kicked out of office', for 'the Church will be disestablished and dismembered in a few years. Harra!'[111] Even accounting for the extreme nature of this letter, factual documentation from this period is much more vehement than Trollope's discourse.

In *Clergymen of the Church of England*, Trollope is more even-handed, and stresses how important it is for an archbishop to be free from doctrinal bias, and for the community to have both high and low church bishops, for, without this, 'we should miss much that we feel to be ornamental to the Establishment and useful to ourselves'. He later surmises that '[p]erhaps it would be well if High Church, Low Church, and Broad Church could be allowed to have their turns in rotation', adding that 'the bishop's own predilections matter little, perhaps, if the man will work with a will'. Trollope has been criticized for his poor opinion of the low church, yet he asseverates that there are few people 'now who remember much of the Low Church peculiarities of the Bishop of London, having forgotten all that in the results of his episcopate'.[112] His awareness of the danger of schism to the Church and to Christianity as a whole is all too clear in this work, although it is often overlooked by critics seeking only to identify Trollope's clerical stereotypes.

Prior to 1867, there is no openly expressed concern for the Church as an enduring institution, but after that there are strong hints that Trollope is fearful for the Church's future. Harry Clavering's refusal to consider the Church as his profession is the initial fictional complication in *The Claverings* (1867), but the situation itself reveals Trollope's growing pessimism with the Church. Not even the humour comparing the indolent Henry Clavering with the sombrely industrious Mr Saul can obliterate the impression that the Church does not command the same respect as it had formerly. Henry Clavering 'smoked cigars in his library', too 'fat and idle' to walk. Mr Saul, by contrast, 'was very tall and very thin' and 'went about his parish duties with grim energy'.[113] Neither rector nor curate inspires confidence that any strength might remain in the Church.

Similarly, in *The Last Chronicle of Barset* (1867), the initial problem of Mr Crawley's supposed thieving sounds alarm bells more than his shabby gentility and gloomy intransigence. Crawley's brickmaker parishioners may love him but the Barchester community is already questioning the Church's representatives, regardless of faction. The warring among the clerical groups simply aggravates matters, for there is no block of loyalty willing to oppose an increasingly secular and material society. The community's questioning of the integrity of a church official indicates that the popular view of the Church is no longer one of blind respect. It is Trollope's 'castles in the air' – his plots – rather than his character portrayals which reveal his underlying anxieties. Liddon mirrored Trollope's gloom, for he was particularly nervous in 1866, just before Trollope's novels change to a more sombre key, that anyone leaving the Established Church for Rome might encourage others to pursue dissenting theologies or, worse still, a totally secular life.[114]

The post-1869 novels mark an even more sombre gradient in the Church's decline. The increasing gloom can be seen in the fictional themes as well as in the behaviour and opinions of fictional characters; at times the pessimism is stated, at others it is illustrated. In *The Vicar of Bullhampton* (1870), the division in human relations is not within the Church but between the Church of England and the dissenting Methodists. While Trollope amusingly upbraids the community for regarding Mr Frank Fenwick as a ritualist complete with cross and candlestick, and pointedly states that Mr Fenwick's tolerance of Mr Puddleham's Methodism is not reciprocated, the two church buildings symbolize the stark reality of Christianity for England. The Established Church has a Norman door, Early English windows, and is picturesque. The Methodist Church is poorly built, looks as if it would tumble down and is ugly. But neither establishment is shown in a good light. The rift is one of class, explains Saint George, who acts as peacemaker between his father the Marquess of Trowbridge, supporter of the Methodist Chapel on account of his low church daughters, and the Vicar. Dissent, Saint George avers to his father, does not owe its genesis to pure motives. Worldly ambition, not heavenly salvation, fills the Methodist Church; belief does not enter into it. Dissent was inevitable, for 'men like to manage themselves', since in the Methodist Church the ordinary man in the street has more status than he could ever hope to attain in the Established Church. The Church of England, too, receives censure, however indirect. Accusing Mr Puddleham of being a 'very meddlesome man' in his futile and clumsy attempts to curb the 'youthful iniquity' of a young man by warning his father, the Vicar cannot seem to check his own deep community involvement. He plays matchmaker with his wife to a young couple unsuited to each other, and interferes in the upbringing of a family's (the Brattles') troublesome pair of siblings – the son accused (wrongly) of murder, the daughter of sexual impropriety. This family is the same one approached earlier by Mr Puddleham. There is even a very faint whiff of amatory scandal, and a slightly stronger one of clerical questioning of faith. The Vicar's possibly suspect feelings for Carry Brattle are suggested, and Mr Brattle, berated by Trollope for most of the story for his lack of Christian devotion, makes the Vicar himself acknowledge that 'the unbelieving old man' would meet his death without a tremble. The reserve exercised by the Barchester clerics in the earlier novels and practised in this novel by the older style Anglican clergymen, Parson Marrable and Mr Chamberlaine, seems impossible for the Vicar to maintain, despite his belief that '[h]e was the last man in the world to adopt a system of sacerdotal interference'. The Vicar's awareness that 'of the three millions of people [in London on a Sunday] not a fourth... attend divine service' might possibly account for his failure to adhere to his own dictum.[115] Trollope knew that Christian belief was on the wane and appears to be showing panic in the Anglican clergyman, whose dignity shrinks in inverse ratio to his community activity.

Increased secularism troubled Liddon two years before the publication of *The Vicar of Bullhampton*. He visited Russia with an avowed intention to avert disaster within the Church by securing from a Suffragan Bishop of Moscow wishes for Christian *rapprochement* and unity across Europe.[116] Trollope's increasingly negative portrayals of Christian officials and communities are thus not concomitants of the disillusionment which might come with age; they are deeply ingrained anxieties shared by the Church's leaders.

The secular themes of *The Eustace Diamonds* (1873) continue Trollope's vision of a downward moral spiral in his society, if not in his Church. Beautiful Lizzie Eustace, niece-in-law of a bishop, consanguineous niece of a dean and countess, as well as sister-in-law and first cousin to a member of parliament and daughter of an admiral, is described, not without good reason, as 'a dishonest, lying, evil-minded harpy'. Her preference for lies over the truth, as long as she can manipulate a situation to suit her own ends, matches her contempt for her clerical relatives – 'these old fogies of the Church' – who 'preach now and then in the cathedral' while, she adds with relish, 'everybody takes the opportunity to go to sleep'.[117] This very long novel, with its emphasis on greed and lust, dangled as a badge principally by Lizzie Eustace but contemplated seriously by 'good' and 'bad' characters alike, who, when under Lizzie's spell, cannot discern right from wrong, captures a society clinging to respectability by the flimsiest of gossamers. Lizzie, after rejecting the older generation of churchmen, her relatives, and failing to trap into matrimony other possible suitors, finally marries a member of the new generation of clerics. The Church's representation by the unpleasant Rev. Joseph Emilius, a Hungarian Jew, makes the modern reader shudder, not least for its imputed 'anti-Semitism'.[118] But discussions of 'racism' would constitute several book-length studies in themselves. Nineteenth-century society generally disliked 'foreigners', and Trollope's views on this matter were not uniform. Jewish Rebecca Loth in *Nina Balatka* (1867) is almost saintly in her support of the heroine of the novel's title. More significant for this study is the fact that, although the Established Church was still linked to the state, Trollope could see that the nation's church was no longer necessarily being run by people belonging to the nation. It had lost its identity, seemed lacking in direction and was being represented, he suggests, by clerics like Joseph Emilius, whose moral fortitude was found to be as sadly wanting as that of his most materialistic character, Lizzie Eustace. The eventual marriage between these two flawed characters in Scotland, and not England, ends the novel on its only cheering note. At least the fictional couple was sufficiently respectful of the Church of England to venture beyond its borders for their nuptials.[119] That the 'good' characters are rewarded and that the 'bad' may be facing their just desserts, hinted at by the notorious reprobate the Duke of Omnium, does little to redeem the overall picture the reader has of a nation tumbling into its temporal temptations, uncurbed by its Established Church.

Surprisingly, in the midst of his increasing gloom, Trollope reveals a glimmer of optimism. Regarded as a very pessimistic novel, for its focus on greed and lust is even more vehement and pervasive than that of *The Eustace Diamonds*, *The Way We Live Now* (1875) actually shows the Church in a brief redeeming light. Uninterested in creeds and labelled as a 'time-server' by those who were 'very high' or 'very low', 'because he would not put to sea in either of those boats', the Bishop of Elmham was 'an unselfish man' and perhaps 'more loved and more useful in his diocese' than any other bishop in England.[120] It is this happy contrariety of human nature within an institution losing its way that could possibly, implies Trollope, be its saving grace.

But Trollope's despondence returns. The world of *Is He Popenjoy?* (1878) engages relatively unblushingly with the issues of extra-marital liaisons, illegitimacy and the general pursuit of pleasure and wealth. Neither the high nor low church escapes Trollope's censure. The wealthy high church Dean's fondness for hunting, despite episcopal and community disapproval, is far less of a problem than his worldly ambition. His determination to make his daughter a Marchioness, 'whether he made himself, her, and others happy or unhappy', and his 'pagan exultation at the death' of the young heir to the Marquessate of Brotherton, expressed by Trollope as his winning 'the great stake for which he had been playing', is chilling. Trollope's talent for combining positive and negative elements in characters actually darkens the ultimate view received by the reader. Somehow the Dean's perfect drawing-room manners and the latent respect and liking between him and his 'notoriously low' bishop casts the Church in an even gloomier light than if their factional differences had been of the bitterest.[121] The Dean's popular urbanity makes him appear like an upstart ruffian, reminding the reader of his modest social origins, when he thrashes the Marquess for insulting his daughter, intolerably provoking and untrue though the slur is. The reader, after all, has already seen multiple examples of the Dean's indulgence towards his daughter: his negligence of her regular attendance at church at home; his insistence that she and her husband spend the London season in a fashionable house of his purchase; his neglect to ask her which church she would attend in London; his encouragement of her to join the metropolitan 'fast set'; his lack of interest in influencing her on serious matters, and his reluctance to act as moral guardian of her 'perceived' behaviour in sybaritic society. His worldliness attracts no more respect from the reader than the low church bishop's chaplain Groschut who, having strenuously criticized the Dean for his lax churchmanship, is banished to a poor parish for reneging on a promise of marriage.

Equally depressing is Trollope's view of the Church in *John Caldigate* (1879), where it appears to be increasingly sidelined by a community simultaneously fascinated and scandalized by a court case involving cohabitation and/or bigamy. The search for evidence is hampered by the vast distance between England and Australia, where John Caldigate's 'first' marriage is alleged to have taken place and by the supposed casual attitude to cohabitation and formal nuptials in the new country, the old country more intrigued than horrified by this possibility. The two clergymen, the one quietly supportive of the couple, the other condemnatory and stridently intrusive, despite his awareness that 'the ordinary life of gentlefolk in England does not admit of direct clerical interference', scarcely seem to be heeded by the community. The accused's father, labelled a 'pagan' by a mild-mannered clergyman and an 'infidel freethinker' by a zealot, refers to 'the antiquated absurdity of a State Church', but acts more like a Christian than most of the believers when his son's wife needs protection during the court case. Of the remainder of the principal characters, only the fanatical Mrs Bolton seems concerned with religion; her low church fear of 'giving some foothold to Satan', should she not cling to the 'rules of religion fitted [more] to prejudice' than ideology, is perhaps even more abhorrent than the Dean's hedonism in *Is He Popenjoy?* (1878). Convinced that she is right, on religious grounds, to shun her daughter and grandchild when her son-in-law is on trial for bigamy, she cannot bring herself, even once the matter has been happily resolved, to visit her daughter in her marital home, for she 'cannot readily give herself to new affections'.[122] The power of inner reason over parental instinct for a child's well-being, whether acknowledged as religious or not, can be tragic, and Trollope demonstrates that both high and low factions were guilty of favouring abstract principles over personal claims.

The remarkably similar issue in *Dr Wortle's School* (1880) creates an even deeper pessimism, for here is a schoolmaster in a Church of England school actually living with a woman who is not his wife. Dr Wortle's protection of Mr Peacocke has been seen as indicative of Trollope's sympathy for the couple. Yet what the modern reader tends to overlook is Trollope's emphasis that Dr Wortle's naive visits to Mrs Peacocke and his resistance to his bishop's remonstrations and those of his fellow clergyman Mr Puddicombe and his wife are in danger of dividing the community and of bringing the Church into disrepute. As cleric he needed to be *seen* to be above suspicion, as his worried bishop advised him, for he 'could not do altogether as other men might' and, as for forgiving a wrongdoing on the part of others, he was 'not entitled' to do so, as Mr Puddicombe recalled for him; nor could he be blind to the fact that '"[a] woman should not live with a man unless she be his wife"', as Mrs Wortle reminded him.[123] A clergyman unheeded by a community gives rise to complacency about moral issues, but a clergyman scorned for imputed amorality at best and immorality at worst can only precipitate moral degeneracy, as Trollope hints will be the case in the fictional world of Bowick.

That precipitation towards moral degeneracy, led rather than unchecked by the Church, looms large in *Marion Fay* (1882), published in the year of Trollope's death. It is only the peripheral position of the chaplain Mr Greenwood to the central concerns of romance, radicalism and inheritance that rescues Wednesbury's society from moral decay.

The Marchioness of Kingsbury's active Christianity as well as her boundless ambition to have her own son succeed as heir, in place of her stepson, throws her into an unholy alliance with Mr Greenwood, whose insidious influence over her encourages her to contemplate possible thoughts of murder. Mercifully, the chaplain's power over her is perceived by her husband to be too repellent, and he dismisses the old churchman – a clergyman who was 'not religious' – from his employ. Significantly, the chaplain's presence contributes largely to the Marquess's illness; his absence helps to restore his health.[124] The possible superiority of a dissenting sect over the Church of England and the possible superiority of non-practising Christians over the hypocrisy and dishonesty of certain Church officials is pessimistically blatant. The Quaker father and daughter, Zachary and Marion Fay, display far more impressive Christian virtues than the Anglican Kingsburys, in whose gift is a family living. And George Roden, even with his doubtful origins and radicalism, is much more to be trusted than the Kingsburys' chaplain. This novel, among Trollope's final works, exhibits the writer's continued and developing criticism of the Church as an institution. His criticism in no way prevented his active participation in the Church of England until his death, as has been attested by the vicar of his parish,[125] but he fervently believed that the Church, in turning its attention inward to fight futile battles of doctrine, was in danger of overlooking the weaknesses of some of its representatives and of neglecting the community, who in turn might regard the Church itself as irrelevant.

Finally, Trollope's year of death coincided with Pusey's, proponent of the high church; with Tait's, leader of the broad church; and with Darwin's, to whom the secular beliefs of later generations are often, if erroneously, attributed. None of these men lived, therefore, to see the infighting between ecclesiastical factions cease, for ritualism cases continued to be tried in the courts in the 1890s. With the aid of a century of hindsight Trollope's fears that schism would cause the Church's decline can now be fully understood. So too can his descent into pessimism.

2
Patronage versus Philanthropy

Trollope's pessimism about the Church's survival did not just derive from his irritation over its internal dissensions. The image in his works of sharp schisms cleaving the Church apart is countered by the Church being unevenly buttressed by the tradition of patronage. Trollope was a firm opponent of this tradition. Yet without access to patronage an Anglican clergyman of few private means found it well nigh impossible to fulfil his charitable duties, for he himself needed to be the recipient of philanthropy. Any clergymen finding himself in this dire position was in danger of losing community respect, in addition to his own self-respect. This chapter argues that Trollope criticized both ecclesiastical patronage and philanthropy, which share certain elements, because he believed that, by preventing the Church from accommodating the changes taking place in Victorian society, they conjoined to aggravate its problems. As far as Trollope was concerned, schism was causing the Church to implode from within, while patronage and philanthropy, as it were, conspired to risk its reputation in the wider world.

Since neither patronage nor philanthropy was the exclusive property of clergymen, it is useful to draw a general comparison between the two in order to explain Trollope's attitude. In some ways, they are two sides of the same coin. Both practices are carried out with the intention of helping others. Both are gifts handed from a social superior to an inferior. They differ, however, in their intended outcomes. Philanthropy is an act of benefaction usually executed on behalf of strangers; the beneficiary is not intended to be placed under any obligation. The process of patronage, on the other hand, requires that the benefactor and beneficiary have a reciprocal and enduring obligation, with the participants invariably known to each other even before the question of patronage arises. Patronage involves an ongoing dialectic; it is often part of a wider network of relations and assumes that at some point in the future the gift will be reciprocated. Both patronage and philanthropy are age-old practices, but in the nineteenth century patronage fell into disfavour, while philanthropy increased its scope so greatly that it became transformed into a kind of monolithic monster. Trollope was wary of patronage and philanthropy, both of which, in his estimation, augured ill for the Church, despite their long associations with it.

Trollope's wariness derived from the very bases on which patronage and philanthropy were founded. Patronage seemed to set up birthright over merit, while Trollope felt strongly that merit should always be rewarded. Who could help one's birthright? Philanthropy seemed to be motivated more to enhance the donor's sense of self-worth than that of the recipient. Who would ever wish to humble himself in order to gratify another's self-aggrandizement? A look at these principal foundations should suffice to explain why Trollope feared that the Church's apparent unconcern about these issues would ultimately hasten its own decline.

Patronage, birthright and merit

Trollope was not alone in setting up merit against birthright, and affirming that patronage seemed to favour the latter. As early as 1836, W. L. Bowles, a canon of Winchester, complained about the iniquities of ecclesiastical patronage. He was concerned not so much for himself, he said, as for his brethren, 'who have mostly large families to support'.[1] It is significant, though, that Trollope, who gained his Post Office position, albeit a lowly one, through Sir Francis Freeling's patronage, did not believe competitive examinations in the Civil Service to be useful in evaluating merit. Yet he was adamant about ecclesiastical patronage preventing merit from being rewarded in the Church. Men should be paid for their endeavour and abilities, not their family name, he believed. He cites in *Clergymen of the Church of England* (1866) the common case of a rector whose living is £1000 a year, does a quarter of the parish work and employs a curate to do three-quarters for £70 a year. He allows that this was not so reprehensible when the curate had no family to support, but now that the population was so large and the number of beneficed rectors and vicars could not be increased *pro rata*, 'the clerical babe must become a clerical old man on the same pittance'.[2] Trollope wrote *The Last Chronicle of Barset* (1867) a year after *Clergymen of the Church of England*, so it is not surprising that he should persist with the same concern in his fiction. Mr Crawley is a perpetual curate of nearly 50 years of age, earning £150 a year.[3]

No doubt Trollope decided to give Mr Crawley twice the income he accorded to the perpetual curates in English parishes in order to avoid the kind of angry response which Henry Alford, Dean of Canterbury, had made to him after the publication of his non-fictional work in 1866. Alford accused Trollope of wanting to 'tickle the public ear' by relying on 'hearsay and superficial acquaintance with facts', and stated that the lowest stipend for a curate was £80 a year, although Alford acknowledged that the curate's lot was unhappy and that the Church had to improve conditions for its clerisy. Charging Trollope with inaccuracy and suspecting his frames of reference, Alford conceded that his concerns were shared by the Church itself.[4]

To drive home his point about clerical poverty without even mentioning the word reform, Trollope made the pivotal incident in *The Last Chronicle of Barset* (1867) the supposed theft of a cheque by Mr Crawley. What reader could fail to be struck by the injustice of an erudite, conscientious clergyman, well versed in the classics and loved by his working-class parishioners, clothed in rust-coloured black, struggling in vain to feed his wife and children, while his bishop lived in a palace? The man's innocence becomes irrelevant in Trollope's suggestion that the reform of clerical payment would obviate the need for clergymen themselves to be the recipients of philanthropy. In *Clergymen of the Church of England* (1866), he argues that unless a more equitable salary structure, not based on patronage, is introduced, decent families will cease to consider the Church as a profession.[5] His unproclaimed belief, then, is that certain philanthropic reforms would not be needed if people were paid properly for their labour. He is aware that this would involve changes to the social structure, but avoids direct discussion. Trollope could never regard himself as an active reformer, for he could not bring himself to interfere in the affairs of others. Nonetheless, he hoped that his written nudges would stir the community's conscience to effect change. The charge of inaccurate figures for clerical incomes in *Clergyman of the Church of England* made Trollope sufficiently incensed to write to the *Pall Mall Gazette*'s editor to point out that his critic's figures were wrong, for they related to curates who worked 'without any other resident clergyman', whereas his own figures had referred to 'ordinary curates...whose work is done under a vicar or rector'. He denounces the Church for allowing its curates to remain in this demeaning situation 'for ten years, – for twenty years, – for life'.[6] Significantly, the *Quarterly Review* urges help for the poor on the grounds that 'poverty tempts to crime'.[7] Trollope, evidently, subscribes to this view, even though Mr Crawley is ultimately proved innocent.

The difficulty faced by Lady Lufton in *The Last Chronicle of Barset* (1867) in persuading Josiah Crawley to accept help when illness strikes his family underscores the danger of the Church relying on means outside its payment structure to enable its poor clergymen to survive. Subterfuge circumvents the fact that Mr Crawley would in no way accept money in *Framley Parsonage* (1861), so 'a bill here and there was paid, the wife assisting', and clothes for the children were placed 'surreptitiously' with gifts of food, accepted as essential for his family's health.[8] These measures may have prevented tragedy, but the psychological impact on the clergyman known to the brickmakers of Hogglestock for his own philanthropic deeds – practical involvement in clothing clubs and benefit societies, common activities among Victorian clergymen[9] – was such that he was ashamed to feel like a pauper. There is much evidence that recipients of charity generally resented help. One woman, '[a]sked by passers-by why she was washing the new flannel, . . . replied, "Why, I bin washin' the charity out on it"'.[10] Not surprisingly, in light of these secular duties expected of clergymen, Trollope devotes much narrative space to explaining Lady Lufton's deliberations as to how she can help Mr Crawley without meeting his point-blank refusal, for she realizes that '[i]t is ever so much easier to proffer kindness graciously than to receive it with grace'.[11] In this instance, Trollope intimates that the very proximity of the relationship between donor and recipient is vital for the exercise of true charity.[12] But the implication is that no clergyman should be subjected to this kind of humiliation.

A mirror image in some ways of an early prototype for Barchester's Mr Crawley appears in *The Kellys and the O'Kellys* (1848). The Irish Church rector of Ballindine, Mr Armstrong, like Mr Crawley, is the father of several children, and has a wife who has slipped from middle-class comfort into penury because of meagre clerical stipends, and becomes nothing short of a beggar. Unlike Mr Crawley, he is physically dirty and not too proud to ask Lord Ballindine for a cheque for £20 to pay 'for the emergencies of the road' to enable him to plead his superior's matrimonial case, although he 'had still a gentleman's dislike to be paid for his services. But then, Necessity – how stern she is! He literally could not have gone without it'.[13] As Trollope realized, this incident could not help but demean the rector and his office. His unstated criticism is that a clergyman should not be placed in such a penurious position as to have to ask for simple expenses and be placed in the role of suppliant. Even ten years later Trollope links mendicancy with clerical work, this time in England, in his bitter narratorial comment in *The Three Clerks* (1858) about the rarity of finding a man 'who will work ... seen begging for his bread', unless 'he be a clergyman'. His arraignment of the Church of England for not providing adequate salaries for its clergy is the most trenchant in all of his work. His ensuing remark that working men 'may generally trust to God's goodness' is his way of turning the knife in his attack on the Church.[14] Trollope knew that his readers would conclude that no institution claiming allegiance to God should have allowed its system to fail its employees so badly. His pessimism for the Church's future spurred Trollope to be as hard-hitting as possible, in the faint hope that the Church would react sensibly to community disapprobation. As Chapter 3 will show, his pessimism about the Church's payment structure, which continued throughout his writing career, was in no way alleviated by its changing recruitment policy.

Trollope believed clerical work to be worthy of being paid at its full value, rather than being paid according to birthright under the protection of patronage. The Church should perpetuate its role as dispenser of charity and not force its representatives to receive it on their own behalf. Trollope's concern for poorly paid clergymen, illustrated by his repeated comments, disclosed his belief that the Church's charitable energies should be expended more at home than abroad and that patronage did nothing to close the yawning gap between the just reward for merit and the random dice of fortunate birthright.

Motivation and origin of philanthropy

Where the impetus for patronage was secular, the impetus for philanthropy was religious. Indeed it would not be too extravagant to say that the Church was the initial patron of philanthropy. Its motivation and origin lay with the Church. Altruism, however, was not the Church's main motivation in philanthropy. One of the motives behind acts of charity, Trollope suggests in *The Warden* (1855), is the pleasure derived by the donor from the recipient's gratitude. If gratitude is not forthcoming, an act of charity may be regretted, even if the donor's desire for recognition is subconscious. As Trollope says, '[c]harity may be given with the left hand so privately that the right hand does not know it, and yet the left hand may regret to feel that it has no immediate reward'.[15] This is a biblical reference: the donor's reward is more important than the recipient's benefit. The belief was of long standing, since

Catholic charity prior to the Reformation involved the doctrine of repentance or 'poenitentia': '[t]he effect of almsgiving on the soul of the donor was theoretically more important than its effect on the body of the recipient.'[16] The motive, initially derived from religion, later became inscribed in law.[17] Trollope's emphasis on the motivation of donor satisfaction in *The Warden* is therefore of both religious and legal origin.

It is on these early links between religion and law that Trollope relies in *The Warden* (1855) for putting to his readers his dual-sided argument about charity to show the Church's dilemma. Is there any good reason why Hiram's Hospital, a centuries-old charity with sufficient investments to produce a healthy profit surplus to requirements, should disperse its profits among its almsmen who are already comfortably accommodated? Why should its patron, the Church, and its Warden, Mr Harding, not benefit? That is the Church's tacit position. But surely a charity's *raison d'être* is to help those in need? That is the community's position, instigated and articulated by the *Jupiter*. Trollope balances both claims throughout the novel. To this day the law remains helpful to Trollope's fictional case, since '[i]f . . . the purpose indicated is legally charitable, the Court is not concerned to inquire whether it is actually beneficial'; nor have legal charities always accorded with popular notions of charity.[18] Without a doubt the purpose of Hiram's Hospital was charitable, but its 'corrupt' administration (the unequal distribution of monies) was beyond the purview of the law. The Church's philanthropy, Trollope feared, would be part of its undoing, because increasing public scrutiny among social reformers would utterly discredit it.

In Trollope's era, as indeed today, there was no precise legal definition of charity; the preamble to the 1601 statute simply gave a list of charitable purposes,[19] so the legal position on what actually constituted a charity was vague. Dr Grantly in *The Warden* (1855) depends on legal loopholes like this to defend Mr Harding's ever-increasing revenues from the charity of St Cross, in contrast to the bedesmen's fixed incomes. He is delighted to learn, for instance, that 'there is a screw loose in their case', and that Mr Harding is only a 'paid' servant of the Church;[20] presumably, he cannot be held accountable for decisions made concerning the distribution of emoluments.

The ever-growing wealth of the fictional Hiram's Hospital and similar charities in Victorian society was also due to the links between religion and law.[21] A charity could enjoy manifold pecuniary advantages, since taxation privileges were granted to a legacy *'ad pias causas'*; charitable bequests took precedence over private bequests. If there were insufficient assets to satisfy the testator's charitable stipulations, 'debts were first satisfied from private rather than from charitable legacies', and if the testator's wishes could not be carried out 'in a lawful manner', the private legatee might lose his legacy to charity.[22] Not surprisingly, therefore, charities like Hiram's Hospital had become embarrassed by their riches. It was not until the nineteenth century that law and charity became less intertwined,[23] and Trollope illustrates part of this disengaging process through the quest for 'social justice' in investigations like that of John Bold and the *Jupiter* in *The Warden*. Balanced though Trollope's arguments are for both sides of the case, he doubtless hoped that the Church's inordinate pecuniary advantage over its almsmen would touch its own conscience. Its guardianship of the wealthy legacy, whereby it augmented its wealth to the apparent disadvantage of its poor dependants, did not enhance its public image. On the one hand, the Church looked mean because many of its poorly paid clerics had to receive charity; on the other hand, the Church looked greedy, because its own charitable organisations were viewed as not dispensing their emoluments evenly.

Linked to the growing separation between law and charity was another change in the nineteenth century in the competition between religious and secular philanthropic societies. The primary motivation for a religious charity was for a 'theological end'; that of secular foundations was for the relief of a physical or social ill.[24] While Trollope does not directly touch upon secular philanthropy, he shows that motives for charity can spring from secular rather than religious causes, even when the philanthropist is a clergyman. And this, too, acts as a warning to the Church.

For instance, Trollope hints that a hidden motive behind philanthropic generosity can be the donor's desire to appear attractive to a recipient of the opposite sex. When the donor is a vicar and the recipient a fallen woman the motive remains invisible to both donor and recipient, but obvious to the world at large. Mr Fenwick's help to Carry Brattle in *The Vicar of Bullhampton* (1870),[25] despite his wife's assertion that ' "[s]he should be put into a reformatory" ', seems genuine to the vicar and his errant parishioner, but imprudent to his wife and downright suspect to his community. The narrator speculates that the vicar would have been better able to execute his duty 'had some harsher feeling towards the sinner been mixed with his charity'.[26] Similarly, Dr Wortle, the reverend headmaster in *Dr Wortle's School* (1880), invites newspaper scorn by championing the bigamous Mrs Peacocke. The newspaper labels his nocturnal visits during Mr Peacocke's absence '"amo" in the cool of the evening', and there is speculation whether the reverend doctor would have been so willing to find 'shelter for [Mr Stantiloup or Sir Samuel Griffin] in their ignominy and trouble' had they been found to have 'prior wives'.[27] The implication is that the vicar would not have been so generous had the woman been less attractive.

In both examples Trollope knew that it was the practice for women in more fortunate circumstances to come to the aid of their 'castaway' sisters, and that the vicar is acting out of line. Several influential women had involved themselves in penitentiary and reformatory work, which was on the increase in the latter half of the nineteenth century.[28] Trollope's depiction of clerical men carrying out this task was bound to strike a note of warning, for clerics interested in this kind of charitable work tended to act through institutions, referred to by Mrs Fenwick. Hamilton, in his time as bishop, had helped to found a penitentiary for fallen girls in his diocese of Salisbury.[29] But Gladstone, with whom Trollope was acquainted, had attracted some notoriety through his rescuing of fallen women. His wife, Catherine Gladstone, also played a role in the reclamation of prostitutes in her establishment of a women's refuge in Paddington, and Trollope would have known of this. Trollope, by having vicars help fallen women in a private capacity, is drawing attention to their possible secular motives as well as to the salacious interpretation which will be made by the community. Public scorn, Trollope implied, could relabel one of the Church's so-called virtues as one of its vices.

Never one to overplay a point, Trollope moves throughout his fiction to illustrate the unintended consequences of originally good intentions. The Church was not alone in promoting philanthropy; nor was it alone in its patronage of philanthropy. Its influence was broadly scattered over its congregations, but the confusion of the theological and the secular often led to the predominance of the secular. Human nature seemed to dictate this. Trollope was especially suspicious of the motivations behind corporate charitable societies, which were initiated by members of the Church's congregations in the spurious belief that they were following the Church's teaching. As opposed to the altruistic attempts of the heroine to provide private philanthropy for her brother's family, it is the subscribers' veritable need for social advancement that prompts the Negro Soldiers' Orphan Bazaar in *Miss Mackenzie* (1865). The august names connected with its organization read like a 'Who's Who' of London society in its 'list of lady patronesses which included some duchesses, one marchioness, and half the countesses in London ... It was even rumoured that a certain very distinguished person would have shown herself behind a stall, had not a certain other more distinguished person expressed an objection'.[30] The bazaar is an excuse for social-climbing and acts as a vehicle for fulfilling 'the love of power' that motivated so many organizers of charities.[31] Social advancement and power are obviously linked, and Trollope equates both motivations with entertainments posing as charity events. His article on Ladies' Bazaars in the *Pall Mall Gazette*, a year after the publication of *Miss Mackenzie*, indicates that his views on collective motivation remained unchanged.[32] An anonymous article *not* written by Trollope in the same journal suggests that the novelist was not unique in holding these pessimistic views.[33]

In Trollope's socially conservative view, the proliferation of philanthropic societies was dangerous because they tended to intervene as substitutes in roles which were better handled by the extended family. They, perhaps unwittingly, undermined both the traditional function of the family as a safety net for relatives and weakened the ideal of personal responsibility. Private charity targeted those genuinely in distress; the scatter-gun approach of corporate charitable institutions was likely to be founded more on middle-class fears of the poor than on an altruistic sympathy for the distressed and unfortunate.

Equally reprehensible for him was the motive of hatred which sometimes deprived relatives of their inheritance in favour of a charity, simply because the deceased had quarrelled with them, even if the Church became the beneficiary. Brooke Burgess, a clerk from the office of the Ecclesiastical Commissioners in London and the recognized heir to Jemima Stanbury's fortune, speculates in *He Knew He Was Right* (1869) – a tale depicting irrationality of grotesque proportions – that Miss Stanbury, out of spite, might spurn her kith and kin in her will and leave her money to a hospital. He speaks of this as a common occurrence in an old lady who hates everybody and imagines that 'people around her are all thinking of her money', so decides to 'indulge herself in a little bit of revenge, and solace herself with large-handed-charity'. Trollope strongly disapproves of revenge disguised as philanthropy, not only in Hugh Stanbury's spirited defence of his aunt, but also in Brooke Burgess's revelatory rejoinder: ' "How else did the Church get the estates, of which we are now distributing so bountifully some of the last remnants down at our office?" ' This prediction, based on a decades-old quarrel, proves unfounded when Jemima Stanbury confesses that she ' "would wish that all animosities might be buried" ' between her and Brooke Burgess's kinsman Barty Burgess.[34] But Trollope's point has been made. Devout though he was, Trollope believed family to be more important than the Church; charity should be given to relatives in due order of blood ties before it was extended beyond hearth and home.

Another motivation for philanthropy for which Trollope had no respect was that propelled by sectarian interests. He strongly disapproved of competition among Christian denominations to help others merely to swell the congregation or score points against each other. The potato famine of Ireland in the 1840s and the philanthropic measures taken to alleviate the situation dominate the narrative of *Castle Richmond* (1860), which counterpoises the tragedy of Ireland with a serpentine tale of threatened ruin for a landowning family involving love and loss, bigamy and blackmail. Against an almost biblical backdrop of famine (Trollope actually refers to pestilence and plague), two young cousins, one of wealthy, the other of modest means, determine to marry the same young woman, only to have their fortunes temporarily reversed by the former's estate being inherited by the latter because of an alleged bigamous marriage. When the charge is proved false, the philanthropic magnanimity of the one cousin, equalled by the noble pride of the other, prevents an embarrassing situation, but not misery for the rejected lover. The rivalry between the cousins for the hand of the young woman emulates the rivalry between the Roman Catholic and Protestant clergy for the souls of the poor. Although they manage eventually to work together as a relief team, the Roman Catholic priest, Father Bernard, suspects '[w]hat he called the "souping" system of the Protestant clergyman', whereby, he was convinced, Mr Townsend used the lure of food to encourage people 'to leave their faith'. Trollope despairingly describes the hatred between the two men, but adds that 'neither of them were [*sic*] bad men'. Most revealing of all are the rival sectarian intentions and the compromises reached. The Roman Catholic priests favour giving the dole to the poor; the Protestant clergy prefer the poor to work for it. Levelling Ballydahan hill by transporting wheelbarrows of dirt from top to bottom is the work-for-the-dole scheme finally devised by the relief committee. The Protestant clergy want the poor to be paid in food; the Roman Catholic priests want them paid in money. The project begins and the men receive money, despite Protestant suspicions that '[t]he priest will get a penny out of every shilling'. Doomed from the start, owing to the inexperience of the young English engineer and of the men with regard to regular labour, the project made the roads impassable with slimy mud, '[b]ut the great object was gained; the men were fed, and were not fed by charity'. For all their buried differences, the churchmen of opposing doctrines are less effective than the landowning gentry who, even in the face of their own ruin, manage to build a mill to grind the donated Indian corn properly for the poor. It is the active competition between the clergy of both denominations, rather than their sectarian motives, that Trollope finds difficult to reconcile amid the plight of a starving population, thousands of whom became 'famished living skeletons',[35] prior to perishing prematurely.

In Trollope's descriptions of a wide range of motivations underpinning the charitable impulse, he distinguishes between private and corporate philanthropy, but shows that individual motivations can vary from the purely altruistic to the self-serving, however the charity is distributed or organized. If a human being was in need of financial assistance, Trollope believed that a close relative was better placed than any other individual or organization to assess the kind of aid needed and, aside from kinship quarrels, was likely to be motivated by genuine concern. He was supportive of the Church setting an example of Christian charity, but not of the Church intervening unnecessarily, whether swayed by altruism or by its own greed to augment its potentially 'charitable' coffers. Instead it should set an example by precluding the need for philanthropy among its own dependants – thereby leaving itself wide open to possible charges of hypocrisy – and begin its charity at home through an improved payment structure for its clergymen, rather than continuing its haphazard, unequal practice of patronage. This strong conviction, expressed with increasing doubt as to whether the Church was likely to listen, is paramount throughout Trollope's oeuvre, and can best be appreciated by examining the different kinds of ecclesiastical patronage and philanthropy manifest in his writing.

The varieties of ecclesiastical patronage

Trollope referred in his novels to four kinds of church patronage: patronage in the gift of private individuals; patronage in the gift of collegiate bodies; patronage in the gift of bishops and other ecclesiastical dignitaries; and patronage in the gift of the Crown.[36] His detailed references to ecclesiastical patronage convey his knowledge of this practice and his interest in its effect on donors and recipients. As far as he was concerned, the practice denigrated merit, inevitably produced an underclass of poor clergy dependent on the philanthropy of others and, as a result, imperilled the Church. He firmly believed ecclesiastical patronage to be an outmoded custom, and he returned to this theme several times, desperate for the Church to attend to him.

Patronage in the gift of private individuals

Ecclesiastical patronage was often in the hands of private citizens having no connection with the Church. Trollope's view of private patronage, although mildly expressed, was not positive. There is a dismissive mention in 'Christmas Day at Kirkby Cottage' (1870) that, had not young Maurice Archer, with an Oxford degree 'not high enough to confer distinction', 'positively refused to be ordained', he would have had a living when his 70-year-old cousin died.[37] Archer's later kind gift of Christmas fare to a poor widow's family (possibly to help woo the girl he loves) in no way annuls Trollope's alluded disapproval of the ease with which young men, with no interest in the Church, could obtain livings from private individuals.

Patronage in the gift of private individuals had been common for a number of centuries and was a direct result of the Reformation and the sale of church lands to laymen. The right to present livings had consequently been taken, in part, out of ecclesiastical hands. By the nineteenth century this category was the largest form of patronage and still increasing, making up half of the total benefices.[38] From the middle of the nineteenth century until about 1878, the number of patron-incumbents rose, particularly in the rural counties extending from Devon to Lincolnshire and East Anglia. These incumbent patrons purchased their own livings, rather than inheriting them. This did not prevent the patron from passing on his living from one generation to the next in order to ensure that family members could remain within the clerical profession, more securely in fact than in any other profession.[39] The opportunity for such a legacy is apparent in Trollope's fiction. Had Maurice Archer in 'Christmas Day at Kirkby Cottage' decided to become ordained, he would have inherited, not bought, his cousin's living, for, Trollope carefully remarks, the living 'would be at his disposal'.[40]

By raising the question of the credentials of private individuals having the right to present livings in 'The Lady of Launay' (1878), Trollope queries both the lay patron's judgement and the consequences of that judgement, whereby a young man could supersede more experienced and more worthy candidates. The Rev. Alexander Morrison was 'an excellent young man; but it may be doubted whether the patronage by which he was put into the living of Budcombe at an early age, over the head of many senior curates, had been exercised with sound clerical motives'. The motive of the lay patroness, Mrs Miles, Trollope disapprovingly notes, was to provide 'a husband for Bessy ... who ... might probably make her happy'.[41] Bessy was an orphan adopted by Mrs Miles.

The comedy lies in the young man's acceptance of his living and Bessy's acceptance, not of the clergyman's marital proposal, but of that of Mrs Miles's own son. Comedy notwithstanding, Trollope's repudiation of lay patronage is abundantly clear.

More oblique is Trollope's comment on lay patronage in *An Old Man's Love* (1884). The Rev. Montagu Blake could confidently anticipate receiving the living of Little Alresford from the squire 'who, being patron of the living, might probably bestow it on him', especially as the living 'was worth only £250', a pound for each of the parishioners, among whom there was not one Dissenter and 'as pretty a little parsonage as could be found in England'. Blake's contentment with the modest living is sealed by his private fortune of £300 per year and an income of £5000 belonging to his fiancée, 'the daughter of one of the prebendaries of Winchester'. Blake is presented as an over-confident young man, whose high opinion of himself as 'the happiest young man in Hampshire' does not coincide with that of the other characters, who certify him variously as 'that ass Blake', 'the most conceited young man I ever came across' and 'a general idiot', whose ordination could probably not have been 'refused' by a bishop on that account alone. His former Oxford friend calculates that, 'of all the fools who were ever turned out in the world to earn their own bread, he is the most utterly foolish', yet 'he will perform the high work of a clergyman of the Church of England indifferently well'.[42] Although Blake possesses redeeming features, as does every Trollopian character, he in no way merits his life of ease. Patronage, Trollope believed, obviated the need for personal endeavour, and to have this need removed in one's youth was wrong.[43] Nor did it help the Church.

Lay patronage in nineteenth-century society became increasingly associated with commercialism and simony, with patronage treated as a form of property. Simony was the buying and selling of livings. Livings were 'bought and sold, and the newspapers often contained advertisements extolling the trout stream and salubrious climate of a particular benefice the nomination to which was up for auction'. Despite the fact that simony was illegal, clergymen could overcome this by having a relative, friend or agent nominate him to a benefice. This abuse incensed the Liberation Society, although patronage reform 'which was sensitive to all infringements on the rights of property', particularly of the kind belonging to peers, failed repeatedly in the House of Lords during Trollope's lifetime.[44] The Liberation Society was founded by Dissenters who, not surprisingly, loathed ecclesiastical patronage. The militant Dissenters, headed by Edward Miall, founded in 1844 the Society for the Liberation of Religion from State Patronage and Control, which became known as the Liberation Society.

Simony was such a delicate subject that Trollope felt compelled to review this process by slightly circumspect means, and this he does in *The American Senator* (1877). Cleverly taking a leaf out of his mother's book, *Domestic Manners of the Americans* (1832), in which she criticizes American habits and mores, and turning the leaf on its reverse side, Trollope has an American, Senator Gotobed, criticize English practices and institutions. In spite of his official status forming the novel's title, the senator seems to float on the periphery of two narratives involving matrimonial aspirations: one a traditional halting romance; the other a decadent aristocratic hunt for a husband who really is a lord and master. The former ends happily, the latter unsuccessfully for the lady, who fails to snare her 'fox' Lord Rufford, aptly named and hair-coloured though he is. While matrimonial machinations and lawsuits absorb the other characters, nothing diverts the senator from his caustic analysis of English traditions. In the same way as the Americans felt stung by Frances Trollope's sharp comments, the fictional English characters in *The American Senator* are infuriated by Senator Gotobed's insensitive remarks. Trollope, through the mediation of a gauche 'foreigner', is able to condemn ecclesiastical patronage much more pointedly than he could otherwise have done had the condemnation emanated from another English character or from the narrator. More subtle a writer than his mother, Trollope takes a further step – typical of his narrative method. He makes the perpetrator of the 'crime' of simony much more likeable than the critic. Parson Mainwaring was the guilty recipient of simony, for his living 'had been bought for him with his wife's money during the incumbency of an old gentleman of seventy-eight'. Yet the reader cannot help but sympathize with Mainwaring who, having invited Senator Gotobed to a special dinner with the best food and wine, waits with baited breath while the senator asks 'pressing questions as to church patronage', and, on gleaning the details of his host's good fortune, tactlessly conjectures that '[t]hese kinds of things, I believe, can be bought and sold in the market'. Mr Gotobed expresses surprise in a letter to a fellow countryman that his fellow guests as well as his host have been angered by his bluntness; their anger, he judged, was 'unreasonable'. His subsequent public criticism of British institutions includes Church patronage in his barrage of complaints. When his lecture launches into an attack on the army, the police are brought in to control the crowd, and yet, Trollope deliberately tells us, the audience let his strong censure of the Church pass, silently agreeing with him, since '[i]t is not often that the British public is angered by abuse of the Church'.[45] However ill-mannered and ill-timed the Senator's comments on the Church are, Trollope leaves the reader with the final impression that the country as a whole is impatient for church reform, but that the clerical beneficiaries of patronage are not to be blamed personally. He did not approve of *ad hominem* attacks where the issue at stake was a fault in the system, but nor was he hopeful in the late 1870s that the system would change.

Patronage in the gift of collegiate bodies

Patronage was often a collective responsibility. Trollope seemed ambivalent about this kind of patronage, and two of his novels illustrate opposing viewpoints. A corporate decision was not necessarily any more efficacious than a personal one, and there was a deal of difference between the principle of accepting clergymen appointed by a collegiate body and the fact of living with that choice, as is demonstrated in *The Small House at Allington* (1864), the name of which he took from family annals. Indeed Trollope's choice of Allington for his novel might have been a veiled reminder in itself of the wrongs of ecclesiastical patronage.[46] Allington is in the gift of the collegiate body of King's College, Cambridge, and the Dale family, while 'steady supporters of the Church [and] graciously receiving into their parish such new vicars' as the college wished to appoint, were so 'imperious' to their own families and 'hard' on their tenants that they had forever perpetuated 'unpronounced warfare against the clergyman' appointed; the result was that 'the intercourse between the lay family and the clerical had seldom been in all respects pleasant'.[47] Having the choice of parson removed from all personal considerations could provoke prejudice in itself. At the same time, a corporate decision could liberate individuals from difficult interpersonal situations. The eponymous hero's benefice in *The Vicar of Bullhampton* (1870) is in the gift of a collegiate body, St John's College, Oxford. This fact saves Mr Frank Fenwick and the Established Church from being eclipsed by the encroachment of the Methodist Chapel. Mr Fenwick is informed by his barrister brother-in-law, Mr Quickenham, that it is his duty to protect the glebe land on which the Chapel has been built, for the glebe 'was only given to him in trust', and that he was 'bound to protect it as such, on behalf of [his] successors, and of the patrons of the living'. The chapel's continued existence would mean that the vicar's successor would be left with the task of demolishing it.[48] In this instance Trollope acknowledged the advantages of collegiate patronage over private patronage, since its impersonal nature pre-empted the embarrassment of individual sanctions.[49] The two contrasting situations in these novels underscore Trollope's ambivalence as to whether collegial patronage was the lesser of the two evils of corporate and lay patronage. On the one hand, corporate patronage could upset the traditionally cordial relations between squire and clerical incumbent which lay patronage could avoid; after all, lay patronage often resided with the squire. On the other hand, corporate patronage could abrogate an awkward duty for a clergyman wishing to relieve himself of the burden of personal responsibility.

Patronage in the gift of bishops and other ecclesiastical dignitaries

Trollope laments in *Clergymen of the Church of England* (1866) that patronage remains 'the private property of the bishop', and he speaks of this as having 'much of the sweet mediaeval flavour of old English corruption'.[50] Episcopal patronage, partly as a consequence of the subdivision of parishes, did in fact double during this century and has been seen as an improvement on lay patronage, for bishops were able to use patronage to promote deserving diocesan clergymen.[51] Howley had over one hundred livings at his disposal as Bishop of London (1813–28) and, as Archbishop of Canterbury (1828–48), had a further fifty.[52] Both lay and episcopal patronage, therefore, multiplied in this period.

Yet this increase in episcopal patronage occurred at the same time as 'Old Corruption' in general declined dramatically, following the 1832 Reform Act and subsequent Whig decade of reform.[53] Trollope's Whig friend, Sydney Smith, revealed to Bishop Blomfield (1786–1857) of London that this may have been due to the church hierarchy's reluctance to surrender its patronage privileges. He praised the bishop's act of dividing livings to lessen the scandal of pluralities and thereby reduce bad feelings between high and low church extremists, but reminded Blomfield that the policy could be taken further. Bishops, he noted, seemed reluctant to give away 'their own superior emoluments to the improvement of smaller Bishoprics'. Smith was a noted wit and this may have been a joke, for he conceded that the Church did not possess 'enough of property... to pay each man a decent competence; they must therefore be paid by a lottery of Preferment, some more, some less'.[54] It has to be remembered that Smith's own very successful career was not due solely to his unquestionable talents. He had his influential patrons to thank: the Archbishop of Canterbury, who presented him to the living of Worth with an income of £623 a year, and William IV, who presented him to the prebendal stall of Mora in 1831 until his death. Smith was a man 'driven by high principle... very ambitious

... Complete lack of vanity coexisted with enormous pride'.[55] Moreover, he was happy for his daughter to marry a clergyman, and sought preferment from Rev. Dr Charles Wordsworth for his son, who wished for a place at a Cambridge college.[56] Notwithstanding these paradoxes, Smith felt the same way as Trollope, and was perturbed about the Church's treatment of its clergy, for it subverted the Church's community role as principal philanthropist.

Despite his hostile feelings on preferment, Trollope does reveal ambivalence to radical change. He warns the Church, through his favourite fictional characters, not to submit to pressure by resorting to extreme measures. In *The Warden* (1855), Dr Grantly advises Mr Harding, his father-in-law, not to surrender the preferment from his bishop, for in acting on his conscience, he would 'inflict a desperate blow on' his 'brother clergymen', and would encourage 'every cantankerous dissenter in England to make a similar charge against some source of clerical revenue', thereby failing the Church, which, if 'so deserted ... must fall to the ground altogether'.[57] Trollope, therefore, clearly sees changes in preferment as a threat to the Church. Disliking patronage, he is nonetheless concerned that its sudden cessation could strengthen the Dissenters' cause at the expense of the Church's survival.

Gaskell shared Trollope's disdain of patronage and also voiced this through her characters. Mr Hale's small living at Helstone in *North and South* (1855), published in the same year as *The Warden*, had not been augmented or exchanged by his bishop in 20 years, yet his wife knew that he was 'more learned' than Mr Hume and 'a better parish priest' than Mr Houldsworth, to both of whom the bishop had given preferment. There is, of course, the additional problem that Mr Hale decides that he cannot accept the Thirty-Nine Articles, so putting himself forward for promotion would have been impossible. Nonetheless, Gaskell has Dixon, a servant to the Hales, declare that '[m]any a one who never reads nor thinks either, gets to be Rector, and Dean',[58] implying that patronage was not conferred on merit, but predilection. Gaskell felt as strongly as Trollope about the iniquities of preferential treatment through patronage.

Patronage in the gift of the Crown

Trollope is equally critical of royal patronage and his laconic checklist of ways and means of becoming a bishop in *Clergymen of the Church of England* (1866) includes being 'a charmer of the royal ear', as well as marrying a bishop's daughter, editing a Greek play, and becoming a tutor to a noble pupil, while quickly adopting 'the political bias of the pupil's father'.[59] Trollope particularly disliked royal patronage because it promoted obsequiousness, sycophancy and fawning, qualities which impeded independence of thought and action. In reality, royal patronage was divided between the Crown and the ministry. The state, in this case, was the Church's direct patron, as one would expect of an established church bearing the name of its nation state and having the monarch as its head. Dr Proudie, for example, a Whig bishop appointed by a Whig ministry, almost certainly achieved his pre-eminence because he lived in an age where 'high church principles... were no longer to be surest claims to promotion'.[60] Trollope's lack of respect for Dr Proudie's accommodating personality, which helped him to win royal patronage, is manifest throughout the Barchester series.

Trollope attributes the attenuation of high church supremacy in the 1830s to one statesman, presumably Lord Melbourne, but for later decades far more influence has been accorded to Queen Victoria than to either Disraeli or Gladstone, since Victoria's 'female side of the question' mostly seemed to prevail.[61] She could be *very* fickle; although she publicly favoured the broad church, she privately preferred the Evangelical to the high church. In *Barchester Towers* (1857) not only is an Evangelical cleric made bishop, but also, through indirect royal patronage, the high church Mr Arabin is promoted to the position of Dean, rather than the disappointed Evangelical Mr Slope. Mr Arabin's patron, Dr Gwynne, through his own web of patronage, succeeded in his protégé's name being mentioned at Windsor, and thus secured for him the coveted position.[62] Mr Arabin seems amiable, but Trollope pointedly refers to his constant travelling. Royal patronage, according to Trollope, is no more efficacious than any other church patronage. Every one of these categories of church patronage in Trollope's fiction seems defective in some way, indicating his lack of faith in this means of selection and promotion. But he never suggested a convincing alternative.

The varieties of philanthropy

Trollope was as aware of the varieties of philanthropy as he was of the varieties of ecclesiastical patronage, and he featured both private and institutional philanthropy in his works. On balance, Trollope favoured private over corporate charity, mainly because the former was more likely to result from genuine Christian benevolence and an informed knowledge of the recipient. For Trollope, the face-to-face relationship of personal philanthropy gave it a superior moral dimension over organized charitable exertions, which could be indiscriminate, potentially demoralizing for the recipient and open to fraud, as well as threatening to undermine the duties and responsibilities of the family. Trollope's approach to philanthropy was in fact extremely complex and, while he constantly engaged with the subject, he rarely mentioned it by name. A compassionate man, he recognized the need for philanthropy, but he also recognized one essential ingredient: the retention of human dignity. The degree to which this ingredient could be destroyed through either the denial or the imposition of philanthropy primarily coloured Trollope's attitude.

Philanthropic institutions

Hiram's Hospital is one of the most famous charitable institutions in English literature. For Trollope, it represented some of the best features of the ancient charitable hospitals, almshouses and endowed schools which were established after the dissolution of the monasteries had left the question of charitable provision mainly in the hands of private individuals. It was small; it was local; and it allowed the possibility of intimate, though hierarchical, social relations between the charity's officers and its beneficiaries.[63] Its longevity, too, appealed to Trollope: as for another social conservative, Edmund Burke, before him, the age of an institution was confirming evidence of its usefulness.[64] In short, Hiram's Hospital – partly based on Winchester's St Cross Hospital, founded by Henri de Blois in 1160 – was a relic of a more paternalistic age, a sitting target for the new reform ideologists.

Trollope's philanthropic ideal is perhaps best shown in the closeness between Mr Harding and his bedesmen in *The Warden* (1855). Harding's friendship adds greatly to the bedesmen's well-being; with the cessation of the 'abuse' of the charity, this social nexus is destroyed. The grandiose plans to have provision 'extended to the fair sex', to have a matron and to have schools attached for the poorest of the children of the poor' do not all come to fruition.[65] Nonetheless the bedesmen gain more in monetary terms and receive more Church 'services' under the wardenship of Mr Quiverful, but they realize that their loss is greater than their gain. The more the Church concentrated on supplying material wants in its philanthropy, Trollope hints, the less it actually improved the human lot.

Trollope was by no means the only novelist of his generation to be inspired by St Cross. Indeed, his positive portrayal of the hospital may have encouraged Gaskell to incorporate it as the Hospital of St Sepulchre in *Sylvia's Lovers* (1863), when Philip Hepburn, a disfigured marine, is given the wayfarer's dole and offered a position as bedesman. Later, in memory of him, Hester Rose founds an almshouse in Northumberland for poor disabled sailors and soldiers.[66] Unlike Trollope, Gaskell avoids any possibility of malversation and dwells only on the hospital's benefits.

Similarly inspired was Mrs Oliphant's defence in *Phoebe Junior* (1876) of Reginald May's appointment as warden to the College, where six old men are housed, fed and clothed. Its detailed description with its 'picturesque old building' closely resembles St Cross Hospital, and Horace Northcote's attack on the Church's encouragement of 'idle pauperism' in Carlingford's branch of the Disestablishment Society presupposes a knowledge of Trollope's *The Warden* (1855) for full comprehension.[67]

St Cross appealed to Gaskell and Oliphant for the same reasons that it attracted Trollope; for its 'quaintness', its paternalism and its resonance of a bygone age, even though charges of charitable abuse punctuated its long history.[68] As an institution, however, it was seen to be obsolete in the new age of large, impersonal charitable enterprises. These Trollope found many reasons to despise. Missions, at home or abroad, particularly provoked his irritation; he saw them as a waste of resources. In *Framley Parsonage* (1861) he mocks Mr Harold Smith's charity lecture in aid of the missions in 'Sarawak, Labuan, New Guinea and the Solomon Islands' by emphasizing the man's obsessiveness and the transient nature of his obsession: 'As is the case with all men labouring under temporary specialities, he for the time had faith in nothing else, and was not content that any one near him should have any other faith.'[69] Missionary work often involved secular as well as spiritual objectives, for the missionaries' secondary purpose was to bring Victorian civilization to the world.[70] Certainly, Trollope doubted the efficacy of missionary work and philanthropy in *South Africa* (1878), remarking that '[o]ne is tempted sometimes to say that nothing is done by religion and very little by philanthropy'. He believed, instead, that 'European habits', like working for money at the Kimberley mine, for example, would 'bring about religion' and that the 4000 Africans working there were 'growing Christians'.[71]

Similarly, Trollope's ironic conclusion in *Miss Mackenzie* (1865) sums up his scepticism as to the success of the Negro Soldiers' Orphan Bazaar, for its 'expenditure in gloves and muslin had been considerable', but its 'returns ... had been very small'. In short, the philanthropic enterprise had made 'more than eight hundred pounds ... but whether any orphans of any negro soldiers were ever the better for the money I am not able to say'.[72]

While most denominations were engaged in missions overseas, the Evangelicals added home missions to their list of philanthropic institutions. Strangely, these missions proliferated at a time when, according to the most recent calculations, the proportion of paupers in England and Wales was falling, from 8–9 per cent in 1841–2, to 4–5 per cent in 1850 and to only 2½ per cent by 1900.[73] Others besides Trollope wondered why such an effort was necessary. William O'Hanlon, in his examination of medical charities, asked whether philanthropic measures did 'the recipients more harm than good'.[74] In 1869 the *Quarterly Review* expressed anxiety over the £7 to £8 million per annum being spent on charitable activities. Per capita, it was enough to 'gild poverty with comfort'. Apparently, however, it was having no effect on what was seen erroneously to be an increase in poverty: 'pauperism increases yet faster than either charity or wealth.'[75]

O'Hanlon had suggested that 'abuses' were partly responsible for the ineffectiveness of the charitable medical societies; modern commentators, although agreeing in part with him, have pointed more to boardroom inefficiency than to corruption as the main cause of waste. It now appears that '[m]ost charities were honest and well intentioned, but anomalous and inefficient';[76] if charities had spent less on public buildings, relief for the poor would have been greatly augmented.[77] Perhaps the societies took on too great a task, as a cautionary analogy implies: 'The Philanthropist is like the ingenuous youth who does not recognise the distance immensely stretching between purpose and achievement.'[78] Trollope, for his part, also seemed more inclined to charge philanthropic institutions with inefficiency than with abuse. For that reason alone he had strong grounds for his pessimistic view of philanthropy.

If the great Evangelical enterprise was not successful, it may be attributed primarily to the Evangelicals' self-defeating conviction that poverty was in part the consequence of the poor's lack of interest in religion. Poverty, they thought, was best attacked with a mixture of soup and sermons. In London, the Evangelicals inaugurated a home mission in the form of sermons at Exeter Hall, attracting many with the prospect of simple refreshments. The *Pall Mall Gazette* asked Trollope to report on the sermons, but he loathed the experience, went only once and pointedly called his report, 'The Zulu in London' (1865). His title linked missions at home with those abroad, and he drew attention to their fruitlessness, for the 'Zulu' is horrified by the prohibition of any discussion and the assumption that the ladies present were 'ignorant'.[79] The *Quarterly Review* described the city mission in London as 'an invasion of the parochial system', confirming the simplistic message offered as brooking no discussion and assuming a high degree of ignorance.[80] An article in the same journal explains that the Exeter Hall sermons in particular and home missions in general conflicted with the parochial system's main rationale, the preservation of traditional relations 'between the incumbent and his parish'.[81] The *Quarterly Review*, of course, was the major Tory anti-reforming journal of the day. It is significant that its main defence of the status quo and its criticism of modern philanthropy corresponded closely with Trollope's own concern that missions both at home and abroad tore asunder the close social attachment that almsgiving had traditionally created between donor and recipient.

The provinces did not resort to the tactics of Exeter Hall, but relied on the proliferation of Sunday schools for children and Dorcas meetings for women to provide philanthropy through organized outlets. As Trollope illustrates in *Barchester Towers* (1857) and *Rachel Ray* (1863), both Sunday schools and Dorcas societies were run primarily by the Evangelical party. Sunday schools had actually been a product of the Enlightenment, and had been a 'secular activity designed to teach reading and writing to children' but they very soon attracted the attention of the first generation of Evangelicals, and by the time that Trollope was writing, they had turned this institution into its own kind of 'nursery'.[82] Sunday schools were a replacement for charity schools and their original educative role soon diminished in importance. Instead, they became a means of 'reforming the behavior of the lower orders and implanting in them a reverence for the Christian religion'. They were also an effective way of keeping children off the streets, where they made 'the Sabbath hideous for others'.[83] The controlling role of Sunday schools over the children of the poor was admitted by Sarah Trimmer, a contemporary Evangelical.[84] Like Sunday schools, Dorcas societies seemed to be institutions of instruction. 'Dorcas Discipline' in *Rachel Ray* (1863) is 'inflicted daily' by the local Dorcas society's founder and patron on her younger sister, the heroine of the title, for 'standing under the elms with a young man'. The 'Dorcas view of . . . virtue' extended beyond 'works of charity' to life in general and to the female Ray family in particular, under the dominion of the elder widowed daughter, who had approached 'that stage of [Dorcas] discipline at which ashes become pleasant eating, and sackcloth is grateful to the skin', for '[f]ine raiment and dainty food tempted her not at all', but whose 'giving in charity was her luxury'.[85] These societies did not just involve charity work, but also provided opportunities for the Scriptures to be read to poor women at all-female gatherings, during which tea and simple comestibles were served.[86] Dorcas meetings also served a philanthropic purpose, for those assembled would make clothes for the poor.[87]

Trollope was equally dismissive of both institutions. He relies on Mrs Proudie's strident voice to betray his distrust of Sunday Schools in *Barchester Towers* (1857). It seems to be the coercive nature of the enterprise which annoys Trollope the most. Mrs Proudie's assertion to the visiting Master of Lazarus, in the middle of a light-hearted festivity, that children '[o]n weekdays... belong to their parents, but on Sundays they ought to belong to the clergyman', followed by her raised finger, was bound, Trollope knew, to raise the hackles of his readership.[88] Mr Harding's reluctance and Mr Quiverful's willingness to add Sunday school to the duties of warden to 12 old men mock the zeal and effectiveness of this enterprise. Just as corrective and useless, Trollope suggests, are Dorcas societies. According to Rachel Ray's reaction, '[t]he Dorcas meeting had become distasteful to her because the women were vulgar', having, under its influence and that of her sister's, 'learned to think that the world was all either ascetic or reprobate', but never having succumbed totally to its 'asceticisms', even though 'she had half believed herself to be wrong in avoiding the work and the vulgarity together'.[89] What Trollope appears not to have noticed, although it would have supported his opinions about ulterior and self-serving motives behind much philanthropic activity, was that 'charity needlework acted as a mischievous competition to force down women's wages'.[90] Rather than finding a solution to poverty, or even merely seeking to alleviate its worst features, the Dorcas enterprise tended to spread poverty more thinly among a larger number of families.

Private philanthropy

There is no doubt that Trollope believed private philanthropy to be preferable to institutionalized philanthropy, but he does not claim private philanthropy to be necessarily more successful, especially if the recipient is a clergyman. He demonstrates, though, that the proximity of the donor to the recipient enables the donor to gauge how, when and what to give. A philanthropic act is only successful, Trollope reveals, if the recipient willingly accepts the gift. In *Dr Thorne* (1858), Mary Thorne's upbringing, provided by her uncle, Doctor Thorne, and her social and music education, given by Lady Arabella, constitute successful acts of private philanthropy and examples of *noblesse oblige*, because Mary Thorne is happy to receive Doctor Thorne's benevolence. For his part, he determined to 'be father to her and mother to her'. He promised the child's mother, who had been seduced by his now deceased brother, that '"[o]f what bread I eat, she shall eat; of what cup I drink, she shall drink"'. Yet the duty was all pleasure for when, after being 'kept at a farm-house till she was six' and at a 'school at Bath' for a further six years, Mary came 'home' to Greshamsbury, 'the doctor was like a child in his glee'. Nor did the novelty of having her as part of his life wither or fade away. On being asked to share her with her other uncle, the doctor retorts: '"She lives with me, and belongs to me, and is as my daughter".' For Mary's part, the doctor's views on their relationship are more than accurate. When she learns that she is heiress to a fortune, not 'a nameless pauper', and can therefore marry the aristocratic but impecunious Frank Gresham, she wonders how she can repay 'that uncle of hers, who had been more loving to her than any father!'[91] Doctor Thorne's adoption of his niece was a fictional replication of Trollope's own philanthropy. He and his wife Rose raised three nieces as daughters after their mothers' deaths. These were Edith Tilley, Beatrice Trollope and Florence Bland. Edith Tilley was the daughter of Trollope's beloved sister, Cecilia. Beatrice Trollope was the daughter of Trollope's brother Tom, and Florence Bland was the daughter of Rose's sister Isabella.[92] Florence became Trollope's amanuensis in the late 1870s until his death, and was Rose's companion until she predeceased the old lady.

Adoption of this familial kind appears again in *Ralph the Heir* (1871) and seems to represent Trollope's indictment of the alternative institutional care for orphans, often under the auspices of the Church, when extended family is available to help. The attendant problems of private adoption, as well as its advantages, are not brushed lightly aside, however. Sir Thomas Underwood makes a point of stressing in this novel concerning the problems of inheritance that his niece Mary Bonner, now orphaned, must regard herself as one of his daughters to share their 'cup' and their 'loaf', but privately he ruminates on the difficult fact that he will have to make a new will which, in the event of his death, will 'take something from his own girls in order that he might provide for this new daughter', and yet 'she was not his daughter'.[93] Trollope was careful enough in his own life to leave a small legacy of £4000 to Florence Bland on condition that she made Trollope's sons her heirs.[94] In his adherence to the Church's teaching of charity, Trollope did not ignore the prior claims of direct progeny.

The significance of face-to-face relations was shown, perhaps surprisingly, by a very prominent Victorian who, following the death of her husband in 1861, was not renowned for her gregariousness, but who was certainly aware of the importance of *noblesse oblige*. Queen

Victoria's account of her visits to cottages in the north of Scotland highlights the importance of the traditional personal touch in the charitable process. She recounts how she and her daughter Vicky gave a dress and a handkerchief to 'old Mrs Grant' and warm petticoats to Mrs Farquharson, 88, and Kitty Kear, 86, the latter of whom expressed surprise 'at Vicky's height'.[95] In each cottage, there was a dialogue between donor and recipient exchanging family news. About six or seven cottages were visited and not every account mentions a gift; the visits obviously provided the opportunity for a social interchange between sovereign and subjects that benefited both sides in the classic manner. As Supreme Governor of the Church of England, Queen Victoria rightly believed herself to be setting that institution's example of philanthropy exercised on a private level.

Queen Victoria undoubtedly set the tone, for '[v]isiting the poor was one of the commonest forms of charity throughout the Victorian period'.[96] Visiting the poor had long been an honourable Christian duty, 'enjoined as it was by Scripture and practices by the deacons of the Early Church'.[97] Trollope, himself, according to the vicar of Harting, was well known for his kindness to the sick and poor.[98] But a degree of status and wealth was vital in order to dispense such kindness. So straitened in circumstances, while her mother had been trying to prove the validity of her marriage to the Earl of Lovel, the heroine of *Lady Anna* (1874) had believed herself to be 'just one' of the poor. She is not introduced to 'visiting the poor' until she stays at the rectory of Charles Lovel, among 'the luxuries of a rich, well-ordered household', where 'to dress for dinner with silk and gauds . . . had made life beautiful to her'. Having thus removed the 'stern hardness in [her] life', the rector's sister recruits her help in going 'among the poor'.[99]

Out of this age-old paternalist practice in the Victorian era there emerged a vigorous offshoot, usually known as district visiting, which neatly reflects the private/individual-organized division within contemporary charitable endeavours. Unlike the traditional visiting of the poor, which was small-scale and highly directed, district visiting was the organized philanthropists' solution to the perceived problem of mass urban poverty. It was like a massive (and inefficient) door-knock campaign; every house in an area was visited, the assumption being that every family was in need of help. The seeds of charity were to be sown broadcast. Both high and low church parties visited the poor; only the low church, however, sold Bibles, sometimes giving them away if the need arose.[100] District visiting also allowed the middle classes to peer into the working-class abyss, to confirm (rarely to deny) their fears of the urban unknown. It also gave them the opportunity to detect, and perhaps even to suggest removing, the 'sources of malignant disease', which might at any time burst the boundaries of the poorest districts.[101] Trollope repudiates this hidden agenda in *Miss Mackenzie* (1865). Desperate for society and torn between her enjoyment of the good things of life among the 'sinners' of the smart Paragon district of Littlebath and her desire to do good among the 'saints' of the Evangelical Stumfoldian circle, the heroine begins 'a system of district visiting and Bible reading', only to be stunned later by Mrs Stumfold's admission that *no* social interaction, either through one's own hospitality or through another's, could ever be 'looked upon as an end in itself', but was 'one of the most efficacious means of spreading the gospel teaching' and of 'admonishing', if necessary, 'some erring sister'.[102] By contrast, the distinction between visiting the poor and district visiting was the distinction between Lady Lufton's extra care and thought in her execution of *noblesse oblige*, both on the spiritual and secular levels, to the Rev. Josiah Crawley and his family in *The Last Chronicle of Barset* (1867), mentioned earlier, and the zealotry and self-centredness of organized philanthropy that Trollope so abhorred. Trollope's approval nonetheless of Lady Lufton's thoughtful private philanthropy was countered by his vexation that she needed to do this in the first place. The Church, he believed, should not usurp its philanthropic role in the community; nor should it, through its haphazard stipendiary and patronage system, *create* a need for philanthropy to be meted out to its own clerics. As the century wore on, and both the former and the latter seemed to be on the increase, his pessimism grew in equal measure.

Trollope's growing dismay that the combination of patronage and philanthropy was adding to the Church's woes originated not only from their principles and practices, but also from their abuses. The Church had long tried in vain to curb the abuses of patronage; the abuses of philanthropy proliferated in proportion to its multiplying forces, although Trollope in this area was rather more circumspect in his criticism. The abuses of both, although manifest in different ways, fuelled his pessimism for the Church's future.

The abuses of patronage

Ecclesiastical patronage induced the abuses of pluralities, absenteeism and nepotism, in addition to simony. Trollope's complaints about curates' salaries led him inevitably to scorn the absent cleric. In *Barchester Towers* (1857) Mr Crawley's patron, Mr Arabin, before he becomes dean, undertook to his patron, Dr Grantly, that, although he 'intended to keep his rooms at Oxford, and to have the assistance of a curate at St Ewold . . . he promised to give as much time as possible to the neighbourhood of Barchester'.[103] Yet in *Doctor Thorne* (1858) Trollope makes a point of noting that Mr Arabin was absent from Mary Thorne's wedding,[104] and when he is needed to confirm Mr Crawley's innocence in *The Last Chronicle of Barset* (1867), he is thought to be in Palestine, for '[a] dean can go where he likes'.[105] And, since a dean could be peripatetic, he could also marry young people in exotic places. In *Ayala's Angel* (1881) Trollope mentions that the Anglican marriage ceremony in Rome between Nina Baldoni and Lord George is officiated by the groom's uncle, the Dean of Dorchester, who comes to Rome specifically 'for this purpose'.[106] His absence from his duties at Dorchester was presumably no problem.

Absenteeism was often excused ostensibly on health grounds. In *An Old Man's Love* (1884) Mr Harbottle, the vicar of Little Alresford and the holder of its living for nearly 50 years, lived almost permanently in San Remo on account of his asthma, having for nearly 'a quarter of a century' only visited his parish '[o]ff and on in the summer time'. Even then, 'he could not take much of the duty, because he had a clergyman's throat'. Instead, his curate, Montagu Blake, ran the parish and waited for Mr Harbottle's death which, of course, came eventually!'[107]

Prebendaries, too, enjoyed a life of ease, comfort and even riches. Their absence from parish duties could be achieved without too much trouble, since many employed curates to perform their daily tasks. Charles Lovel, rector of Yoxham and prebendary in *Lady Anna* (1874), 'keeps two curates', is 'a much richer man than the peer', his nephew, maintains only the best cellar and larder in his rectory, does not breakfast before ten o'clock, and takes 'his own carriage' on the occasions on which he needs to be 'with the dean and his brother prebendaries'. A wealthy beneficiary of patronage and pluralism, Charles Lovel's sense of class is acute to the point of snobbery. As to the right of his nephew's cousin and aunt to the titles of 'Lady' and 'Countess', despite a lengthy court case deciding in their favour, he remains steadfastly sceptical and continues to nourish his prejudices against them. Though he accedes to his nephew's request to invite the young heroine and her betrothed to the rectory prior to his acting as the officiating parson at their wedding, he is reluctant 'to pollute his own rectory by the presence of that odious tailor',[108] and ensures he has as little contact with the couple as possible. He is obviously not one of Trollope's favourite characters, nor would he have enhanced the Church's reputation.

Deanships and prebends were both notorious sinecures, and Trollope was fond of pointing this out. The leisure time enjoyed by prebends enabled them to indulge their weaknesses; not that these weaknesses were necessarily unattractive. The Rev. Augustus Horne in 'The Relics of General Chassé' (1860) was '[l]oved by his friends [and] he loved all the world'. But then '[h]e had known no care and seen no sorrow'. His career had been meteoric. Having become a deacon at 24, a priest at 27, a rector at 30 and a prebendary at 35, 'his rectory was rich and his prebendal stall well paid', and neither of these required his constant attendance. Under this beneficence, 'his corpulence exceeded even those bounds which symmetry would have preferred'; he nourished his love of travel and 'was rather inclined to dandyism'. His Belgian holiday, however, would never be forgotten, either by himself or others. Tempted by his love of dressing up to try on the clothes of General Chassé, which are displayed within the walls of Antwerp Cathedral and are not sufficiently ample to cover his own capaciousness, he is disturbed by five of his 'countrywomen', whose knowledge of history is so deficient that they mistake his clerical clothes for the famous General's 'relics', and proceed to cut them into small pieces to take home as souvenirs. Though sweet revenge is wrought and though the reverend gentleman himself possesses enough aplomb to survive his hilarious appearance in borrowed 'red plush' not quite meeting his 'black silk stockings', there is an obvious inference to be drawn.[109] His opportunity for being in this comical situation is because of his 'sinecure' in the Church of England. Small wonder that Mark Robarts in *Framley Parsonage* (1861) almost sells his soul to the Duke of Omnium to obtain a prebendal stall and gain its privileges. The absenteeism afforded by this position proves too seductive to refuse. Lucy's remark, 'It does not seem very hard work' is countered by Mark's wife, Fanny, 'But it is very dignified'.[110] Trollope's implied question is, how long could a church survive on so feeble an expenditure of effort?

Yet deaneries and prebends, often called 'golden prebends', were actually popular for incumbent and community alike, for neither required the incumbent to reside nor the community to pay tithes.[111] Non-residence required little from the incumbent, which was why deanships and prebends were regarded as sinecures. As to whether large or small benefices led to pluralities, there is now disagreement. One belief is that small benefices were likely to lead to plurality in order for the incumbent to make ends meet,[112] but there is statistical evidence suggesting that pluralism was more likely with incumbents of large benefices, and that patrons with more than one advowson promoted pluralism more frequently than patrons with *only* one.[113]

Reasons given for non-residence often involved the disrepair or size of the domestic establishment. Sometimes the suitability of the rectory had less to do with its physical state and more to do with the expectations of the clergyman, as Trollope indicates in *The American Senator* (1876–7). Parson Mainwaring, on his arrival at Dillsborough, 'having a wife with some money and perhaps quite as much pretension, had found the rectory too small', so had taken Hoppet Hall 'on a lease for seven years'. Not until he had 'spent a little money' did the parson find 'that the rectory would be large enough for his small family'.[114] While this may not have been uncommon, the reasons for non-residence were sometimes as a result of genuine need. The diary of the Rev. Francis Witts (1793–1854) mentions signing a certificate 'that the glebe house at ... Bledington was on account of its meanness unsuitable as a residence for the incumbent, so that he might obtain from the Bishop licence for non-residence'. Witts, rector of Upper Slaughter, had an invalid wife. He was himself the beneficiary of patronage, having succeeded to his living on his uncle's death. His wife was the daughter of the Rev. Vavasour, rector of Stow-on-the-Wold,[115] of which Trollope's cousin, Edward, became Archdeacon in 1867, remaining there until he became Suffragan Bishop of Nottingham in 1877. Edward was also Prebendary of Liddington.[116] Thus Edward, too, was a pluralist and provided Trollope with a real-life model for non-residence.

Nepotism within patronage is a practice to which Trollope refers directly and indirectly. Archdeacon Grantly is the son of the bishop, Dr Grantly;[117] Mr Arabin, Archdeacon Grantly's protégé, is Grantly's brother-in-law;[118] the Rev. Henry Clavering presents his living to his future son-in-law, Mr Saul; and Edward Fielding, Henry Clavering's other son-in-law, holds a family living belonging to his uncle.[119] Trollope's casual acceptance of this practice may have derived from the many examples of nepotism in his extended family, one of the most intriguing examples of which is the story of the three Rev. John Trollopes. The first Rev. John Trollope (1729–94) was given the perpetual curacy of Little Marcle by his second wife's uncle.[120] On his death his livings went to his son-in-law, the Rev. Thomas Daniel Trollope who, a year before his own death, inherited the estate of his 98-year-old cousin, Jane Trollope. His son, the second Rev. John Trollope, inherited his ancestor Jane's estate, and was presented with the rectory of Crowmarsh Gifford by his patron, Lord Barrington. The third Rev. John (Joseph) Trollope (1817–93), the son of the first Rev. John Trollope's youngest son, was Prebendary of Hereford and had two patrons, the Bishop of Hereford and Sir W. Rause Boughton. This branch alone of his family would have acquainted Trollope with the role of chance in birthright and ecclesiastical patronage.

Trollope's oblique references to the coincidences of names in families, and the confusion that can arise from these indicate his knowledge of his extended family, and suggest that he drew on this knowledge in the writing of his fiction. Parson John in *The Vicar of Bullhampton* (1870) was 'always so called to distinguish him from the late parson, his cousin ... the Reverend James Marrable'.[121] In *Ralph the Heir* (1871), written only a year later, there are two Gregory Newtons, an older one and a younger one, and three Ralph Newtons, an older one and two younger ones who are cousins. The older Ralph Newton was a rector of Peele Newton and the younger Gregory Newton is the current rector of Peele Newton, and the plot concerns the thorny problem of inheritance and illegitimacy. Gregory Newton, the heir of the deceased Ralph Newton, also practises nepotism by bestowing the living of Newton on his nephew, the Rev. Gregory Newton.[122] Shared names in families at this time were not unusual; in Trollope's family they were common because of intermarriage. The parents of the second Rev. John Trollope were first cousins, and Trollope's father's sister married her first cousin, so he was accustomed to such confusion. It is also more than possible that he had his ancestors in mind when he commented sardonically in *Clergymen of the Church of England* (1866) that a cleric who has an aunt highly placed, or a father well-placed and is not himself 'of too tender a conscience', may well 'hope to rise' in his profession.[123]

Family examples of nepotism would have made a vivid impression on Trollope, but he would also have known that nepotism in ecclesiastical patronage was widespread. The Marquess of Bath had three livings of £1236 in his gift, all of which he gave to his son; the Duke of Beaufort did the same with his four livings, valued at £2422 and including two sinecures.[124] Nor was nepotistic patronage less common among the Evangelicals. William Wilberforce's sister was the mother of John Bird Sumner, later Archbishop of Canterbury, and of Charles Richard Sumner, Bishop of Winchester. Charles Sumner acted as patron to both Samuel and Henry Wilberforce in their early careers.[125] Of more influence for the Evangelicals was the selective patronage by aristocrats. Lord Dartmouth, Lord Smythe and Lady Huntingdon gave patronage to several Evangelical clergymen.[126] The Second Earl of Dartmouth bought advowsons to give them to selected men, and obtained 'nearly a dozen livings'.[127] The most famous Evangelical patron was Charles Simeon (1759–1836), who 'used money inherited through a brother's death to buy the patronage of some livings'.[128] This was developed into the Simeon Trust, mentioned in Chapter 1. Abuses of this nature were indirectly responsible for impoverishing the stipends meted out to clergymen at the lowest end of the pecking order of ecclesiastical patronage, a fact of which Trollope was also all too aware from his own family, for it contained the full range of clergymen, from those entitled to wear the mitre to those condemned to rusty black. His gloom was the deeper for knowing how impossible it was for the Church to eradicate such an entrenched practice.

For his Barchester and Palliser novels showing interconnections between the Church, politics and land ownership, his relatives provided actual models. The Trollope, Thorold and Welby families were connected through marriage, patronage and support, through the Church and politics. Sir John Thorold nominated Sir John Trollope (1800–74) in 1852 as tory MP for South Lincolnshire. Sir John Trollope, who in turn supported W. E. Welby as his successor, owned land abutting that of the Trollope and Thorold families,[129] and often played host to his novelist kinsman. George Trollope (b. 1802), great-great-grandson of Sir Thomas Trollope, married Walter William Welby's daughter Alicia, and was friend as well as cousin to Trollope. Trollope, therefore, had family connections with some of the highest levels of the Church, as well as with the political and landowning classes. His first-hand knowledge would have sharpened his insight *and* his depression.

Ecclesiastical patronage was in truth a way of life for Trollope's family, and he had, within his extended family, examples of pluralists of the two extreme opposing factions. His high church cousin Edward had Sir John Thorold, a maternal relative, as his patron for the Leasingham living, which had an income of £977. Trollope's Evangelical relative by marriage, Anthony Wilson Thorold, bishop of Rochester and later of Winchester, had the Lord Chancellor as his first patron to the St Giles-in-the-Fields living with an income of £663, and the Dean and Chapter of St Paul's as his second patron for the St Pancras living with an income of £1,150. Both bishops were pluralists with influential patrons – living proof of preferment on a grand scale.

At the other end of the scale, two of the three great-great-grandsons of Sir Thomas Trollope (3rd baronet) became clergymen: William Trollope (1798–1863) and Arthur Trollope (1799–1848). William and Arthur had more modest careers in the Church than their relative,

Edward Trollope. William, a scholar whose patrons were the Haberdashers' Company and Christ's Hospital, became the vicar of Wigston Magna in 1834 with the small income of £109, which may have been the reason he decided to emigrate to Tasmania, where he died nine years before Trollope was to visit. Arthur remained curate of St Mary-le-Bow in Cheapside, London, for 21 years until his death and it is more than possible that Trollope was thinking of Arthur when he wrote about curates in impecunious London boroughs. In *Clergymen of the Church of England* (1866) he notes how small is the payment and unpleasant the location for the town incumbent, and foresees that, if life does not improve, 'we shall hardly find that sons of English gentlemen will continue to seek the Church as a profession'.[130] Trollope's family grapevine would have constantly reminded him of the abuses to which ecclesiastical patronage could lead; it is no coincidence that he returned again and again to this theme, increasingly dejected that the Church could not eliminate its iniquities.

The abuses of philanthropy

Rather more complex was Trollope's attitude to philanthropic abuse, which involved his practice of seeing both (or all) sides of an issue. His interest in this subject is confined to a small part of his writings, whereas his concern for the motives behind charitable works is more widely spread. An instructive comparison is with his mother's novels. Both she and her son lived in an era when controversy stalked the boardrooms of charitable institutions. In 1818 Charity Commissioners had been appointed in response to 'the abuses, maladministration, and ignorant management of the schools among other forms of endowed charities'.[131] Fanny Trollope took up the cause. She became well-known in the 1840s for writing novels with a social purpose, and was one of the first writers to expose the deplorable working conditions of the lower classes in *Michael Armstrong, the Factory Boy* (1840), and *Jessie Phillips* (1843), which concerns the cruelties of the New Poor Law of 1834,[132] particularly its bastardy clause. This clause was amended a year after the book's appearance had led to a shocked response from the journal, *John Bull*.[133]

In contrast to his mother's iconoclasm, Trollope's reforming impulse was muted, constrained by his conservative social philosophy and his suspicion of all-embracing ideologies. He also followed the practice of many other nineteenth-century realist writers of effacing his personal views from his fiction.[134] Only once did he set out to write a novel with a specific cause in mind. This resulted in *The Warden* (1855), but even then he could not help giving both sides of the story. Not surprisingly, Trollope's treatment of charity abuse has inspired many discussions comparing the real-life Rochester, Dulwich and St Cross cases with the fictional Hiram's Hospital. The most well-known of these investigates the Earl of Guilford's contribution as Master of the Hospital to the abuses of the St Cross charity.[135]

Yet literary critics have tended to sympathize with the progressive position, the very attitude lampooned by Trollope in his attack on the popular press. A glance at other contemporary commentators reveals, however, that not all voices clamoured for an end to charity abuse, and that, as the century wore on, commentators increasingly condoned Trollope's ambivalence. The *Quarterly Review*, for instance, observed that '[a]ll human institutions have a tendency to collect abuses as seaweed gathers damp', adding that '[e]very man sees the dishonesty of his neighbour's trade, but defends similar malpractices in his own on the plea of necessity'.[136] In Trollope's lifetime, reformers insisted on the strict maintenance of original endowments, 'restoring old rights rather than creating new ones'.[137] After his death they demanded the adjustment of endowment provisions to match the needs of the day. Both positions would have been too ideological for Trollope's taste; as always, he perceived the shades of grey between the extremes of black and white. But he was worldly enough to realize that even the palest shades of grey encompassing a charge of abuse could do irreparable harm to the Church's fragile position as the community's moral arbiter. The Church had to be seen to be as pure as Caesar's wife.

Interestingly, in an aside that has never before been noticed, there is a possible ancestral source for the subject of *The Warden*. Trollope's ancestor William Trollope of Thurlby, Lincolnshire, left an endowment of £70 in 1636 for the Free Grammar School of King Charles,[138] now known as Bourne Grammar School. Private financial records of the school reveal that the endowment did not provide an adequate maintenance for the school. Significantly, the records become more detailed after the publication of *The Warden*, possibly because the custodians of the endowment were fearful of charges of abuse. Trollope's ambivalent approach to charitable corruption in *The Warden*, noted by many commentators, perhaps may be explained by factors in Trollope's family history.

Not until 1880 did Trollope again take up the subject of institutional corruption. In *Dr Wortle's School* (1880) Trollope does not mention the word endowment, but shows the headmaster to be scrupulous in the charging of his accounts, despite newspaper and parental criticism. The school may not be Hiram's Hospital and the inhabitants may be a great deal younger than the warden's bedesmen, but community criticism and Trollope's countering of criticism are remarkably similar to those in *The Warden*. Through *The Times* and other newspapers, a parent claims that £200 a year was too much to charge for a little boy but, as Trollope points out, the success of Dr Wortle as headmaster was such that he had to refuse admittance 'to a dozen eligible pupils', because the school was in great demand.[139] If Dr Wortle is a successful headmaster, so, too, is Mr Harding a worthy warden, even if his emoluments seem to be the product of corruption.

Before the law was changed, the courts in the early nineteenth century had continued to favour institutions claiming right to profits. Trollope's ambivalence to Hiram's Hospital and changing court decisions remind us that labels like 'abuse' depend for their currency on prevailing attitudes. The acknowledgement that 'modern London ... has done well from the old City endowments' is further evidence that a charity's profits can be viewed either as a virtue or a vice and that prosperous societies can evolve in this way, for good or ill.[140] Many philanthropic enterprises were of a capitalist nature,[141] and Chancery in its deficiency could not cope later in the century with cases involving charity abuse.[142] Perhaps, for that reason, an excess of ardour towards charity abuse might have struck Trollope as a waste of energy?

Whether or not he genuinely disliked Dickens' opportunism, as his reference in *The Warden* (1855) to Mr Popular Sentiment suggests,[143] or was envious of his success, Trollope usually avoided Dickens' kind of caricaturing when fictionalizing philanthropy. In no way was Trollope tempted as Dickens was in *Martin Chuzzlewit* (1844) to portray a Miss Charity 'making impracticable nightcaps for the poor',[144] or in *Bleak House* (1853) to depict a Mrs Jellyby, whose neglect of her multiple offspring matched her devotion to worthy causes in Africa.[145] The closest Trollope came to this kind of criticism was in his very first novel, *The Macdermots of Ballycloran* (1847), with his caustic comments about the energetic philanthropy overseas of Lord Birmingham, the absentee Irish landlord. In this case Trollope is unusually direct, censuring 'the squalid sources of wealth' which his fictional lord used to help 'Poles' and 'poor Blacks' to the neglect of his starving Irish tenants.[146] He was, most likely, still under the influence of his mother at this early point in his literary career.

Significantly, Trollope was more willing to express firm and unequivocal comments on philanthropy in his non-fiction than in his fiction. In *North America* (1862), for instance, he admires the 'eager and true' philanthropy of the United States, sharply counterbalancing this with his condemnation of the country's political corruption, which 'stinks aloud in the nostrils of all men'.[147] Indeed, in an article of the same period, 'Public Schools' (1865), Trollope appears to support the position of his fictional *Jupiter*, for he condemns the practice of allowing fewer scholarships to 'poor scholars' in public schools founded as Church 'charity schools'.[148] That there was a genuine problem cannot be doubted. The *Quarterly Review* had stressed in its definition of 'pauperes scholares' and in its insistence on increasing charity places in schools and colleges that '[p]overty is not want of blood, it is not want of position: it is want of means'.[149] By the nineteenth century many public schools 'bore little resemblance to the intentions of their founders', and Harrow, which had been founded for the free education of local scholars, had in 1816 only three free scholars among its 700 fee-paying pupils. This supports Trollope's argument that Winchester College's 1382 charter stipulated its main aim to be 'free education in Latin for the sons of the poor people', intending them for the Anglican priesthood.[150] In this instance, therefore, and following in the footsteps of the fictional Tom Towers, Trollope appears to be calling for the restoration of the social justice and philanthropy of an earlier age.[151] In reality, however, there is a distinction important for an understanding of Trollope's attitude to philanthropy: differing motivations. Trollope is focused on the redress of a particular grievance; Towers is using an 'abuse' as a vehicle for his wider political purposes.

Trollope's focus on motivations as the key for understanding the value of charitable activities is best displayed in *The Warden*, one of literature's most famous accounts of clerical corruption, in which much of the comedy comes from his counterbalancing of the reforming clerics from London with the existing complacent Barchester clerics.[152] Trollope begins his critique of philanthropic reform by stressing the ubiquity of the cry for reform in contemporary society. John Bold is keen to bring about 'the reform of all abuses'. It so happens, hints Trollope, that Hiram's Hospital was, for Bold, a convenient cause, and he, in turn, was for Tom Towers, the *Jupiter*'s editor, a young man gullible enough innocently to promote the media's selfish interests. Trollope shows that Towers's ambitions instigate Bold's actions, and thus that philanthropic reform is a current topic of interest attracting unscrupulous as well as genuine involvement. Towers, when Bold wavers in enthusiasm for effecting public reform at the expense of his putative father-in-law, quotes from Dr Pessimist Anticant and gives him a pamphlet declaring that modern charity does not live up to the standards of ancient charity.[153] Mr Popular Sentiment's novel, 'The Almshouse', is thrown in for good measure. Dr Pessimist Anticant and Mr Popular Sentiment are commonly known to be Trollope's fictional names for Thomas Carlyle and Charles Dickens. Trollope's point is that reform is a fashionable topic, support for which does not necessarily demonstrate a sincere desire for social amelioration. Again, personal motivations determine the moral value of a charitable action. Whether right or wrong, however, the reformers succeeded in harming the Church's reputation; limiting this damage was integral to Trollope's narrative design.

Trollope continued his critique of movements for philanthropic reform in subsequent Barchester novels, albeit indirectly. The low church faction, led by the Proudies, plan to reform philanthropic activity in Barchester. Picking up the threads of the Hiram's Hospital saga in *Barchester Towers* (1857), Trollope suggests that the reformers' intent may not match their rhetoric. Mr Slope's reforming passion is unmasked in his change of heart about the wardenship question. His agreement to install Mr Quiverful, a poor clergyman with 14 children, as the new warden of Hiram's Hospital, satisfies the low church's plan for philanthropic reform. When the plan risks ruining Mr Slope's matrimonial ambitions with regard to Eleanor Bold and her inheritance, it is dismissed. Nor is Mrs Proudie's insistence on making Mr Quiverful warden prompted by pure motives; it is her revenge against Mr Slope and her thirst for power.

On the need to rectify the abuses of ecclesiastical patronage and philanthropy Trollope is eloquent, but he is silent as to the best possible means of effecting reform in these areas. In the case of philanthropic reform, he is actually nervous that remedial measures might aggravate, not ameliorate matters for the community. At the same time, the consequences of a *laissez-faire* policy on these issues, he believed, would hurt both Church and its society.

The consequences of patronage and philanthropy

The confluence between patronage and philanthropy can be appreciated in the resentment often shared by *protégés* of patronage and beneficiaries of charity, since both could feel robbed of their dignity – considered by Trollope to be one of the most important factors in social arrangements and ignored at the Church's peril. Collectively, individual personal affronts had a habit of fuelling doctrinal dissension. If the seething remained latent, the damage sustained was the more difficult to undo. In *The Last Chronicle of Barset* (1867) Dr Proudie is furious at Mr Crawley's lack of deference, assuming rightly that Mr Crawley's sense of obligation to his patron must cement his high church affiliations. He fumes that '[n]o dean should have any patronage';[154] Mr Crawley's patron is Dr Arabin,[155] who had also paid for his curate's son to go to Marlborough.[156] While Mr Crawley's partisanship to the high church faction may remain firm, his personal feelings towards his patron are not warm, for he could not forgive his friend for paying his debts and giving him a living. His friend had been dearer to him when he had been 'as penniless as the curate himself' and Crawley's advice concerning Rome had made him the creditor and Arabin the debtor.[157] Certainly the poor clergyman's support of the high church does it no favours in Barchester, for the man's intractable nature attracts him more foes than friends. The dangers of ecclesiastical patronage were rife in Victorian England: 'for every friend that a single appointment could make there might be made a hundred enemies',[158] for there was often an unwelcome debt stored up by patronage.[159]

Stirring bad feeling on the personal level, patronage on the collective level, Trollope showed, actually exacerbated doctrinal struggles. Lady Lufton's continued support of Mark Robarts in *Framley Parsonage* (1861) is as much part of her war against the low church bishop, Dr Proudie, as it is of her refusal to admit that she had made a mistake in her choice of *protégé*. In *Barchester Towers* (1857) Archdeacon Grantly patronizes the high church Mr Arabin, knowing that his new living of St Ewold's will annoy Dr Proudie who 'would be forced to institute into a living, immediately under his own nose, the enemy of his favourite chaplain', for Mr Slope and Mr Arabin have been 'engaged in a tremendous controversy . . . respecting the apostolic succession'.[160]

Trollope lived at the time of a famous example of patronage inflaming factional fighting, and realized its consequences for the Church. The Gorham case in 1850, outlined in Chapter 1, was not so much over Gorham's refusal to accept the doctrine of baptismal regeneration as it was over the patron's right 'to present whomsoever he liked'.[161] Had Gorham lost, the Church's decline would have been accelerated.

Factional battles did not confine themselves to the dioceses. Since the Reformation, the appointment of bishops within the Church of England had been a royal prerogative. But Prime Ministers could not resist choosing men whose political allegiance would help them, and tried to persuade the monarch to endorse their partisan decisions in a form of state patronage. Gladstone's knowledge of the Church and high church allegiance drew him into several clashes with Queen Victoria over the selection of bishops, but Disraeli, whose ignorance of the Church as a whole made his task laborious, has been said to be 'responsible for the advancement of some of the most eminent churchmen of the century'.[162] There were, however, some appointments which, through Disraeli's inexperience and Victoria's intransigence, led to continued dissension in the Church. Victoria insisted that the broad church Tait become Archbishop of Canterbury, totally against Disraeli's advice. Although Tait came to be regarded as one of the most powerful and hard-working archbishops, his insistence on continuing links between Church and state has been seen, as noted earlier, to have contributed to the Church's gradual downfall.[163] Patronage, therefore, from the highest to the lowest levels endorsed factional divisions.

The desire for position could annihilate any sense of moral rectitude in the seeking and conferring of patronage, which was commonly done through letters. Trollope alludes to the practice in *Marion Fay* (1882), one of Trollope's last novels and well known for its pessimistic depiction of the Church, which is represented by the unscrupulous Mr Greenwood. Lady Clara Kingsbury writes to her sister to ask if her husband could find something for the indolent Mr Greenwood.[164] The petition is unsuccessful. This was not always the case in real life. There are several letters from Liddon requesting Hamilton's patronage. In one he alludes to Hamilton's patronage for himself for a prebendal stall at Salisbury Cathedral, remarking that it does not have preaching duties,[165] even though sinecures were said to have disappeared by 1835,[166] and the Dean and Chapter Act of 1840 had 'suppressed all non-resident prebends'.[167]

Yet it is now argued that patronage did not necessarily preclude merit since, even in the eighteenth century, bishops could come from humble origins through patronage.[168] Certainly, Liddon was universally admired. Patronage did not necessarily entail undeserved appointments, in the same way as under the unreformed Parliament, patronage often brought into politics young men of ability but no fortune.

Was Trollope right in his assessment of ecclesiastical patronage? His acute awareness of the gradual decline of the Church is illustrated by his increasingly pessimistic portrayal of it. *The Warden* (1855) ultimately supports the Church's strength and integrity, having initially drawn attention to its eleemosynary abuses, but each subsequent novel questions more and more the Church's unassailable supremacy, partly through the human failings of its representative officers, but mostly through its rigid structures and practices. One of the practices stimulating his fear of the Church's decline is that of patronage. The reforms of his century sought to eliminate the power and practice of patronage in the Church as elsewhere, so that merit could prevail as a means of advancement. Yet historians of the last two decades believe that patronage did not necessarily preclude merit as a determinant, and one argument is that the reforms which modified ecclesiastical patronage, followed as they were by the depression of the late 1870s and 1880s, perhaps precipitated the decline of the Church, while not necessarily halting patronage.[169] Trollope himself had admitted in 'The Civil Service as a Profession' (1861) that '[t]he noviciates of the bar and of the church are costly and cannot be endured by slender purses'.[170] Perhaps, albeit with regret, he realized that patronage was necessary after all.

Trollope was equally conscious that philanthropy, too, was necessary, despite his wariness of some of its consequences. The main reason for his repugnance for organized philanthropy was that it so often deprived the recipient of pride, just as patronage could fill the *protégé* with acrimony or encourage a vacation of principles. Philanthropy, mismanaged, could encourage begging, which robbed an individual of self-respect. Begging as a practice, said to have begun in the Church with St Francis of Assisi and his followers, was deemed to have produced 'a rich crop of permanent evil'.[171] If acceptance of philanthropy from an individual was difficult for both donor and recipient when the recipient was reluctant, the situation was aggravated if one assumed the role of suppliant. To have to seek help lessened a suppliant's sense of self-worth. To be importuned to provide succour diminished the donor's regard for the suppliant. The relationship between donor and recipient was therefore soured from the beginning.

Begging as an evil manifests itself in *Castle Richmond* (1860). While the Roman Catholic and Irish churchmen compete for fresh congregation members, a young mother slips through their hopelessly inadequate philanthropic net and openly begs,[172] 'waiting with the patience of poverty', by the wayside for herself and her starving children to importune a young couple belonging to the Irish gentry. As Herbert Fitzgerald knew, '[w]hat money each had to bestow would go twice further by being brought to the general fund – by being expended with forethought and discrimination', and yet, 'from the first moment of his interrogating the woman, [he] had of course known that he would give her somewhat', for 'it was impossible not to waste money in almsgiving', however indisposed he was 'to give promiscuous charity on the road-side'. This particular incident has the effect of placing not the famished woman, but the other protagonists *and* the reader in a demeaning light, so abject is the picture of the two-year-old child, whose legs 'seemed to have withered away', and whose teeth could be seen through his 'emaciated lips'.[173] That such human torment could eventuate and only possibly be alleviated by mendicancy could not fail to humiliate any onlooker. Begging and the need to beg, implies Trollope, is simply wrong.[174]

At one polar end of philanthropic consequences lay begging; at the other end, *because* human beings preferred to retain their dignity, lay self-help. Trollope approved of self-help, for no one lost face. Even the poor could help themselves by helping others. Fanny Clavering is attracted to Mr Saul in *The Claverings* (1867) through his ability to give: '"He has nothing but his curacy, and what he gives away is wonderful".'[175] His own philanthropy makes him less of a recipient than an awardee when the Clavering living is given him. Following in the tradition of philanthropy as one of the prime responsibilites of English cathedrals, a prebendary of Winchester Cathedral, Frederick Iremonger, devoted himself to charity, both spiritual and secular.[176] Trollope's Mr Saul continues this tradition.[177] The novelist was clearly aware of humanity's need of private philanthropy which did not humiliate, but encouraged self-sufficiency.

While Trollope disliked ecclesiastical patronage and institutionalized philanthropy, he believed in *noblesse oblige* involving patronage and private philanthropy. Thomas Noel created the following rhyme in 1841: 'Rattle his bones over the stones; he's only a pauper, whom nobody owns.'[178] Seldom did Trollope use the word pauper. A glance through Trollope's work even suggests that poverty did not exist in his world, for he wrote mainly for the middle classes about the middle classes. Yet closer examination discloses that poverty appeared in almost all of his novels. Careful inspection shows that poverty was not only hidden in the middle classes in the shape of poor clerics like Josiah Crawley, but that the alleviation of poverty was assumed to be the responsibility of the Church and of the middle classes. The pauper, as far as Trollope was concerned, *was* owned by someone, in the sense that his welfare was the responsibility of those capable of giving help. The pauper, Trollope believed, should not be passed on to impersonal institutions, for only the private individual could determine the nature and degree of succour needed. He was wary of bureaucracies grown too complex to function effectively. Charity, he illustrates, can only operate on a personal level, where private judgement can be exercised by both donor and recipient.

Neither patronage nor philanthropy and their consequences have entirely vanished. *The Spectator* (1994) spoke of an uncanny living legend of patronage: the Rev. Henry Croyland Thorold (b. 1921),[179] direct descendant by marriage of Trollope and the bishops Edward

Trollope and Anthony Wilson Thorold. The Rev. Henry Croylan Thorold died in 1999, but until his death he not only lived in Marston, which has remained the family seat for many centuries, but was also known as a scholarly antiquarian bachelor clergyman, whose co-patronage of five livings would have made Trollope shudder that the practice of ecclesiastical preferment could so continue a century after his death. Or, with the benefit of hindsight, would it? Thorold was a kindly gentleman, well loved by local inhabitants and known simply as 'Henry'. Nor has the abuse of philanthropy escaped the public eye. More than a century after Trollope's death, *The Spectator* (1996) betrayed the embarrassment of philanthropic institutions grown too fat. The Charities Commission, begun in the nineteenth century, admitted that the top 200 charities in the United Kingdom were to be 'monitored' because they had become too large and did not 'know what to do with their money'.[180] Four years on, *The Spectator* (2000) bemoaned the fact that the Charity Commissioners were still powerless to prevent philanthropic abuses, reliant as they were on four vague classifications of charitable purposes in the legislation dating from 1601.[181] As Trollope cautioned throughout his writing, the larger the distance from donor to recipient, the larger the abuse of funds and the smaller the benefit. Despite his *caveats* the solution, in Trollope's view, rested with the individual – in *noblesse oblige*. But his greatest regret was that officers of the Church had to be recipients, rather than donors of *noblesse oblige*. Since, for Trollope, 'given bread is bitter bread',[182] whatever its source, neither ecclesiastical patronage nor philanthropy could relieve the Church from an expedient plan of reform. On *that* issue his pessimism seems to have been well founded.

3
Gentlemen Clergymen

Patronage and philanthropy assume that members of a community belong to different levels of a social hierarchy. As this chapter will demonstrate, Trollope, in his advocacy of a more equitable distribution of clerical incomes, was in favour of social strata becoming less uneven, thus precluding the need for patronage and philanthropy and an assumed superiority of patron over *protégé* and donor over recipient. Nor did he limit his comments to the Church. He constantly argued for the need to recompense the labourer according to output rather than social rank. This is one of the main reasons for his documentation in *An Autobiography* (1883) of income received for his writing. Unfortunately, some commentators have concluded that Trollope's pride in financial reward was due to his preoccupation with mercenary details. It is easy to forget that Trollope was, as a child, the victim of sharp downward mobility, even though his father's failure as a barrister is well documented, as are the family's problems with debt, about which all of Trollope's biographers have written with vivid detail. Trollope, trapped in middle-class poverty in a hierarchical society, realized that the only escape was through hard work, and was proud that his toil was rewarded. His financial documentation, therefore, reflects his relief that, for every pound and shilling earned, he could reascend the social ladder from which his family had fallen. His attitude to social rank was understandably coloured by his experiences.

The word 'gentleman' is rarely used today except as a public mode of address. In the Victorian age, however, the word had great currency, and was used to denote both background and behaviour. Unlike our own age, '[t]he word "gentleman" became in Victorian times a subject of dialectical enquiry and nerve-racking embarrassment'.[1] This chapter will argue that Trollope charted the changing definitions of gentlemen clergymen, that he measured society's modes of exclusion, and that he changed his mind over time about the importance society attached to this term.

The chapter challenges previous views based on more general studies of the gentleman in Trollope's fiction. One view, for example, emphasizes moral conduct as Trollope's guiding reference point, and refutes the definition of a gentleman as '"a man of ancestry"', since English people have always married across social boundaries to such an extent that few families can safely claim noble ancestry *throughout* their history. Since the practice of primogeniture in the laws of inheritance sometimes left younger sons having to descend the social ladder, mixed marriages were often imperative. Cardinal Newman's definition of gentlemanly behaviour as conduct which fits in easily with other people and never causes embarrassment or negative feelings is cited as evidence of Trollope's stance,[2] but this ignores the fact that Trollope, initially, defines a gentleman as '"a man of ancestry"' as *his* point of departure. This may be because the examination of Trollope's fiction is thematic rather than chronological. There were actually subtle changes in Trollope's attitudes in his writing from the 1850s to the 1880s. Another view suggests that Trollope's view of a gentleman possessing worthy qualities, rather than 'high social position',[3] is one which he had always held, although these observations are, admittedly, directed to the later novels. Trollope's ideas on gentle birthright did not remain fixed, as suggested, but changed over the years.

Trollope's use of language is a key to unlocking his thoughts on this subject. One of the reasons why he has taken so long to be accepted into the literary canon is his genius with language. In the twentieth century most new critics, structuralists, poststructuralists and postmodernists despaired of using Trollope's texts as quarry, because his language seemed so straightforward. Unlike Dickens and George Eliot, he deliberately eschewed figurative language. Yet it is Trollope's apparently straightforward use of language which illuminates his ideas on the gently born. His writing appears deceptively simple, and critics have even reproached him for this, comparing his unadorned style unfavourably with writers like Thackeray.[4] Trollope's writing style resembled the report writing which he was taught at the Post Office under Francis Freeling, and which was based on legal writing, 'laconic, informed, and objective', as well as 'plain, simple and unadorned'. Trollope's use of metaphors is sparing and of the sort 'to put the reader at . . . ease – the courteous and conciliatory passwords that bespeak a common ground'.[5] Trollope adopted the kind of language a gentleman would use in the attempt to make his interlocutors feel comfortable. Trollope's very modes of expression reveal his attitude to the concept of gentleman.

The gentleman and birthright

Every one of the clergymen in *The Warden* (1855) is a gentleman. Every one of its principal male characters is a gentleman. Only the bedesmen of Hiram's Hospital, recipients of charity, are not gentlemen. Yet the category of gentleman is never mentioned, for, in the early 1850s, people were unlikely to cross social boundaries, since widespread professionalism had not yet facilitated social mobility. A term only requires special mention if categories are not clearly drawn. The distinction between the bedesmen and Mr Harding, the Warden, lies in modes of address since, with the occasional exception of Mr Bunce, the bedesmen call their warden, 'your reverence'.[6]

Much of Trollope's comedy relies on contrasting characters. The unctuous Obadiah Slope in *Barchester Towers* (1857), one of the novels of the 1850s, encourages Trollope to exhort the reader with mock pomposity: 'Think, oh, my meditative reader, what an associate we have here for those comfortable prebendaries, those gentleman-like clerical doctors, those happy well-used well-fed minor canons.'[7] The syntactical patterns mimic the supposed speech of Bishop Grantly's clerical gentlemen, when engaged in ecclesiastical duty, and alert the reader as to the humorous proposition that the new clergyman is perhaps not *quite* a gentleman. Trollope's subtlety in depicting distinctions of rank was not necessarily typical. The Rev. Witts, a broad churchman of comfortable social standing, notes in his diary of 1832 that he attended the parish church of Cheltenham, and thoroughly enjoyed the 'eloquent, impressive' sermon of Francis Close, an Evangelical clergyman, on whom some critics believe Mr Slope to have been founded. Although Witts concedes that 'there was a large proportion' of 'the lower order', there were also 'many elegant females of the higher order' listening attentively.[8] These facts closely corroborate Trollope's portrayal of Slope as a favourite of the ladies of all social classes, and as a persuasive preacher, but do not endorse Trollope's depiction of Slope's hypocrisy. Nor do they correspond to the reader's impression that Slope is not a gentleman. Furthermore, even though Witts is confiding these thoughts to his diary, and feels no compunction to moderate his reactions, there is the sense that he is not at all self-conscious about referring to class.

Closely following Slope's description in *Barchester Towers* comes that of Archdeacon Grantly, whose autocratic governance, Trollope stresses, is 'not unpalatable to the gentleman', his popularity demonstrating his wisdom in dealing with all classes. The understatement, 'not unpalatable', expresses the gentlemanly qualities of moderation observed by Newman which a gentleman uses to adapt to immediate company; it also appeals, through its *own* understatement, to the reader's sympathies. Nor are Trollope's contrasts necessarily binary, for Mr Arabin's gentlemanly ancestry is indicated by justifying his conduct in terms of his patrician background. Mr Arabin's decision to remain in the Church of England was because he was 'a conscientious man' and, 'as the archdeacon had boasted of him, a thorough gentleman'.[9] This last phrase, attributed to Dr Grantly to deflect possible accusations of partisanship, underscores Mr Arabin's 'gentlemanly' ancestry.

Mr Arabin's attributes accord with those of the early Victorian era, when 'the ideal priestly *persona*, [was] that of an unworldly gentleman whose moral qualities placed him apart from the society to which he ministered'.[10] His gentleman's victory in winning the lady in *Barchester Towers* is shown to be dependent on gentlemanly attributes due to birth, not chance. The marriage proposal is indicative of this: 'Men we believe seldom make such resolves. Mr Slope and Mr Stanhope had done so, it is true; but gentlemen generally propose without any absolutely defined determination as to their doing so. Such was now the case with Mr Arabin.' The supposed spontaneity of the gentleman, Mr Arabin, thus won over the wealthy widow, Eleanor Bold. Fortunate in love, the gentleman is fortunate, too, in worldly position, for Mr Arabin's promotion to dean was decided by a marquess suggesting the appointment. The impersonal construction, 'And so the matter was arranged',[11] underlines the casual means by which ladies and gentlemen of high birth converse with each other. The casual manner in which the decision is made parallels the understated language. This scene completes the novel.

By contrast, the narrative had relied hitherto for much of its comedy on the ungentlemanly Mr Slope's overtures to Eleanor Bold *and* Signora Neroni, and Bertie Stanhope's overt coveting of Eleanor Bold's income. Trollope thus illustrates in this novel of the late 1850s the triumph of gentlemanly breeding, which excludes men and women of inferior lineage from attaining worldly success and personal happiness. Bertie Stanhope's lineage may have been impeccable, but he (as well as his sister) had supposedly been corrupted by their life of ease on the continent. Significantly, one of Trollope's critics, Joseph Cauvin, wrote to William Longman in 1856 after reading the manuscript, but prior to the book's publication, to comment that '[t]here is hardly a "lady" or "gentleman" among them'.[12] Trollope's restraint in exaggerating the lack of gentility of some of his key characters has to be appreciated in light of Cauvin's remarks, which assessed wrongly the fictional situation.

Aphorisms in *Doctor Thorne* (1858) render more explicit the idea that gentlemanly qualities are inherited. Frank Gresham's tacit respect for the pedigree of birth is the reason for his dismay over Mary Thorne's supposed doubtful origins: 'A man having it need not boast of what he has, or show it off before the world. But on that account he values it the more.' The aphorism uttered by Dr Thorne earlier in the novel may challenge Frank's beliefs but cannot negate them: 'A man raises a woman to his own standard, but a woman must take that of the man she marries.'[13] Yet Dr Thorne's words, intended to reassure Mary, are never tested, for she conveniently discovers that her lineage is not humble, and can marry Frank Gresham without concern that any offspring might inherit a doubtful descent.

The questioning of inherited integrity

In the 1860s, Trollope was more explicit in questioning the equation of gentlemanly birth with integrity, and this correlates closely with contemporary articles written on gentlemanliness which emphasize that most writers from the 1860s until the 1880s believed that a gentleman should be defined, not according to birthright, but according to 'self-respect, integrity, generosity, thoughtfulness, tact, and ease of manners'.[14] Trollope was beginning to show clergymen whose 'pedigree' genealogy had not necessarily endowed them with gentlemanliness or with a gentleman's standard of living.

Mark Robarts in *Framley Parsonage* (1861) is a gentleman on account of his father being a doctor, and receives Lady Lufton's patronage at a young age. Yet he becomes associated in the reader's mind with paper IOUs, smart modes of transport and additional servants like a footman, gardener and groom. In the same novel, the plight of the poor scholarly cleric, whose unquestionable gentlemanly origins and integrity exacerbate his situation, is explored in some depth. Mr Crawley's poverty is vividly illustrated through family illness. The clergyman's unwillingness to receive help annoys his more fortunate fellow clergyman, Mr Arabin, who tells him, 'I would rather beg than see my wife starve'. Crawley's bitter retort explains his pride: 'Gift bread chokes in a man's throat and poisons his blood, and sits like lead upon the heart.'[15] Crawley's repugnance at the thought of philanthropy is not only characteristic of common attitudes to charity discussed in Chapter 2, but also illustrates that the very act of philanthropy is a reminder of

Crawley's diminished status, even though he is a clergyman who has received a gentleman's education at Oxford. Trollope's unstated suggestion, in the case of Mark Robarts, is that gentlemanly birth is no guarantee of gentlemanly behaviour and, in the case of Mr Crawley, that, if the Church wishes to maintain gentlemanly rank for its officers, it should exercise social justice, and reward all delegates with an income commensurate with their education and duties.

Crawley's plight and character struck a chord with readers *and* other writers. Having said of Crawley that 'we cannot easily find a parallel in fiction',[16] Oliphant replicated aspects of his situation in *Phoebe Junior* (1876) in her depiction of Mr May, incumbent of St Roque. Mr May, too, was a gentleman, well educated, with a tiny income for his large family and debts.[17] His situation is constantly compared with that of the wealthy Dissenting butterman, Tozer, of humble origin, whose signature he forges. Clearly, Oliphant transformed the alleged crime in *The Last Chronicle of Barset* (1867) into an actual crime to illustrate further the social decline of clergymen. Social rank in the Church reappears in Oliphant's *A Son of the Soil* (1883) in Colin Campbell's disappointment that his Oxford prize and double first could not obliterate his modest origins whereas, had his father been a Duke, his 'glories . . . would have been a graceful addition to the natural honours of his name'; instead, he 'was entirely at liberty to pursue his vocation' in a Scottish parish.[18] Trollope's attention to clerical position and rank had thus provided thematic seeds for other narratives.

More attention is drawn to this in *The Small House at Allington* (1864) – a story which hinges entirely on balancing the merits of noble birthright, wealth and common decency, and finally rewarding common decency after the poor heroine Lily finds to her cost that her betrothed is able 'to jilt the niece of a small rural squire; but it was not in him to jilt the daughter of a countess'. When Lily questions the assumed equivalence of gentlemanly birth and integrity, Trollope expresses this through one sister echoing the other's words. Lily's remark that Mr Crosbie 'is only a mere clerk' is countered by her older sister: 'I don't know what you call a mere clerk, Lily, Mr Fanfaron is a mere barrister, and Mr Boyce is a mere clergyman . . . You might as well say that Lord de Guest is a mere earl.' The echoing illustrates Bell's gentle mocking of Lily and suggests that the accident of birth is not an indicator of personal worth, her own constancy to a struggling doctor finally rewarded by marriage *and* a supplementary allowance from her uncle, although her wedding was 'not a thing to be talked about much' for, still in the 1860s, '[p]arsons' marriages [were] often very grand affairs. They c[a]me in among county people'.[19]

The questioning of inherited prosperity and inherited integrity

In two of his novels of the mid-1860s, Trollope's fictional characters come from modest backgrounds, and gentle birth is no guarantee of worldly prosperity. Mrs Ray's deceased husband in *Rachel Ray* (1863), though 'not a clergyman himself, had been employed in matters ecclesiastical' – as a lawyer. He was also 'a gentleman' who had not been able to leave sufficient means to his family to keep them particularly comfortable. The modest meals of 'cold mutton and potatoes' provide evidence of their humble finances and make them prey to Evangelical proselytizing. As in his early novels, Trollope continues to depict Evangelical clergymen from families having no claim to gentle birth. He admits that he is at a loss to define the indicators of gentle birth, denying that it is just a matter of morals, manners and language, for Mr Prong, who was 'not a gentleman', was not a 'thief or a liar'. Although Rachel disparagingly remarks that Mr Prong 'had been educated at Islington, and that he sometimes forgot his "h's"', Trollope says it is not a question of whether or not he 'picked his teeth with his fork' or 'misplaced his "h's"', for he could be identified through 'a word' or 'a glance' as someone who was 'not a gentleman'.[20] Rachel's reference to Islington is to Mr Prong's education at a theological college, rather than Oxford or Cambridge. Theological colleges were increasing and were often treated contemptuously by those who were horrified by their democratic selection processes and the absence of Latin and Greek in their curricula.

Not only was '[u]niversity graduation ... generally thought to guarantee gentility', but there was also a belief at this time that even the graduate clergy should forget their Oxford and Cambridge education and adopt a simpler approach to pastoral preaching, so that their largely illiterate congregations could understand them.[21] Moreover, the generally held opinion that Evangelicals lacked a university education has been disputed, for some Evangelicals were noted scholars. The Evangelical Isaac Milner's university degree had the distinction of being *'incomparabilis'*, and the Evangelical Samuel Lee, a carpenter's apprentice and autodidact, mastered Greek and Hebrew, as well as learning some 'Chaldee, Syriac, Samaritan, Persian and Hindustan before being sent to Cambridge at CMS expense in 1813'.[22] And Charles Richard Sumner, the low church bishop to the Winchester diocese, stated in his charge of 1862 that it would be 'a national loss' if clergymen ceased to be educated at 'our Universities', allowing that the theological colleges, which he called 'supplemental nurseries', could only supply 'another class of students' for certain ministerial work.[23] The nuances between birthright, education and social distinction were therefore as complex as Trollope depicts.

Another mark of social distinction appeared to be the capacity to exercise emotional restraint. Trollope seems to indicate in *Rachel Ray* (1863) that Evangelicals of humble origin were unable to conceal extreme emotion for, when Mr Prong is annoyed by Mr Comfort's advice, 'the mouth assumed a would-be grandeur, the chin came out, and to any one less infatuated than Mrs Prime it would be apparent that the purse was not made of silk, but that a coarser material had come to hand in the manufacture'.[24] This kind of attitude was not atypical, for Liddon remarked on the gaucheness of the low church clergy at the Wesleyan conference, alluding to them as children, interested in spite of themselves, 'altho' too awkward to be correspondingly well mannered'.[25]

Trollope offers a further sign of Mr Prong's doubtful background in his overt interest in money and courtship of Mrs Prime to augment his finances. He 'did not covet money, but he valued it very highly'. Moreover, the inclusion of 'that' in his profession of love for Mrs Prime hints that he lacks the spontaneity, which Trollope, referring to Mr Arabin, stressed in *Barchester Towers* was the hallmark of a gentleman's proposal of marriage: 'I entertain for you all *that* deep love which a man should feel for her who is to be the wife of his bosom.' Luke Rowan, by contrast, is a gentleman despite his family's humble finances, for his mother had told him so, although she could never 'define the word'.[26] He is, nonetheless, ultimately given the promise of prosperity and personal happiness, for he is assured of the brewery and Rachel Ray as wife.

The second of the novels in the 1860s is *Miss Mackenzie* (1865). Miss Mackenzie finally marries a man who is a gentleman with an income as well as a title and happens to be her cousin, but the comedy arises from her two suitors, who may have one attribute but not the other. Mr Maguire was 'by profession a gentleman', since he was a clergyman, argues Miss Mackenzie to herself, but 'he was afflicted by a terrible squint' *and* by a terribly low income. God might excuse him the first, but Miss Mackenzie was unlikely to excuse him both. Mr Rubb, though, 'was very good-looking', but 'not a gentleman'. Miss Mackenzie's dilemma is comically outlined through the supposed sentiments of her friend, Miss Baker: 'She would have broken her heart rather than marry a man who was not a gentleman. It was not unlady-like to eat cold mutton, and she ate it. But she would have shuddered had she been called on to eat any mutton with a steel fork.' Miss Baker disapproves of Mr Rubb, and Trollope again laughs at the vagueness of the term, gentleman: '... Miss Baker, from an early age, and by all the association of her youth, had been taught to know a gentleman when she saw him'. The opinions, attributed to Miss Baker, are not to be taken seriously. Always desirous of approval, Miss Mackenzie realizes that she will not encounter social exclusion if she were to choose the doubly-afflicted Mr Maguire, whose gentlemanhood, she allows, has been decreed 'not only by Act of Parliament, but in outward manners', and yet he squinted 'so horribly'.[27]

Juxtaposed with Trollope's caricaturing of the Evangelical squint is the deciding factor of Mr Rubb's lack of good taste in his yellow gloves. Miss Mackenzie's anguish in weighing the two features enhances the mockery of the dilemma: 'This was beyond her, and there he sat, with his gloves almost as conspicuous as Mr Maguire's eye. Should she, however, become Mrs Rubb, she would not find the gloves to be there permanently; whereas the eye would remain. But then the gloves were the fault of the one man, whereas the eye was simply the misfortune of the other.'[28] Fortunately, Miss Mackenzie is saved by her cousin's constancy of love resulting in their marriage.

The questioning of birthright and education

Trollope's questioning of social distinctions in education in his article, 'Public Schools', offers an insight into the education of the gentlemanly class and its original purpose. He describes conditions at Winchester College in 1831 under which young boys lived and learned and draws attention to the founder's intentions. The school was originally designed to prepare boys for the priesthood, for Wykeham had founded the school for 'the sons of needy people, who could not otherwise be educated, and who should receive, without any cost to themselves or friends, an education rare in those days in any class, and of a nature to fit them for the priesthood. But as they were poor and of the poor, so were they to be poorly nurtured'. Their diet and living conditions were certainly spartan. The euphemism, 'dispars', was applied to 'a lump of fat from the breast of a big sheep', weighing about 1 lb, and was a boy's daily ration of meat. Cutlery there was none; 'a small wooden skewer' was thought to be the only utensil needed, but, in the absence also of plates, a boy's 'lump of mutton was [often] lost to him in the scramble' because he would be required to act as fag in the short 'half-hour given over for eating'.[29]

Trollope's argument is that, horrific though these conditions were, they were in keeping with what Wykeham had wanted. Trollope believed that the much-vaunted reforms in public school education had succeeded in posing 'the question whether the rich are not robbing the poor'. He is not so worried that the sons of gentlemen attend these schools, as concerned that they attend them to the *exclusion* of the less fortunate, whose places they should be subsidizing. The great value of these schools, he asserts, is their diverse clientele, whereby the 'son of the squire of the parish and the son of the parson are placed together at the same school, are educated in the same way, enjoy an equal footing, so that in after life they meet together with mutual sympathy, and on an absolute equality as gentlemen, – though the school education of one has cost three times the sum expended on the other'.[30] Trollope had earlier criticized modern education in *Orley Farm* (1862) which, unlike public schools, did not teach a boy 'to measure himself against others' in his conduct rather than his knowledge, with the result that Lucius Mason, for all his knowledge and drive acquired at his new school, found that '[l]ife did not come easy to him'. His efforts were 'conspicuous', since he lacked 'the unpretentious, self-controlling humour' of an ex-public schoolboy.[31]

The article on public schools is one of the most indisputable pieces of evidence that, as he grew older, Trollope believed that gentlemanly status could be acquired through education rather than birth, and that this status should be made an achievable goal through the public school system by the rich subsidizing the poor, so that the poor could enter the Church worthily through education, as Wykeham had planned. It is also clear from this article that he felt that the community benefited from this levelling-up process.

Birthright distinctions and clerical calling

Trollope's non-fictional works of the mid-1860s chart the changes in attitude, customs and fortunes of the gently born. His endorsement of the arbitrary distinction of gentle birth can be found in a letter by him in the *Pall Mall Gazette* (1865). In this Trollope defends the newly formed 'sisters' from high-ranking families of the high Church of England, who wished to tend the sick within a conventual life. Nonetheless his defence of the decision of these 'sisters' is put into perspective when he ends his letter by announcing that: 'I call myself a gentleman and am fond of my rank, – but I would sooner see a daughter or a sister marry a shoemaker than become a sister, because I believe the end sought for is not obtained.'[32] His specific references to social rank were to emphasize his horror of this kind of confinement which, he thought, did not achieve the desired result. Trollope believed that participation in the ordinary dramas of life was preferable to abstention. This is further corroborated by his assertion, repeatedly stated in his work, that employment and industry should be rewarded by pecuniary amounts commensurate with the efforts expended.

For this reason Trollope is dismayed that a gentleman can be assured of social and financial standing only in a limited number of ecclesiastical positions. He explains in *Clergymen of the Church of England* (1866) how some of the changes relating to rank, station and industry in the Church have occurred. The English archbishop was no longer a prince but 'should be a gentleman, and – if it were always possible – a gentleman of birth', so this ecclesiastical position had *descended* to the class of gentleman over the centuries, and gentlemanly ancestry was desirable but not obligatory. The English bishop of the 1860s could be high, Evangelical or broad, but could not indulge in the idleness of his eighteenth-century princely antecedents, for he was 'a working man'.[33] For all the humour directed towards Bishop Proudie in the Barchester series, his industriousness is never in question and is the very reason why the high-and-dry clergymen disparage him. As far as they are concerned, the bishop's energy is dually reprehensible: it diminishes *his* stature and draws attention to their own lack of exertion. In *Doctor Thorne* (1858) Dr Proudie remarks to an earl, who privately acknowledges that he had not shared the bishop's 'martyrdom', that ' "[m]en in high places" ' are compelled to ' "burn their torches not in their own behalf" '. From the Barchester bishop's perspective, ' "[r]est and quiet are the comforts of those who have been content to remain in obscurity" '.[34] Dr Proudie *was* a working man. At this time, a cleric's elevation to the rank of bishop was generally because he had been 'conspicuous as a working parish clergyman', through merit rather than scholarship, for he was 'as ignorant of Greek as his former parish clerk'.[35] Work, not intellect, was his guiding star.

Whereas an archbishop or bishop in the mid-1860s might emerge from humble origins, the dean and archdeacon of this age were likely to be of gentlemanly background. The dean was noted for his scholarship, especially in literature, and had 'often written a book or two', since he had 'little to do and a good deal to get', while the archdeacon of this age was 'almost equal to a dean, and in diocesan power ... much superior to a dean, but ... [had] a great deal to do and very little to get'. By virtue of his relatively small remuneration, the archdeacon was 'generally a gentleman who [was] well-to-do in the world, and who [could] take a comfortable place in the county society'. The archdeacon was 'a bishop in little, and as such ... often much more of a bishop in fact than ... the bishop himself', for the archdeacon held 'court' and made 'visitations'. The dean lived in a cathedral town; the archdeacon lived in the country, a distinction in the nineteenth century which automatically placed the country dweller on a higher social pedestal. More refined yet more remote from society was the college fellow, who had to remain celibate for the tenure of his fellowship. He, like Mr Arabin, often chose the marital state in middle age when bachelor habits had begun to pall. Trollope defines the gentleman fellow as one who had 'nothing of the clergyman about him but the word Reverend attached to his name on his cards and letters', and the fact that his lower vestments enjoy a richer black hue than his married counterpart in a parish.[36] In other words, Trollope argues that the clergyman's worth as a Christian was often in inverse ratio to the newness of his clothes. A 'designer label', to appropriate a twenty-first century phrase, often denoted superficial faith.

The social changes in the role of parson were more complex, for long after the Reformation, 'the rural clergyman was anything but highly esteemed'. His inferior rank was marked by his having to leave 'the dining-room when the pudding came in and that he by no means did badly for himself in marrying the lady's maid'.[37] The Rev. W. G. Jervis, writing in 1856, warns indirectly of a possible return to the years of the Reformation and just after, when the clergy were counted generally among the plebeian class, and the children of clergy were on a par with the peasantry; clerical sons 'followed the plough' and daughters 'went out to service'.[38] Social transformation took place during the reigns of George III and George IV, when, as Trollope says, 'the parson in his parsonage was as good a gentleman as any squire in his mansion or nobleman in his castle'. Trollope blames the sudden rise in theological colleges in the nineteenth century for the parson's re-descent of the social ladder. It is the so-called 'literate', leaving a theological college, who is 'less attractive, less urbane, less genial – in one significant word, less of a gentleman' who was often now becoming a parson. Trollope adds that 'the adult parson of the parish' was nonetheless extant and had been educated at Oxford or Cambridge, and therefore remained 'all but the squire's equal'.[39] When upbraided by the heroine for daring to '"liken Mr Green to Sir Francis"', an indignant retort by Mrs Green in *Kept in the Dark* (1882), that Sir Francis Geraldine and her husband, a minor canon, '"are both gentlemen"', illustrates the continuance of these social pretensions late into the century, despite the unjust stipendiary system in the Church.[40] Even at the end of the century, in an article on the Church as a profession, Douglas Macleane confirmed that the vicar's high status derived from his own private background and income, and that it was not out of his official income 'that the vicar keeps up his pony-carriage, subscribes to the flower-show and cricket-club, sends his children to school, and takes a holiday in the autumn'.[41]

According to Trollope, however, the town incumbent, unfortunately, did not enjoy the same social exclusivity, being regarded as a 'professional gentleman', living in a newly built house overlooking a 'brick-field', his 'flock' constituting his 'hearers, not his parishioners'.[42] As clerk in the Ecclesiastical Commissioners in London, Brooke Burgess in *He Knew He Was Right* (1869) not only had to 'deal with the rents of episcopal properties', but also had 'to correspond with clerical claimants, and to be at home with the circumstances of underpaid vicars and perpetual curates' with much less than £300 a year'.[43] Burgess, of all Trollope's fictional characters, was acutely conscious that the rent-flow paid to the Church, once it filtered down the pecking order to town incumbents and perpetual curates, had virtually dried to a trickle. They could not live as gentlemen.

The real sadness lies, Trollope observes, in the mismatch in the nineteenth century between gentlemanly background and financial reward, especially in the case of the curate of a populous parish. Whereas in the past, 'the poor clergyman mixed with men who were not poor, and received something from his status in the world', the poor clergyman was no longer 'by virtue of his calling, a gentleman', and no longer 'admitted into all families simply because he had a place in the reading-desk of the parish church'. Mothers were afraid of allowing their 'softly' nurtured daughters to slip into penury by being tempted by the calling of such men.[44] Jervis, writing ten years before Trollope, decried 'a system, which pauperises talent, and exalts the artizan above the priest'.[45] Trollope warns the Church that its low stipends may tempt 'men of lower class in life, who have come from harder antecedents', and that this decline in social exclusivity would change the very essence of the Church.[46] He refrains from being more explicit. Trollope's reticence as well as his fear can be understood in light of W. J. Conybeare's famous article, 'The Church of England in the Mountains', which disclosed the existence, in 1853, 'of about one thousand "peasant clergy"', whose livings were in Wales and northern England, and whose own origins were farm homes, 'marked by ignorance, coarseness, intemperance, and immorality'.[47]

Birthright, education and poverty

The indigence of the gentlemanly scholar and clergyman returns as a theme in Trollope's fiction in *The Last Chronicle of Barset* (1867), in which Mr Crawley is older, but no less stubborn than he was in *Framley Parsonage* (1861). Trollope concentrates not so much on Mr Crawley's poverty this time, but on the appalling fact that the community could think of accusing a Church of England official of theft. Trollope's concerns, expressed in *Clergymen of the Church of England* (1866), about the increasing correlation between the gentlemanly curate of the populous parish and extreme poverty extend his unarticulated but damning thesis that the Church will have problems if its iniquitous system of remuneration attracts clergymen of too humble an origin. The drama of the novel hinges on the community's willingness to believe that a clergyman could be a criminal. The possibility of such a terrible situation arising is overwhelming. Crawley's conversation with his wife about community interest in his case echoes in fictional terms the fears expressed by Trollope one year earlier in *Clergymen of the Church of England*:

> 'They have come to see the degradation of a clergyman,' said he; – 'and they will not be disappointed.'
> *'Nothing can degrade but guilt,'* said his wife.
> 'Yes, – *misfortune can degrade, and poverty* ...'
> 'They have not always a clergyman before them as a criminal.'[48]

The conversation relates to Trollope's warning in his earlier work that extreme poverty among the clergy would lead to trouble.

Material means, too, play a large role in the novel in distinguishing Crawley's social exclusion through his poverty. The cheque itself, as paper money, is a financial sign with which Crawley, as a poor man, is unfamiliar. His innocence cannot be proved until Mr Arabin is able to confirm that it was he who gave the cheque to Crawley, but the real puzzle of the case, namely that Crawley could not remember the circumstances, was confused about the piece of paper, and seemed not to understand the situation, can only be explained by Crawley's complete lack of sophistication as to this mode of financial transaction. His intransigence is stressed almost to the point of insanity, but the reader cannot fail to recognize the more tragic indications of social exclusion of a clergyman gently raised but fallen into dire poverty. Macleane confirms that the clergyman, whatever his station, was expected to marry 'a lady, and it is looked for that he shall also be fairly cultivated and abreast of modern thought and books'. Despite these expectations in the late nineteenth century, 'about thirteen hundred curates... [had] been over fifteen years in Holy Orders. Some have waited more than half a century for preferment'.[49] Trollope's picture of clerical poverty was as accurate as it was haunting.

Haunting, too, was the accompanying humiliation. Trollope avows that starvation is almost preferable to 'the angry eyes of unpaid tradesmen', 'the taunt of the poor servant who wants her wages', 'the gradual relinquishment of habits which the soft nurture of earlier, kinder years had made second nature', 'the wan cheeks of the wife', 'the neglected children, who are learning not to be the children of gentlefolk', 'the alms of doles of half-generous friends', 'the waning pride' and 'the hand ... open to receive and ready to touch the cap'.[50] Outside Trollope's fiction, the Rev. Jervis, citing a letter from a poor clergyman, grateful for the 'little frocks' which 'fitted my girl as if they had been made for her', and for the coat which 'suited and fitted himself', condemned a society which could allow such degradation 'for a clergyman and gentleman to have to make!'[51] The aforementioned signs in *The Last Chronicle of Barset* relate to the clergyman's family; his own degraded position is marked out for the world to see by the signs of raiment and mien. Mrs Proudie refers to him as a 'beggarly, perpetual curate', mostly because his demeanour and dress so identify him on his memorable visit to the bishop in his 'dirty boots', 'rusty pantaloons', covered with mud from his long walk, and 'deep furrows on the cheek', while in stark juxtaposition the bishop is 'sleek and clean and well-fed'. Crawley's social exclusion is all the more unjust, Trollope suggests, since the poor curate, in contrast to the low church bishop and the high church dean, bears other hallmarks of gentlemanly distinction in his knowledge of Hebrew *and* Greek, the dean knowing 'very little Hebrew' and the bishop knowing no Greek.[52] In stark contrast, Mr Casaubon in Eliot's *Middlemarch* (1872), set in the 1820s, is both a scholar *and* a wealthy gentleman with a mansion and few duties, since his curate did these.[53]

Times have changed, as the archdeacon regrets to Mr Harding, while the latter reminisces about the former hallmarks of clerical gentlemen, which included good knowledge of port, tobacco, dancing and cards: '"Men were men, and clergymen were gentlemen"'.[54] Nor were expressions of this kind of regret confined to Trollope's fictional clergymen. He had other characters remark that the immediate recognition of a gentleman by means of his clerical cloth could no longer be assured. Jemima Stanbury in *He Knew He Was Right* (1869) mentions briefly but pointedly that '[i]t used to be the case that when you met a clergyman you met a gentleman'.[55]

If, however, clerical calling itself could not act as an identifying feature of social rank, other markers of social distinction could be used. Included among these was the choice of wine, the social significance of which is manifest in Trollope's fiction. Mr Harding's offering of port to his bedesmen in *The Warden* (1855) is egalitarian, and his lament, having tasted the inferior sherry at a London supper-house, reveals 'the discrepancy between the standards of living enjoyed by the lower and upper classes'.[56] The implication was that the older kind of clergyman, as a gentleman, had a discriminating palate.

Even the ultimate restoration of Crawley to gentlemanly dignity through his established innocence and appointment to St Ewold's at the end of *The Last Chronicle of Barset*, marked outwardly by new clothes for him and his wife,[57] fails to erase the image of the perpetual curate, whose indigence provides the sharp antidote to much of Trollope's comedy. This image never quite disappears. References in Trollope's later novels may be slight, but they persist and share significant details. Both Mr Surtees in *The American Senator* (1876–7) and Mr Greene in *Ayala's Angel* (1881) have a salary of £120 per year. While Mr Surtees hopes to marry Mary Masters – a hope that is vain because of prior claims of the heart *and* because her mother 'disliked clergymen, disliked gentlemen, and especially disliked poverty' – Mr Greene does not even entertain false hopes, for he knows that his salary is too small to support a wife and family. To Jonathan Stubbs, Ayala's 'Angel of Light', excited on the eve of his marriage at which Mr Greene will officiate, the obstacle of a small salary could be overcome '"with a little money"', but Mr Greene does not '"want to have to look for the money"' and, even if he did, knows that he '"shouldn't get it"', so '"very unfairly"' is everything '"divided in this world"'.[58] The impression given by Trollope is that, if Mr Crawley's familial situation is less likely to be repeated in the 1870s and 1880s, it is only through the perpetual curate's undesirability as a suitor. No girl without a martyr's tendencies would consider a future on so slender a budget and no curate with any sense of realism could contemplate it, whether or not he was a gentleman.

Birthright and indolence

New gradations in gentlemanly station first appear in *The Claverings* (1867). This suggests that the Church is in some way responsible for this change, possibly through its unmeritorious means of financial remuneration, possibly through its recruitment of a wider range of cleric, which had itself come about from the unequal stipendiary system. Mr Clavering, an old-style rector, is disappointed that his daughter wishes to marry Mr Saul, indisputably a gentleman, but who '"isn't quite one of our sort"'. The distinction lies in various outer and inner signs. Like Mr Crawley, Mr Saul is poor, has 'rusty clothes' and an 'awkwardness of . . . gait'. His habit of dusting his boots 'with his pocket-handkerchief' makes Fanny's brother, Harry Clavering, question whether he is 'fit to be his friend!' Harry Clavering compares the mean pieces of furniture of Mr Saul's single room with those of his own comfortable home. Mr Saul has 'a small rag of a carpet', 'a large deal table', which is 'unalloyed . . . without any mendacious paint', trying to pose as mahogany. There are three chairs in total, a 'small bed', a 'small dressing-table' and 'a rickety deal press in which he kept his clothes'. The simple statement, '[o]ther furniture there was none' is as indicative of the clergyman's poverty, squalor and social exclusion from Harry's class as the mice which had attacked his collection of books, the ubiquitous covering of dust among his piles of papers and the necessity of his eating solitary meals of 'chop', 'broiled rasher, or bit of pig's fry' on his dressing-table. In contrast to Mr Saul's humble domesticity, Harry recollects his own home with its 'Brussels carpet', its 'capacious chairs', its 'ormolu, damask hangings and Sèvres china', which Harry unashamedly acknowledges as the signs 'of the first-class clerical world'.[59]

Despite the Clavering men repeatedly mentioning that Mr Saul is a gentleman, his inner qualities mark him out to be different from *their* kind of gentleman, although their kind in no way appears attractive, for Trollope stresses their indolence, carelessness and prodigality. Mr Saul is hard-working, but goes about his duties with a solemnity which the Clavering men find puzzling. His lack of 'hand-pressing and the titillations of love-making', together with his absolute refusal to accept that his small income is an impediment to their marriage, makes even his putative fiancée Fanny wonder at his kind of gentleman, for '[i]t could not be her duty to marry a man who would have to starve in his attempt to keep her'. Even after Mr Saul's acquisition of Mr Clavering's living the Clavering family continues to be perplexed by the new breed of gentleman who can worry, as Mr Saul does, that 'the riches of this world... [might] become not a stumbling-block... and a rock of offence'. Mr Clavering's hope that marriage may encourage him 'into the way of drinking a glass of wine like anybody else' is as faint as Florence's hope that marriage may enable him to 'moderate his views'.[60] Thus the outer and inner signs of Mr Saul's clerical gentlemanhood stand him well apart from the older category of gentleman clergyman, and yet the older category is now presented by Trollope to be unattractive.

So uneven was the clerical stipendiary system in the 1860s that marriage could make or break a young clergyman. Marriage to Florence Clavering rescues Mr Saul from indigence and will provide him with at least the outer appurtenances of gentlemanhood. Mr Gibson in *He Knew He Was Right* (1869) is not so fortunate. Presented as a bit of a puppet and handed around from one marriageable young girl to another, Mr Gibson is so inert in his courting that he can only win the least eligible 'prize' and, because he has infuriated so many people in Exeter through his dithering, is forced to take his bride 'somewhere in Cornwall' – always designated by Trollope as a county of poor and obscure parishes.[61] His prospects as a gentleman clergyman are bleak.

More tragically figured in the same novel, despite the humorous pun in his name, is Mr Outhouse,[62] a town incumbent not dissimilar in manner of living from Trollope's prototype in *Clergymen of the Church of England*. Marriage to the sister of Sir Marmaduke has given him a loyal wife but no extra income. His sole means of subsistence derives from his parish, St Diddulph's-in-the-East, which lies 'very near the river', is 'very populous, very poor, very low in character, and very uncomfortable'. A man of stern character, 'most kind to the poor', but also 'strongly-biased' and 'obstinate withal', he is dismayed when called upon to shelter a baby and his two nieces, one of whom has been wrongly accused by her husband of encouraging the amorous advances of a 50-year-old family friend and duly cast out of the marital home. That he would not shirk his duty, everyone knew. But his parsonage, 'for the abode of a gentleman', was 'a dreary place' and 'a poor residence for his wife's nieces'. When his guests' visit stretches into months, his financial situation becomes desperate. Having, as a gentleman, 'resolutely refused all payment from Mr Trevelyan' (his niece's husband), his 'hand-to-mouth existence' makes him even more dependent on the patience of the neighbouring tradesmen, among whom the butcher 'would often hint' when 'a little money ought to be paid', although 'it was never expected that the parsonage bill should be settled'. Eventually, even that mode of survival cannot be sustained and the gentleman rector is compelled, when the lengthy visit has drawn to an end, not to reject the '[t]wo bank notes' that are tactfully 'put on his table', for 'he knew that unless he took them he could not pay for the provisions which his unwelcome visitors had consumed'. In the same novel, Jemima Stanbury's rigid opposition to change obliquely conveys the plight of clergymen caught between the Church's widening net of social inclusion and its reluctance to reform its method of payment. Jemima Stanbury, living within the Cathedral Close, judges that, generally, the birthright of '[g]ood blood' belongs to clergymen of the Church of England, who 'are allowed within the pale', although 'by no means' is it as certain 'as used to be the case', now that there are 'literates' (men from theological colleges) and, in contrast to when she was young, 'they've taken to ordaining all manner of people'. Her reactionary attitude is clearly not shared by Trollope, for she regrets that the Church has abolished its feudal system of exacting the 'special holiness' of a 'tithe'.[63] If, in *He Knew He Was Right*, Jemima Stanbury's prejudices are indicated as unacceptable, the living conditions of the fictional clergymen expected to conduct themselves as gentlemen are shown to be even more intolerable if they have not married 'well', whether or not they have the energy and capacity for hard work, and whether or not they are gentlemen through birthright. But Trollope does not offer these clergymen as sympathetic models, in spite of their difficulties.

Birthright and laissez-faire

Even though the gentlemanly ancestries of Mr Fenwick, vicar, of Harry Gilmore, squire, and of Mr Chamberlaine, bachelor prebendary of Salisbury, are stressed in *The Vicar of Bullhampton* (1870), Trollope indicates through their weaknesses that the gentleman clergyman of the late 1860s does not command the same respect as his predecessor, and that he probably does not deserve it. Frank Fenwick may have 'more of breeding in his appearance than his friend', Harry Gilmore, but his reckless 'rat-killing matches' with Sam Brattle, 'with a ferret in his hand, grovelling in the dust' somewhat diminish his 'pastoral dignity'. Harry Gilmore's extreme despair over his rejection by Mary Lowther reduces his stature in the reader's eyes, if only because of his long disappearance from the narrative. Mr Chamberlaine's almost 'golden prebend' of £800 a year and a house, his gift for oratory and the great esteem which everyone from the 'boy who blacked his boots' to the bishop who was wary of him felt for him, could not atone for the fact that, according to Trollope, he 'had absolutely never done anything useful in the whole course of his life'. Mr Puddleham, the dissenting minister, is not even accorded the title of gentleman. The signs of gentle breeding, however, are stressed whenever Mr and Mrs Fenwick are compared with Mr and Mrs Puddleham, in order to show their differences, and yet the reader never becomes convinced of a *vast* superiority of the one ecclesiastical officer over the other. The vicarage fruit and cabbages were given to the Puddlehams, Mrs Fenwick 'always inquired after the mother and infant' whenever a new baby was born to the Puddlehams, and Mr Fenwick always made a point of shaking hands with the Methodist minister. Yet the dogged martyrdom of Mr Fenwick, in his refusal to insist that the chapel be built elsewhere, is made to look ludicrous, for the Church is shown later by Mr Fenwick's brother-in-law, a barrister, to own the very land on which the chapel has been built and that Mr Fenwick, the incumbent, had no right to allow the dissenters to build there in the first place.[64]

Birthright and decadence

If decadence in the English clerical gentleman is merely hinted at in *The Claverings* and *The Vicar of Bullhampton*, it is made explicit in *The Eustace Diamonds* (1873). The Jewish clergyman, Joseph Emilius, may, with embarrassing injustice for the twenty-first century reader, be denied any claim to gentlemanly ancestry or any positive attributes, but Frank Greystock's father, the high church dean, fares no better in the writer's estimation, even though his claims to gentlemanly distinction and ancestry are high. The dean, despite his pleasantness, is described in terms of his unashamed prejudices:

> The House of Hanover was bad. All interference with prerogative has been bad. The Reform bill was very bad. Encroachment on the estates of the bishops was bad. Emancipation of Roman Catholics was the worst of all. Abolition of corn-laws, church-rates, and oaths and tests were all bad. The meddling with the Universities has been grievous. The treatment of the Irish land bills were all bad. The treatment of the Irish Church has been Satanic. The over-hauling of schools is most injurious to English education. Education bills and Irish land bills were all bad. Every step taken has been bad.[65]

The prodigality of the Claverings is surpassed by that of the Greystocks, with equal right to gentlemanly status, but without the financial means to support their expensive tastes. There is something of the *fin de siècle* about them and their inability to acknowledge the changing world, either by altering their habits or means of survival. The dean's contentment as long as he may continue to enjoy 'every comfort of life, a well-kept table, good wine, new books, and canonical habiliments with the gloss still on', provided by the Bobsborough tradespeople 'as though they came from the clouds', strikes an unseemly chord, not just for the assumption that debt is unimportant, but also for the dean's advice to his son, Frank, that a prudent marriage is all that is required for the good things of life to endure.[66] Nowhere in the novel does Trollope suggest that the dean's impecunious finances are anything other than of his own making.

The alleged robbery by a poor perpetual curate was an indication in *The Last Chronicle of Barset* that community respect for the Church had lessened, but in *The Eustace Diamonds* (1873) Trollope even jokingly alludes to the possibility, 'some years ago', that the police had placed the bishop under suspicion when 'the altar-plate was stolen from Barchester Cathedral'. Significantly, in the Barchester novels, the last of which was published four years before *The Eustace Diamonds*, there is no mention of such an incident. It is more than possible that allusion to such a suspicion would have been unthinkable in fiction in the 1860s, but was possible in the 1870s, when community opinion of the Church was low. The novel ends on a jocular note of disrespect for the Church's decline in prestige, for the duke jokes about the reduced rank of archbishop from his former princely status.[67]

While the dean of high-ranking ancestry in *The Eustace Diamonds* becomes impoverished, the dean of low-ranking ancestry in *Is He Popenjoy?* (1878) becomes rich by marrying well. Clearly, neither dean gives Trollope confidence in the Church's standing in the community. The dean's low-class origins are referred to throughout *Is He Popenjoy?*, particularly with respect to his aristocratic son-in-law's resentment over his wealth and power, for '[h]e was always conscious of the Dean's low birth' and 'the disposition on the part of the Dean to domineer'. Prior to Lord George's succeeding to the family estate, he was actually 'afraid of the Dean', even though his loud laugh was 'more like the son of a stable-keeper than a dean', and yet he was dependent on him financially. As his older brother, the Marquess, taunted him, '[t]hey used to make gentlemen deans'. The Marquess nonetheless did not expect violence when he insulted the dean's daughter, for '[t]he normal dean is a goodly, sleek, bookish man, who would hardly strike a blow under provocation'. The implication seems to be that it is the dean's humble ancestry that is responsible for the physical response. Yet Trollope has the bishop later defend the dean's actions to his chaplain on the grounds that 'he was justified'. The question of class is raised by the dean himself, who asserts to the bishop that the Marquess 'is a degraded animal, unfortunately placed almost above penalties by his wealth and rank'.[68] Justified or not, the dean's violence and overweening ambition indicate Trollope's diminishing confidence in the Church's ability to maintain social order and retain community respect.

Dr Wortle's search in *Dr Wortle's School* (1880) for a 'gentleman, a schoolmaster, a curate, a matron, and a lady – we may say all in one' is adumbrated as well-nigh impossible, for 'a gentleman, when he is married, does not often wish to dispose of the services of his wife. A lady, when she has a husband, has generally sufficient duties of her own to employ her, without undertaking others'. It is surprising, then, when Dr Wortle does seem to find the perfect couple in Rev. Peacocke and his wife, except that the reader then learns that Mrs Peacocke is the wife, not of Mr Peacocke but of someone else. Dr Wortle's championing of the couple's plight has been assessed by critics as evidence of Trollope's tolerance of human peccadilloes, but the modern reader tends to overlook the fact that Dr Wortle, described initially as a 'well-to-do gentleman', is also known for his laxness, 'made himself wilfully distasteful to many of his stricter brethren', had even 'been heard to swear' and was abrasive with any bishop who disagreed with him.[69] Nonetheless, these factors tend to endear Dr Wortle to the modern reader and Trollope clearly empathizes with him.

Evidence from contemporary sources supports Trollope's depiction of changes in public behaviour and attitude as well as changes in the clergyman's pastoral role. The Rev. John Coker Egerton confirmed the Church's strong views on co-habitation in his diary note of 1857 that he had held a wedding in the morgue and that the 'witnesses were a man and woman living in open sin', and was dismayed that they had had to let the wedding go ahead.[70] Greater public tolerance of human frailties was thus contributing to clergymen modifying their own conduct and approach to duty. The fictional Dr Wortle is therefore just a few steps ahead of the Rev. Coker Egerton on the path to relative morality. Significantly, the bishop in *Dr Wortle's School* goes to great lengths to support his headstrong clergyman and, far from advocating any form of hypocrisy, tries to impress upon Dr Wortle that '[i]t is not enough to be innocent...but men must know that we are so'. The bishop and Mr Puddicombe attempt to apprise Dr Wortle of the importance of maintaining distinctions between ordinary men and gentlemanly clergymen. While Trollope shows Dr Wortle to be impatient with the upright Mr Puddicombe, he never once hints that the stricter clergyman should be ridiculed in the way in which he lampooned the falsely pious Mr Slope of *Barchester Towers*. However unfortunate the situation is for Mr Peacocke and his 'wife', Dr Wortle, in his steadfast support, has, in Mr Puddicombe's words and in the Church's view, 'countenanced immorality and deceit in a brother clergyman'. The final irony is found in Trollope's description of the romance between Dr Wortle's daughter and the young Lord Carstairs. The possibility of their future marriage is shown to delight Dr Wortle, but not Carstairs' father, the Earl, whose self-comforting emission sounds comically hollow: 'At any rate the Doctor is a gentleman.'[71] The reassurance seems particularly lame after Dr Wortle's lapses of gentlemanly forbearance.

The deliberate emphasis on the gentlemanly status of Philip Hughes in 'The Two Heroines of Plumplington' (1882), set in Barsetshire, is telling. Trollope would have had no need to stress Mr Harding's gentlemanhood in 1855 in *The Warden* (1855). But, in the early 1880s, clergymen were not always sufficiently affluent to enable their children to aspire to their father's social status. Philip Hughes was a humble cashier in the bank of which Emily Greenmantle's father was manager. Emily knew that her father disapproved of her choice of husband, even though 'in her eyes Philip Hughes was quite as good a gentleman as her father. He was the son of a clergyman now dead, but had been intimate with [the Rev.] Dr Freeborn'.[72] Philip Hughes has no scandal attached to him, but nor does he have the cachet of high status, and the decline generally in a clergyman's social status is marked in this short story, for Philip Hughes is seen to be ascending the social scale by marrying a bank manager's daughter.

Neither gentlemen, nor gentlemen clergymen in *Marion Fay* (1882) is shown to have positive attributes. A clergyman guilty of theft and a clergyman guilty of immorality may not be acceptable, but to have a clergyman contemplate murder, as *Marion Fay* has, is to commit the ultimate taboo. To have, within the Church, the sanctity of life traded for earthly comfort by a Church official destroys any vestige of ecclesiastical probity. Mr Greenwood, gentleman clergyman, is not accorded any redeeming feature. His greed and guilt are conveyed, invoking Lady Macbeth, by the incessant rubbing of his hands. Lord Hampstead's reluctance to assume responsibility for what he regards as 'a burden and an absurdity to be born to be an earl', even though he *does* fulfil his duty, warns the reader that the concept of *noblesse oblige* is nearing an end. Now that the indicators of birth, wealth and conduct can no longer be equated, the question of social exclusion becomes irrelevant.

The Quakers, Zachary Fay and his daughter Marion, are the only characters in the novel who are drawn to be consistently good. That dissenting Quakers of humble birth and station should evince the very qualities previously ascribed to members of the Church of England and of gentle birth is symptomatic of Trollope's increasingly deep contempt for his own kind. Quakers had long been viewed as people seeking radical social change. The Rev. Witts recorded in his diary, nearly half a century before this novel, that Quakers were seeking the abolition of the death penalty on the grounds that it was 'barbarous and anti-Christian'.[73] The Quakers' understated dress, with 'no variety of colour', and their plain speaking, which Trollope is at pains to point out 'escaped that touch of hypocrisy' in their eschewing of '"thou-ing" and "thee-ing"', are offered as outer signs of their inner sincerity, the kind of sincerity which Trollope used to equate with people of gentle birth within the Church of England, but now equates with a dissenting sect among ordinary people.[74]

Trollope's ecclesiastical concerns span almost his entire writing career. It is not surprising, over a period of 35 years, that a writer should alter his views. What is perhaps revealing is that Trollope, an active participant in the Church of England until his death and constant in his theological convictions, grew ever critical of the Church as an institution. In his early writing he exhibits more nostalgia for past ecclesiastical ways and practices than he does toward the end of his career. While he continues to harbour a covert fondness for the older-style gentlemen clergymen, he increasingly moderates his sympathy for them as the decades of the century proceed towards their three-quarter mark. He realized that they could no longer satisfy the needs of their calling. The Church needed new vigour, new skills and new blood. He was a man who travelled much, socialized widely, and took careful account of what he saw and heard. He was cautious of change, but did not fear it; nor was he afraid to change his mind. Moreover, despite his interest in maintaining social demarcation lines and distinctions, he deplored social exclusion on the grounds of ancestral birthright. Having himself had to reascend with difficulty the steep *échelons* of social rank through hard work, he believed that merit should ultimately determine worldly prosperity and personal happiness. Both his fiction and non-fiction, if read in systematic chronology, increasingly question social exclusion on the basis of circumstantial lineage, and advocate instead reward for personal merit and endeavour.

4
Women and the Church

Gentlemen clergymen inevitably came into contact with women, both in their work and in domestic life. This chapter will concentrate on an examination of those women. Many volumes have been written about the lack of opportunity for productive female employment in the nineteenth century,[1] but few contemporary publications have focused on the powerful contribution of the female population generally to nineteenth-century life and, when they have, have stressed societal limitations rather than female contributions. The concession that a woman could learn to 'manage' her husband, provided that he was 'persuaded' that any new idea was his own, promotes the common judgement that women were treated as inferiors.[2] The recognition of the strong influence of female relatives on their clerical kin in selected case studies of Evangelical and Dissenting families loses its bite by emphasizing that '[s]erious Christians did not doubt that women were and should be subordinate to men socially'.[3] Similarly disheartening is the claim in a study of women writers that, while Anglican sisterhoods and Evangelical sororities did eventuate in the nineteenth century, endowing women with a degree of independence, 'most clergymen wanted them limited to philanthropic rather than sacred functions and kept in strict subordination to the male hierarchy'. To conclude that women did not use their ecclesiastical writing in an influential way, as men did, 'to work through the intellectual issues of Victorian faith and doubt',[4] simply adds to the vast number of works offering a rather dismal picture of women aspiring to achieve emancipation, but not attaining it.

Trollopian scholarship has been rather more positive in its assessment of women's general contribution to Victorian life. There are several excellent views in this area, but none so far has examined the influence of women on clergymen.[5] The closest to a positive statement about female influence on clergymen points out that 'petticoat government' in Trollope's Barchester straddles both low and high church parties.[6] I intend to begin to redress the rather depressing depictions of constrained and helpless Victorian womanhood. Publications hitherto have usually concentrated on cataloguing the limits imposed by nineteenth-century society on women and on showing the dialectical struggle of individual women against societal norms, as in the literature first mentioned. I will take these societal norms as *données*. I hope to demonstrate that Trollope, well aware of society's self-imposed constraints and supportive of women's achievements, actually illustrates the enormous influence of women within socially prescribed parameters. Those parameters determined that women, with few exceptions, could only be defined by their relationship to men, for the public sphere was largely denied to them. My sub-headings thus reflect the limitations placed by society on women. Yet, as I will illustrate, Trollope believed that these domestic roles could actually ameliorate women's effectiveness in society. It is too easy to look no further than the comic surface in his novels. I will show that Trollope's portrayal of the petticoat government of clerical officers, from the most lowly to the most lofty, reveals that women's powerful influence in the private sphere could not but help extend itself into the public world.

Sydney Smith's astute psychology, outlined in 1808, may have been the inspiration for Trollope's portrayal of the clergy and for his methodology. Smith, a friend of Trollope and his senior in age by several years, explained that 'Bishops *are* men; not always the wisest of men', and as they grew older, became more and more 'governed as other men are, by daughters and wives, and whoever minister to their daily comforts', which often accounted for 'a very capricious administration of ecclesiastical affairs'.[7] In other words, Smith suggests that the daily proximity and intimacy shared by men and women in family life ensured that the female confined to domestic pursuits probably had more influence on the public man than any other person, for it was the physical dependence of men on the women close to them which welded the psychological chain of command from the domestic hearth to the public place. Trollope began with this idea and extended it in his fictional work as a powerfully subversive answer to active feminism. His fictional reification was all the more potent because it was expressed through his unique brand of comic realism. His subtlety and popularity are monuments to his success.

In addition to Smith's views was the prevailing attitude of Protestants to womanhood and religion. Trollope could not have failed to know these opinions through his many ecclesiastical connections. Protestants did not, until later in the nineteenth century, have the aid of female devotion; the abolition of the nunneries at the Reformation had seen to that. Instead, they had the services of the wives and daughters of their 'reformed priesthood'. While Roman Catholics could only rely on celibate priests and nuns, Protestants had a family battery of female auxiliaries to strengthen the sacerdotal calling of their clerical menfolk, as well as to assist them, unpaid, in their practical tasks.[8] Trollope based much of his comedy on this understanding and used it to strengthen his thesis that women ruled the Church while the men reigned.

While a number of Trollope's female contemporaries held strong feminist views, some were perturbed by the possible consequences of gender division. Anna Jameson, writing in 1855, urged a note of caution to women contemplating apartheid. When Frederika Bremer, the Swedish feminist and writer, advocated exclusion of 'the cooperation of the masculine brain', Jameson warned that '[a]ll schemes for the public good, in which men and women do not work in communion, have in them the seeds of change, discord and decay'.[9] Trollope endorses this view behind the masks of his comedy.

Female influence began predominantly in the home and Trollope took advantage of this to provide his parsons with a range of female relatives playing a variety of roles as counterparts to their ecclesiastical kinsmen. Sometimes the wearers of petticoats were daughters and sisters, who might later became wives and mothers; at other times they might be single – spinsters or widows. Eleanor Arabin, formerly Bold, née Harding, played all of these roles in the Barchester novels.

Despite Trollope's claim that he was 'an advanced, but still conservative Liberal',[10] his 'natural' conservatism has long been taken for granted, and his dislike of active feminism has been cited as evidence.[11] Yet critics, contemporary and modern, have so far skated around or misconstrued the plentiful evidence in Trollope's writing that his dislike of the feminist movement can in no way be correlated with his belief in the contribution of women to private and public life.

One result of the increasing secularization of higher education, discussed more fully in Chapter 5, was the opportunity for women to attend university. Trollope's lecture, 'Higher Education of Women' (1868), has unfairly been interpreted as a patriarchal Victorian dismissal of women.[12] Certainly, Trollope cautions against sudden change in the universities, and his *tone* seems patronizing, but he often assumes mock pomposity to mask a serious proposition. Even the fairest judge, in allowing that Trollope does not deem women to be inferior, uses a citation without context, and gives the impression that Trollope's statement – that women's occupations 'cannot in the long run be the same' – signifies his disapproval of higher education for women.[13] Careful scrutiny of the lecture reveals that Trollope is very much in favour of women receiving a higher education. Having remarked that Satan finds mischief for idle hands and that the upbringing of children is too lax, he criticizes a young woman of his acquaintance, described as emancipated, for preferring to read novels to studying the German language, and exhorts the women assembled before him not to rely on others to make higher education available to them but to achieve that goal themselves 'by a steadfast adherence to fixed purposes'.[14] His view is that nothing is attained unless those seeking reform actually effect it themselves. Unfortunately, critics have concentrated on Trollope's laconic sense of humour and overlooked his charge to women to prove their worth by fulfilling their own aspirations, rather than leaving it to men to continue to protect them. Since Trollope himself, struggling against his family's diminished finances, had succeeded by his own efforts, and since his mother had done likewise, one cannot dispute his sincerity.

A lecture delivered four years earlier in 1864 to the Leeds Mechanics' Institute provides further evidence of Trollope's genuine interest in promoting higher education for women. The lecture, 'Politics as a Daily Study for Common People', included his belief in the suitability of politics as a subject of study for women. Trollope redelivered this in 1868, the year of his crushing Beverley election and the year of his lecture on higher education for women. It is unlikely that, in the space of a single year, Trollope would have advocated the study of a serious subject for women in one lecture and dismissed the possibility of higher education for women in another. Admittedly, he did not like the American brand of strident feminism, but he liked women to be well-informed. Trollope believed firmly in the Church, but fully supported the secularization of higher education, particularly if its consequences could improve the educational opportunities for men *and* women. Above all, Trollope wished women to take their educational opportunities seriously.

Having received a classical education himself, he did not want a reversion to past practices. A close look at his review, 'Merivale's History of the Romans' (1856), reveals that Trollope vehemently abhorred ancient Roman patriarchy which, '[i]n the absence of all true religious feeling', made the wife 'little better than the chattel of her husband', and ensured that 'mental culture [was] confined to the master sex'.[15] Trollope not only did not subscribe to this view, he also had examples around him to disprove it.

His mother, Frances Trollope, was no ordinary Victorian mother. When his father, Thomas Anthony, could no longer keep his family through his failed barrister's practice, Frances used her writing to provide the family's income. Trollope had great respect for her. In 1848 Trollope wrote to her in Tuscany of the turbulence in Ireland and of the confused interpretations imputed to this. In the year of the Great Exhibition, he refers to the 'Papal Aggression', and is obviously responding to something which his mother has said. Trollope and his mother did not simply write to one another; they had epistolary conversations as equals about politics, religion, literature and topical subjects.[16]

Wives

It is fashionable now to assume that great men's wives were treated as unrewarded drudges. Rose Trollope was no drudge; nor was she an ornament. Trollope's correspondence shows Rose to be actively engaged with the processes of his writing, the financial aspects, and to be his friend. Rose criticized his manuscripts, and Trollope heeded her. A London hostess commented that Trollope knew what women said to each other when men were absent,[17] but this was because Rose 'was his books'.[18] As Trollope's travelling increased, his letters to Rose range from the personal to the literary and financial, and their shorthand communication illustrates a shared responsibility. A letter from Rome in 1875 comprises all elements.[19] It is therefore no surprise that his fictional representations should depict powerful clerical wives. Modern readers need to distinguish between nineteenth-century parameters of power and activity and later ones, for they do not necessarily coincide.

Both publicly and privately, clerical wives in Trollope's novels wield great influence. The archdeacon's two ecclesiastical problems in Barchester are the Ritualists and the Evangelicals. His wife employs successful strategies for overcoming their threatened hegemony. In her husband's absence, Susan Grantly slights a young Oxford clergyman's practice of intoning in *Barchester Towers* (1857) by expressing her 'hope that the young gentleman had not been taken ill', and his ritualist practice immediately ceased.[20] Thus Trollope illustrates that the archdeacon's wife determines the ecclesiastical practices of her husband's clerical subordinates, a position of power gained as much by her status as wife as by her strength of character. The Evangelical threat coming from those in superior ecclesiastical positions in no way deters her. She injures the hubris of Mrs Proudie, the bishop's formidable wife, by feigning surprise in *Framley Parsonage* (1861) at the latter's mock dismay at having to maintain her husband's social position by spending the season in London. Susan Grantly is more than adept at backing her opponent into the murky shadows of social obscurity; her two words – ' "Must he?" '[21] – immediately deflate Mrs Proudie before she proceeds to absolute annihilation. Nor is the archdeacon's wife too proud to enlist more powerful female support in the guise of Lady Lufton against the Evangelical faction. Their friendship heightens aristocratic help in the face of low-church diocesan supremacy, and demonstrates Mrs Grantly's skill in social elevation. There is no doubt that her *private* influence leads to her public influence. To the world at large in *The Warden* (1855), Dr Grantly is forthright, dignified and firm in his convictions, but within the marital bedroom the archdeacon 'talks, and looks, and thinks like an ordinary man', and 'listened to the counsels of his wife'. The archdeacon's nightcap, his yawning and stretching beneath the bedclothes modify the worldly view of him and so, too, does Mrs Grantly's insistence on calling her husband 'archdeacon', even in intimate situations, and even though she obviously has the upper hand.[22] Thus, comically, Trollope indicates the paradoxes of human relationships. Susan Grantly's demeanour is reverential, but she knows that her husband, dismissive of others, listens to *her*. A letter promising Rose, in the year of his death, only to dine with close friends or relatives indicates that Trollope had all his married life been, like his fictional archdeacon, answerable to his spouse.[23] Susan Grantly is the key figure in the archdeacon's social advancement, his early disappointment at not succeeding to his father's bishopric more than compensated for by the tacit understanding that archdeacons in Victorian society were often richer than, and socially superior to, their ecclesiastical leaders.

Mrs Grantly's foe, Mrs Proudie, also holds public as well as private sway, even if the archdeacon's wife can socially outstrip her. One of the most famous clerical wives in his novels, if not in the whole of Victorian literature, Trollope always gives her formal title and surname. She is even granted the role of preacher. While many women among the Dissenters became preachers, women in the Church of England were denied this outlet, although the Evangelicals had encouraged their women to preach, particularly during the 1860s when the belief in pre-millennialism was strong.

Female emancipation, generally accepted in Methodism, was also common among certain Evangelicals. Lord Shaftesbury, a leading Evangelical, was president of the Society for Promoting the Employment of Women. By 1866 many middle-class Evangelical women were involved in preaching, but a growing interest in spiritualism caused much 'controversy within and outside the established church', and the Church of England soon discouraged female preaching.[24] Preaching by Evangelical women in the era of the Barchester novels was not forbidden, and Trollope's Mrs Proudie threw herself into it in *Barchester Towers* (1857), although he does not suggest that she had the authority of the Church. She gave an evening sermon at one of the three Sunday services, held to 'atone for' the congregation's 'dissipation and low dresses during the week', as Trollope ironically puts it.[25]

Her dominion thus extends beyond the domestic household, but it is over her husband that she is the most tyrannical, in public and private. Her assumed guardianship of public morality, particularly when involving a clergyman, is the issue she initially tackles through her husband. Having said that 'submission produces the nearest approach to peace' that the bishop can hope to achieve in his household,[26] Trollope returns on many occasions to the ways in which Dr Proudie bends his will to suit his wife. Mr Slope, the bishop's protégé, whose ambitions are forever thwarted by his fondness for women and by his superior's wife, is often involved, and his visits to young, attractive lady parishioners provide much of the novel's humour and Mrs Proudie's ammunition for criticism.

Trollope's comedy was heightened by his readership's awareness of the dangers of young, single clerics visiting young women without a chaperone. Oxenden, a contemporary commentator, had advised that no clergyman should visit a female without the presence of a third person.[27] Trollope was thus touching a sensitive nerve. Much later, in *Is He Popenjoy?* (1878) Mr Groschut, the Evangelical bishop's chaplain, whose laborious piety is 'worn on his sleeve', is finally condemned by the bishop to the £300 living of Pugsty for 'acting not quite on the square with a young lady'. The reader is not, however, entirely satisfied with this solution as far as Pugsty is concerned, as Lady Sarah wonders, '"What is to become of the poor people?"'[28]

The sharp rise in the number of clergymen and the increase of newcomers to the priesthood from humble backgrounds made the Church itself nervous of maintaining its standards of propriety, and Trollope is stirring matters by introducing comedy into the temptations of the clerical flesh by attractive young women. As mentioned in Chapter 3, Mr Slope is commonly thought to have been modelled on the real-life Mr Francis Close, the Evangelical rector of Cheltenham, who later became the Dean of Carlisle. Close was well known for his oratorical skills and was equally notorious for his susceptibility to female parishioners.

Mrs Proudie also attempts to arrange livings and curtails Mr Slope's activities, as well as her husband's official prerogative. The wardenship question of Hiram's Hospital instigates incidents in which the bishop vacillates between Mr Slope's machinations and Mrs Proudie's demands. The bishop, despite Mr Harding's superior qualifications, finally submits to his wife in *Barchester Towers* (1857), and Mr Slope's disgust prompts him not to 'be the working factotum of a woman-prelate'.[29]

Trollope's depiction of Mrs Proudie as *de facto* bishop may have been inspired by Sydney Smith, who ruefully commented in 1838: 'I have seen in the course of my life, as the mind of the prelate decayed, wife bishops, daughter bishops, butler bishops, and even cook and housekeeper bishops.'[30] It is possible, too, that Trollope remembered Maria Edgeworth's depiction in her novel, *Patronage* (1813), of a bishop's sister, whom Buckhurst Falconer marries in order to acquire a fortune. He lives to regret his decision, for his wife, who has governed the bishop, becomes his tyrant too and refuses to let him have any money beyond the amount which she stipulated.[31]

There were also wives in the dioceses of England who held dominion over their clerical husbands. Henry Carrington (1814–1906) paid a huge price for his preferment. His deanship, won 'by marrying the right man's niece', enabled him to have one of the wealthiest livings in the archbishop's gift. His wife's private income, however, meant that 'it was she who ran the parish', for any documents requiring the Dean as signatory she would remove from the room, sign herself and return.[32] Trollope would not have had to look far for actual models for Mrs Proudie.

Trollope did in fact deny to James Pycroft, clergyman, that Mrs Proudie was 'a freak of fancy', and invited him to look at his ecclesiastical superiors, noting that, because 'diocesan work is too heavy for one man', bishops' wives of Mrs Proudie's ilk will be on the increase.[33] The fact that Mrs Proudie, like Susan Grantly, addresses her husband by his title – ' "What is it about, Bishop?" ' – sharpens the role reversal in *Barchester Towers* (1857) of the apparent patriarchal hierarchy of Victorian society.[34] Several references are made in *The Last Chronicle of Barset* (1867) to Mrs Proudie's assumption of episcopal authority beyond the palace walls. It is, for example, Mrs Proudie's conviction of Mr Crawley's guilt that steers Barchester's opinion, her main qualification being that '[s]he had known much of clergymen all her life'. After her death Miss Thorne tells Mrs Arabin that she does not ' "suppose the poor bishop will count for much" '.[35] Miss Thorne's prediction remains true even years later. On being told in *He Knew He Was Right* (1869) that Dr Proudie is likely to be the next Ecclesiastical Commissioner for the second time – a position in which bishops 'only get blown up, and snubbed, and shoved into corners by the others' – Brooke Burgess scathingly prophesies that the Barchester bishop will 'go into the corner without any shoving'.[36] The bishop without his wife was a spent force.

Humorous though the picture of the henpecked bishop is, Trollope knew that even a faint scent of a strong woman in the Church would propel his contemporary readers into a reconsideration of the controversy surrounding active female participation in various denominations. In a letter to Mr Arabin in *The Last Chronicle of Barset* (1867), in which he calls Mrs Proudie 'that very pestilent woman', Mr Crawley fumes: 'If there be aught clear to me in ecclesiastical matters, it is this – that no authority can be delegated to a female'. He even alludes to the practice in other countries of employing women within the church, but slyly disclaims 'the romantic tale of the woman Pope notwithstanding'.[37] The debate about women in the Anglican Church had engaged the population in England since the founding by Pusey of the first Anglican Sisterhood in 1845, the year in which Newman became a Roman Catholic, the two events striking fear into English people that papal power would return to their shores.[38] The 'Papal Aggression' of 1850 exacerbated this general dread a few years later, since religious life for women was seen to be synonymous with the Roman Catholic tradition. Queen Victoria, in response to a petition signed by 63 peers, 198 Members of Parliament and about 300,000 lay Anglicans, asked the Archbishop of Canterbury 'to maintain the purity of the doctrines taught by the clergy of the Established Church, and to discourage and prevent innovations in the mode of conducting the services of the Church not sanctioned by law or general usage'.[39] By the 1860s Anglican convents were on the increase but were still highly controversial. For many people, their imposition of celibacy pointed to Roman Catholicism. Mr Crawley's emphasis in *The Last Chronicle of Barset* (1867) – that women in England and certain other countries could now legally 'sit upon the temporal thrones of the earth, but on the lowest step of the throne of the Church no woman has been allowed to sit as bearing the authority' – therefore reveals fear within the mainstream Protestant churches of female intrusion into patriarchal preserves, as well as dread of Roman Catholic resumption of power within England.[40]

Mrs Proudie is not the only clerical wife drawn by Trollope who holds sway in the public realm. Mrs Clavering appears all the more powerful in *The Claverings* (1867) after Trollope's mockingly patronizing introduction. Mr Clavering, apparently, regarded his wife 'as the angel of his house', the stereotypical Victorian image of the passive wife, but her fortune yields an income almost twice the size of his. While Mr Clavering's indolence is emphasized, Mrs Clavering's visiting of the poor, accompanied by her daughters, stands in energetic contrast. Mrs Clavering is more down to earth than her clerical husband, who appears slightly decadent. Although her husband is pleased when his son seems to have discarded the impecunious Florence Burton in favour of the wealthy Lady Ongar, he acknowledges that his wife's integrity will triumph, for she is 'imperative and powerful', while he 'lacked the courage to plead'.[41] When her husband inherits the baronetcy, Mrs Clavering arranges the successor to the living by prevailing on her husband to pass it on to Mr Saul, his future son-in-law, and it is she who informs Mr Saul. Mrs Clavering is thus the actual agent of pastoral activity as visitor of the poor and arranger of livings rather than merely 'the angel of his house' – an epithet which draws attention to the ecclesiastical wife concealing her power behind the stereotype.

In addition to the many clerical relatives from whom Trollope could draw his fictional models, there were other sources from which to take inspiration. Francis Witts' diary refers many times to his wife in ways revealing respect for her views and deep emotional commitment,[42] and not once does he disclose that she was an invalid and physically dependent on him. Casual remarks from nineteenth-century commentators also reveal that clerical wives were a force with which to be reckoned. Macleane wrote of the reluctance of incumbents to hire curates of the same age or older, for they knew that older clergymen were not keen to take orders from their rectors, 'more especially if orders are conveyed to him through the incumbent's wife'.[43] The assumption is clear: clerical wives wielded authority of their own.

Mothers

The role of mother within the ecclesiastical family is generally restricted in Trollope's novels to the mother of the parson's progeny. For this reason, the mother's influence is confined to domestic arrangements but, since these concern the matrimonial plans of the children and the future dynasty of the ecclesiastical family, this restriction affects the parson's community standing. Trollope illustrates that clerical wives who were also mothers determine marital matters and that clerical fathers simply acquiesce in their spouse's decisions, however doubtful they may be about their soundness.

Trollope's fictional mothers are strong characters. The Victorian family endowed the mother with extraordinary power. Just as it was expected that the father would be absent on a daily basis from the home in the accumulation of family income, it was also axiomatic that the mother would remain in charge of the diurnal routine and moral welfare of the offspring. Leading Church figures often attributed their calling to their mothers' influence. Pusey, Regius Professor of Hebrew, was the son of the first Viscount Folkestone, known for his domestic autocracy and inflexible Toryism, but it was his mother who 'exercised great influence upon her children'.[44]

Mrs Grantly is the shrewd chatelaine of her daughter's future. She hastens not at all to see her daughter married, being heard to say in *Framley Parsonage* (1861) that 'ordinary ladies are merely married, but those of real importance are established'.[45] Mrs Grantly is triumphant when Griselda becomes engaged to Lord Dumbello, and is deaf to the hesitations of her husband and sister. Significantly, Mrs Grantly's matrimonial ambitions for her daughter lie beyond ecclesiastical ranks. Trollope's point, made through Susan Grantly, is that clerical positions were often used as stepping stones for one generation to reach just the right site from which to elevate the next generation to higher ground. The cleric's wife, as mother to his progeny, was the expedition's leader in this ascension.

For both Mrs Grantly and Mrs Proudie, the continuation of an ecclesiastical dynasty is not uppermost in their minds. Social advancement is their motivation and the competition between them provides comic irony. Both try to win the best prize for their offspring. The bishop's wife has two daughters to marry. Griselda Grantly is beautiful, but the Proudie girls had not 'elicited from the fashionable world any very loud encomiums of their beauty'. Mrs Proudie is mortified at Griselda's engagement to Lord Dumbello, since her daughter has just become engaged to a 'widowed preacher at a district church in Bethnal Green – a man with three children, who was dependent on pew-rents'.[46] Both women engage in controlled but fierce jousting, and both ecclesiastical husbands and fathers are powerless in the matrimonial stakes of their children.

Equally powerless is Parson Rossiter in 'Alice Dugdale' (1878). Even though Alice eventually marries his son, her happiness is due to her own virtues rather than his support. Alice knew at first that 'Mrs Rossiter wanted a grander wife for her son' and that 'Mrs Rossiter would prevail'. Through town gossip rumours waft on the light breezes up and down Beetham. Mrs Rossiter 'was supposed', generally, 'to be of a higher order of intellect' than the parson, 'was of an ambitious mind and had thoughts beyond Beetham'. For her son, surely, a daughter belonging to 'the county people', whose interests were horse-riding, lawn-tennis and archery, would have to be preferable to 'some obscure girl' who acted as unpaid 'nursery girl' to her stepmother and was encumbered with 'perambulator and the constant needle and thread'. The young cavalry officer in question 'was more unwilling to take counsel from his father even than his mother', so Alice herself is caught unawares when the man she loves finally proposes to *her*, for the maternal manoeuvrings had been all but overwhelming.[47] Without exception, the clerical husbands of Trollope's fictional mothers defer to their wives in decisions regarding prospective marital partners for their offspring. Trollope thus stresses that the future financial and social standing of the Victorian ecclesiastical family lies in the hands of the mother within the parson's hearth.

Daughters

Parsons' daughters, like their mothers, are highly influential. Clerical fathers buckle under the decisions of their daughters. Secular models in real life no doubt encouraged Trollope to stress strong fatherly affection for female progeny, insistent as he was to portray clerical men as human rather than divine representatives. Although Trollope had no daughter, he and his wife looked after three nieces as if they were their daughters, as mentioned above. After a long bout of illness in 1881, Florence Bland, one of these nieces, was sent away to recuperate, and Trollope acknowledges to a relative how desolate he will be without her, such is her influence on him.[48] The fact that most of his novels had already been written with the assumption of daughterly authority over the *pater familias* only demonstrates that Trollope had long taken this for granted. Not unnaturally, he translated his own experience of the influence of daughters to family life among the clergy.

There were also well-known real-life examples of strong clerical daughters of which Trollope would have been aware. Mary Stanley, the Bishop of Norwich's daughter, was instrumental in helping Florence Nightingale select nurses to send to Scutari during the Crimean War. Mary Stanley's book, *Hospitals and Sisterhoods* (1854), outlined the high church's position regarding nursing reforms. There was the growing realization that '[i]t was not just a question of replacing drunken Sarah Gamps with a more respectable class of women'; the Church and the author believed that patients' spiritual needs should also be met. Mary Stanley also accompanied nursing sisters of gentle birth to the East, despite attempts by Florence Nightingale to prevent her, since she knew that Mary was making moves to become a Roman Catholic, and wanted neither a strong Roman Catholic presence among the wounded, nor the interference of 'philanthropic, non-professional gentlewomen'.[49] There was no way that Trollope would not have known Mary Stanley, for she was a well-known figure and friend of Sydney Herbert, with whom he had been at Harrow.[50]

Griselda's increasing social authority over her father as an adult is striking. Dr Grantly hints in *Framley Parsonage* (1861) that she is not as mentally alert as her brothers, although his wife squashes this judgement. Comparing his daughter with his sons, he intimates that 'he did not think that Grizzy was quite so clever as her brothers'. His wife's retort is that '"what you call cleverness is not at all necessary in a girl; she is perfectly lady-like"', a fact which her father 'never wished to deny'. Once Griselda has made her marital conquest by becoming engaged to Lord Dumbello, the archdeacon is forced into silent agreement with his wife's evaluation. Such now was 'the family glory' that the archdeacon 'was hardly allowed free intercourse with his own magnificent child'.[51] And so much did he now sense his own inferiority to that of her marquess suitor that he removed himself to the periphery of the wedding arrangements, marvelling at her success. The daughter, then, while not commanding unconditional devotion, overwhelms the clerical father with her social position. As married daughter, while gossip is rife about her alleged affair in *The Small House at Allington* (1864), she is seen by her father as an enigma which defeats him, leaving her mother to admonish her by reminding her that she 'would offend [her] God by the worst sin that a woman can commit, and cast [herself] into a depth of infamy in which repentance before God is almost impossible'. Griselda's strategic quashing of the rumours by inviting her parents to a 'dinner-party' to be attended by 'His Royal Highness', followed by Dr Grantly's assertion that, though he had 'a great respect for his Royal Highness', he did 'not in the least desire to meet him at Dumbello's table', accentuate her social superiority.[52] The archdeacon father, indomitable in his clerical domain, is socially outmatched by his daughter.

Trollope does not confine himself to drawing daughters who are superior in worldly sophistication. Grace Crawley, in contrast to Griselda Grantly, *is* shown to be clever. While the archdeacon wonders aloud in *The Last Chronicle of Barset* (1867) as to her social suitedness to be sister-in-law to Griselda, Henry declares that it is his sister who would find it difficult to appreciate his intended, for she lacks Grace's intelligence. When the archdeacon meets his future daughter-in-law, his prejudices are swept away by her sincerity. Grace also controls her own clerical father's gloom by providing an anchor of relief, for she can read Greek plays to him and he respects her intellect.[53] Grace Crawley, scholar and eligible young woman, climbs the social scale through her intelligence and integrity and reveals herself to be a powerful force for both clerical father and father-in-law, the former of humble station, the latter of fairly high station.

Social scales may be climbed by clerical daughters through a variety of attributes, but their success cannot be maintained without adherence to moral principles. Lady George in *Is He Popenjoy?* (1878), amid the novel's ridiculing of strident feminism, epitomizes the assertive young woman of the 1870s, while retaining the 'purity' of her Christian upbringing. She refuses to share her father's social ambitions for her, even questions his 'pagan teaching' now that she is married, but calmly accepts high rank when it is inherited through her brother-in-law's death. Nor is the power of her father, the Dean of Brotherton, suddenly reduced by the couple's succession to the Marquessate; instead it is gradually attenuated by Lady George's steady maturation into womanhood, and the clerical father at the end of the novel 'almost worships her'.[54] Clerical fathers in Trollope's fiction bow to their daughters' command.

Single women

Every one of Trollope's novels has a romance plot. Romance in the nineteenth century, as indeed in the twenty-first, was a marketing ploy. In Trollope's lifetime, though, the impulse for marriage had a desperation unfamiliar to today's society, and he was fully conscious of this. Spinsterhood without a private income, at a time in which opportunities for female employment were very few, was not an attractive proposition. When the 1851 census revealed that Great Britain had half a million more women than men, the plight of single women took on a more poignant urgency. The worrying surplus of women meant that single women could no longer regard marriage as an inevitable future goal. Marriage was a meal ticket, a roof over one's head and clothes on one's back. Without marriage, Trollope knew, a woman had to be tough. Only a husband could enable a woman to adhere to the Victorian stereotype of helpless femininity, and husbands were in short supply – especially for the middle classes.

A pamphlet in 1855, about a decade after the founding of the first Anglican convent, of which Gladstone was one of the original sponsors, suggested that sisterhoods would provide an outlet and respectable means of survival for spinsters. But many disputed both the cause and the remedy. The word 'sisters' became increasingly associated in the nineteenth century with sisterhoods, or religious orders of women. One of Trollope's sisters, Cecilia, died as a young, married woman in 1849, but during her life was so fascinated by the Oxford Movement that she wrote a high church novel, *Chollerton* (1846), before Trollope had received any recognition for his writing. The novel has been said to favour 'chastity, good works and a life devoted to the Christian religion' over 'love and domestic happiness', and 'virtue' for its hero and heroine 'lay in suppressing desires',[55] but this does not quite convey the fictional situation. It is true that the narrator concludes the book by saying that 'we venture to affirm' that the successful combination of Arthur Fosdyke's spiritual and Anna Marsden's practical labours in the parish resulted in them leading 'a far happier and more tranquil life' than if Arthur had not surrendered his emotions to his belief in monastic celibacy and Anna had not had 'her first youthful wishes ... granted to her'.[56] But, while Arthur's emotional attachment had been to Anna, Anna's had been to Sir Edward Belcomb, and Arthur had long suspected this. Sir Edward's transferred preference to Arthur's sister Charlotte during Anna's long absence from Chollerton, despite the secret understanding between Edward and Anna, had devastated the devout young woman, despite her outward calm. If anything, the novel demonstrates the capacity of high Anglicanism to *overcome* personal unhappiness, rather than subdue private desires. While it does not actually promote celibacy, it does promote religion as a solace as well as a virtue. Above all, it features steely womanhood.

Trollope was interested in the new sisterhoods of the Church and he was intrigued by the burgeoning feminism of secular sisterhoods. He realized that single women could not afford to be helpless, not that he himself had ever been accustomed to helpless married women. Although his attitude to higher education for women, expressed in his article (1868) and mentioned earlier,[57] disclosed his fear of a change in gender roles,[58] he retained his pleasure in the achievements of individual women. His ambivalence on this issue cannot be appreciated without a glance at the sisterhood question in the Church and its pertinence to Trollope's portrayals of strong fictional single women.

Sisterhoods were the ecclesiastical alternative to secular feminism, and were viewed, together with the whole Oxford Movement, as 'the first phases of the drive for the emancipation of women'. The attraction for young women lay in the active participation in liturgical matters and in the practical work in nursing, social work and education carried out by the communities.[59] The Church, with the initial inspiration of Robert Southey, the Romantic Poet Laureate, set up the first female monastic order in England since the Reformation.

The sisterhoods were established by the Tractarians, Pusey, William John Butler and John Mason Neale, and the first sisterhood was St Saviour's, in Regent's Park. Pusey had been so swayed by his 15-year-old daughter Lucy's desire to enter the Church that talks leading to the founding of the first sisterhood began on the day of her funeral. Trollope would have known this famous example of a clerical man under the powerful sway of his daughter, as he had written about the sisterhoods in 1865 and, as noted earlier, was friendly with members of the Oxford Movement to which Pusey belonged.[60]

Nor is his interest in the sisterhoods surprising, considering the strong link between them and literature, for the Tractarians were friendly with the Romantic Lake Poets, Southey, Wordsworth and Coleridge. Moreover, the Devonport sisterhood and the Community of St Margaret at East Grinstead were both subjected to fierce community opposition. The Devonport sisterhood received verbal and written attacks; its St Margaret counterpart was physically attacked and Neale, its founder, was assaulted. Trollope would have been all too painfully aware of these incidents; he had family connections with Devonshire, and Neale and he were correspondents. Parents disapproved of the sisterhoods, believing, as Charlotte Yonge attested in *The Monthly Packet* in 1868, that the Church was trying to increase its revenue through the private income of young girls,[61] and the fear was that sisterhoods would disrupt families.[62]

Trollope, in depicting determined young women *within* the family, reminded readers of this. When Madeline Staveley in *Orley Farm* (1862), mistakenly fearing that Felix Graham does not reciprocate her feelings, seemed to be 'tending in some slight degree to the monastic', her mother, Lady Staveley, says nothing to her daughter. Instead she confides her fears to her husband that her heart would break 'if she were to go and make a nun of herself', adding that she 'would never hold up [her] head again'. She would have preferred her daughter to have accepted the proposal of Peregrine Orme, the grandson of a peer of the realm rather than the young, penniless barrister, but '[w]ould not Felix Graham be better than no son-in-law?'[63] So strong was community fear of wealthy families like the Staveleys losing their carefully nurtured daughters to Anglican convents that there was a stigma attached to any family so afflicted, the supposition being that the family had not provided sufficient protection. In 1851 *Punch* condemned the greed of sisterhoods in a mock-medieval poem, 'Taking the Veil', in which an heiress is enticed into convent life by its abbess and priests, intent on 'catchyng [sic] an Heiress'.[64] Despite this opposition, the sisterhoods developed quickly, partly, it was thought, owing to the demographic imbalance.

Sisterhoods were associated with the high church, but the Evangelicals had 'sororities'. William Pennefather (1816–73) and his wife Catherine founded a deaconess house in 1860. Their patriarchal structure prevented them from attracting the same acrimony as the sisterhoods. The founders of high church sisterhoods, in particular Pusey and Neale, followed the feminist conviction that 'women should govern themselves'; by contrast, the deaconesses regarded themselves more 'in need of men's control and direction',[65] so Victorian society felt less threatened. The deaconess movement in England developed the most strongly in the 1860s, and their absence of vows helped prevent public alienation. Trollope would have known that Bishop Thorold would not have a '"quasi-sisterhood"', but was interested in starting a deaconess programme, which commenced after Trollope's death at Rochester.[66] Women often entered the diaconate with their natural sisters, so the link between sisters and sisterhoods was closely formed in people's minds. Trollope would have known, for instance, of the deaconesses, Cecilia and Elizabeth Robinson, sisters of the Dean of Wells.

Trollope was opposed to any form of community segregation. Nonetheless, his article on the high church sisterhoods in the mid-1860s is even-handed. Trollope is compassionate about the reasons for women wishing to enter sisterhoods, deplores the fact that nursing orders are not paid properly, and defends the sisters' right to choose plain dress as their attire, at the same time as expressing his belief that 'a woman should dress herself as prettily as she can'.[67] The Rev. William Dodsworth confirmed that public opprobrium was caused by 'their peculiar dress', for the dress was 'a very plain, rather coarse, black dress, edged with a little white about the neck'.[68] Despite Trollope's even-handedness about the right to choose such a life, his fictional and non-fictional works provide clues as to his private position concerning conventual life for women as well as monastic life for men. Not until the young sisters-in-law, Marie de Larochejaquelin and Agatha de Larochejaquelin, have lost the men they love to battle in *La Vendée* (1850) do they 'both pass the same holy life', and even then, in Roman Catholic France, they do not choose 'absolutely to seclude themselves', but simply to live 'as though they were within the walls of a convent'.[69] Thus Trollope is at pains to stress that they do not submit fully to convent life. Young men, too, Trollope believed, should marry, particularly if they were Anglican priests. Mr Gibson's pressing need for matrimony in *He Knew He Was Right* (1869) derives not just from personal inclinations but also 'from the hints of his friend the Prebend, from a word or two which had come to him from the Dean, from certain family arrangements proposed to him by his mother and sisters'; in short, he knew 'that he had better marry some one'.[70] Trollope might mock Mr Gibson's vacillations about his choice of bride, but he reveres the very institution of marriage. He is also pleased in *South Africa* (1878) that the high church young men, 'who were perhaps intended to be celebate [sic]', when brought out to Bloemfontein, had all 'become engaged to all the clerical young ladies' who were working at the Home for young girls. For Trollope, celibacy was anathema and he refers to it as a 'negative virtue'.[71] As far as he was concerned, strength was a quality to which *both* men and women should aspire, but autonomy involving celibacy was a thing to be spurned.

It is very likely that Trollope concentrated on showing powerful single women *within* the family because he knew that readers would be alert to the issue of ecclesiastical sisterhoods and sororities. The question of the family versus the institution was one close to Trollope's heart and one dividing the nation. By demonstrating that young single women could exert power and influence over their clerical fathers, Trollope could implicitly question the need for institutionalizing female participation in the Church in a formal way. It is interesting that Trollope, long criticized for his partisanship to the high church, seems to incline more to the Evangelical sorority than to the high church sisterhood, despite his support of the latter in his article.

Believing firmly in marriage, Trollope shows that both Harding sisters, single as well as married, are able to check their clerical father's actions in different ways. Eleanor's choice of betrothed leads to her father's loss of a comfortable ecclesiastical position, and she persuades her father to give up the fight for the wardenship and accept a lesser position, so that they can return to tranquillity. They are clearly devoted, but the father's sacrifice is the greater. Despite Eleanor's early matrimonial victory regarding John Bold, Mr Harding is mindful of keeping the peace between his household and that of his older married daughter, Susan, if only because he believes Susan and her husband, the archdeacon, to be of superior status. An early anonymous reviewer of Trollope's novels in 1858 observes Susan Grantly's ability to 'lecture and hold in awe both father and husband' and admires her strong hold over her father.[72] The significance of this early article is that it does not question this view of young forcible womanhood or its realism. Trollope took great care to prove that women could exert as much influence on their clerical kin whether or not they were married. He did not want to leave the remotest impression with readers that the single state for young women could confer special powers in the Church. The community was especially anxious for the fate of its *young* women. It was not the sisters of actual churchmen who were keen to enter conventual life; it was their daughters, and their families, as noted earlier, were concerned that an institution might usurp their authority.

Widowhood automatically returned women to single status. Trollope's mother became a widow in her fifties, having supported her entire family financially for a number of years after it became evident that her barrister husband was incapable, through illness, of doing this. Widowhood, with no inherited income, would have been grim indeed for her family, but for her indomitable will. Her success as a writer was due as much to her strength of character as it was to any talent. Trollope knew from personal experience that the need of income for bereaved women could uncover invincible powers hitherto undetected.

He would also have known the particular problems faced by clerical widows. His *Clergymen of the Church of England* (1866), while praising the thrift of the parish parson's wife, questions a stipend system allowing indigence among clergymen.[73] The Rev. Jervis wrote in 1856 of the plight of widows and orphans 'left almost, if not altogether penniless, by the sudden or premature death of a clergymen', despite a few societies existing to ease their situation. Their 'abject state of want', he continued, was actually exacerbated by these charities, for they relied on 'a community wearied by the frequency of similar appeals'. He included suggestions for pension funds, which had clauses relating to widows and orphans.[74] *Clergymen of the Church of England*, published ten years later than this work, does not mention pension funds, and the poor clerical widows in Trollope's novels are still dependent on charity, illustrating the Church's tardiness to instigate reform.

Clerical widowhood required adamantine strength for survival. Clerical widows usually had children to support and widowhood was swiftly followed by the deprivation of the family home, since the parsonage belonged to the Church and was needed for the next incumbent. *The Bertrams* (1859) gives two vivid illustrations of clergymen dying and the family home endangered. Mr Gauntlet's death leaves no widow and requires his daughter to vacate the parsonage almost immediately, for, as Trollope observes, 'the moment the rector's breath is out of his body, all right and claim to the castle as regards his estate and family cease instantly.' On the very day of her father's funeral, Adela Gauntlet was compelled to leave the rectory, as '[s]he could not remain alone in that house on the day that her father's body was carried to the grave'. By contrast, Mr Wilkinson's death does not render his widow and five children homeless, for charity is offered by the lay patron, Lord Stapledean. But, as Trollope demonstrates, charity comes at a price, for the patron presents the living to the clerical son, Arthur Wilkinson, provided that the income goes to his 'father's widow'. The widow's situation is therefore relieved at the cost of her son's autonomy. Mrs Wilkinson even comes to regard her son as *her* curate and herself as 'the legal owner of that ecclesiastical income'. Her son's bitter remark that 'I almost think she would wish to take my place in the pulpit' is endorsed later by the narratorial comment that, during her son's absence, the widow 'had reigned the female vicaress' and that the young curate *in loco tenens* had not desired to 'interfere with her power, or to contradict her edicts'.[75] The son's decision to marry and the widow's bitter realization from the patron's own lips that, while the income may have been intended for her, the parsonage belonged to her son, emphasizes the sorry circumstances of clerical widows. Their comfort was at the expense of others.

Such painful charity, though, did not prevent Oliphant's strong-minded clerical widows from holding sway. Mrs Joel, the would-be sexton in *The Curate in Charge* (1876), is a formidable figure,[76] and, in *The Rector* (1863), Mrs Proctor, whose wisdom her clerical son, Morley, trusts implicitly, rules her domain.[77] Oliphant's women in fact tend to dwarf her men, whether or not they are in holy orders. Where Trollope's emphasis is on comedy, Oliphant's is on tragedy.

Not all widows were poor; some were not only wealthy but powerful. Female patrons fell into this category, for they could subject the clergy to their bidding, regardless of blood or marital relationship. The most powerful patron in the land was the crown and this was worn by a woman. Queen Victoria's greatest power was in helping to select bishops and archbishops. Although, technically, as noted earlier, the Prime Minister had this responsibility, the Queen had the right to nominate, and she liked to exercise that right. Although '[m]onarch and minister frequently clashed over nominations to vacant sees' and although Disraeli corrected her illusion that she was merely 'Supreme Governor' not 'Head of Church', Victoria's decisions regarding episcopal appointments were ultimately carried out.[78] Nor, in hindsight, have these appointments been regarded as unsuccessful; on the contrary, modern historians have agreed that Victoria raised 'the calibre of Anglican bishops in wisdom, learning, and freedom from political entanglement', in order to try to free the Church from political schism.[79]

Trollope's favourite female patron was Lady Lufton, who, her husband having died, and her son not having reached his 25th birthday, holds the Framley living. Her living is worth £900 a year, and she has the right to choose its incumbent. Framley lies within Barchester, and Trollope indicates Lady Lufton's broad ecclesiastical powers: she 'did not carry her high church principles so far as to advocate celibacy for the clergy ... she had an idea that a man could not be a good parish parson without a wife'. Thus Lady Lufton's position enables her to participate in the war between high and low church. Her preference for married priests reveals that she does not support the Oxford movement favouring celibacy. Her patronage therefore influences the community. Nor is it limited to the Church. The establishment of two schools, one for boys and the other for girls, 'owed their erection to Lady Lufton's energy'.[80] The novel was published in 1861, by which time the Church still had not been successful with its plans for extensive elementary education, so schools endowed by patrons with church affiliations would have been welcomed by Church and state.[81] Trollope, by showing a widowed female patron providing education, is demonstrating the power of wealthy women who had no need to be tempted, as many widows were, to seek the sanctuary and safety of the new Anglican convents.

There were other outlets, too. Trollope hints obliquely at the Evangelical sororities in *Rachel Ray* (1863), but stresses the possible pitfalls. Dorothea Prime, whose deceased husband was an Evangelical clergyman, has been left with a comfortable income. Her financial status, superior to that of her mother, persuades her that she must control the lives of both her mother and younger sister Rachel. On conduct before marriage, Dorothea believes herself to be an expert. A summer's walk, the withholding of details, yawning in church, the dislike of lengthy second sermons on a Sunday, are all deemed wicked by Dorothea. She becomes the bane of her younger sister's life, for the Ray household is completely under Dorothea's stern rule. An anonymous review in the contemporary journal, *Saturday Review*, pronounced the portraits of the mother and daughters very true to life.[82] Presumably Dorothea had many real-life sisters in the parishes of England. Possibly the principal cause of Dorothea's sovereignty was her private income. So pleasurable and powerful is her single status on 'her uncontrolled possession of two hundred a year' that, when she discovers that she would lose complete control of it, she reflects at length 'on the rights of a married woman with regard to money – and also on the wrongs'. This income, Rachel predicts, 'she'll never give up' and Mr Prong will 'never marry her unless she does', for the amount had been sufficiently ample to enable her to found a Dorcas society, become its 'permanent president' and lead her 'sister labourers', a position she jealously guarded. And sure enough, Dorothea decides 'that she would remain a widow for the rest of her days'.[83] Dull though it may appear to the younger sister and to the reader, respectable widowhood for Dorothea was preferable to undistinguished wifehood. The Dorcas sorority, as Trollope indicates, is Dorothea's solution to life as a single woman, for it endows her with a powerful position in her community and is sanctioned by the Church.

Her income has invested her with the means to found her own sorority without leaving the family nest, thus enabling her to disseminate her influence beyond the family. The wider influence, gained through her Dorcas work, Dorothea does not hesitate to use in order to check her own younger sister. For Rachel to linger late with a young man is, for Dorothea, a sin requiring Dorcas discipline. Trollope's depiction of Dorothea captures the extremes of Evangelicalism. Plain dress and diet became associated with dissenting sects, for their periodicals urged lower- and middle-class readers not to imitate upper-class tastes.[84] Rachel's marriage into 'trade' is a rebellion against the conflict between clerical duty and pleasure. Her older sister, in contrast, has no need to relinquish the single state.

Unlike Oliphant's single reference in *The Doctor's Family* (1863) and multiple references in *The Perpetual Curate* (1864) to the grey cloaks and District Visiting of Lucy and Mary Wodehouse as quasi qualifications for the sisterhoods, Trollope's references to sisterhoods do not directly equate his fictional characters with convents. Oliphant's Mr Wodehouse in *The Rector* (1863) even declares that his daughters are 'both as good as curates',[85] but Trollope is more circumspect. He even refers in *The Warden* (1855) to 'the mortification of papists', allowing nuns to be searched to see if they might be 'in possession of treasonable papers, or jesuitical symbols', provided that the search is carried out by a clergyman 'over fifty years of age'![86] This bill, to facilitate convent inspections, was introduced in May 1853 and dropped in August. Miss Mackenzie in the eponymous novel in the mid 1860s, unable to choose between two undesirable suitors, regrets that she is not Roman Catholic and cannot retire to a convent, eschewing all thought of a Protestant convent, which she deems to be 'bad', especially for Evangelicals.[87] *Miss Mackenzie* was published in the same year as Trollope's article, 'The

Sisterhood Question'. And in *The Vicar of Bullhampton* (1870), Mary Lowther's supposed sentiment that, unhappy in love, she would be so happy 'if her reason would allow her to be a Roman Catholic, and a nun' would not have struck the contemporary readership with the same melodramatic force with which it strikes the modern reader.[88] The 'Papal Aggression' of the 1850s was still feared and Anglican sisterhoods were viewed with suspicion. Trollope was at least kinder than Dickens, whose 'Sisterhood of Medieval Martyrs' in *Bleak House* (1853), casts the new sisterhoods as *outré*.[89]

Sisterhoods may have alleviated the position of single women, but they struck terror into the community. Trollope preferred to offer, through light comedy, his antidote to the fear of Rome. An active social role from within the family structure meant that single women did not need to seek external sororities or sisterhoods.

Trollope's depiction of covert female power over ostensible male sovereignty in the Church, from the wealthiest wife to the poorest widow, transcends his comic design. The comedy is a mask for his serious purpose. In laughing at the subversion of stereotypes, the reader gleans an insight into human nature. Trollope, in his portrayal of clergymen, members of the most powerful institution of the time, is demonstrating that personal opinions, formed in the private sphere, motivate public actions. The public man is thus strongly influenced by those close to him. In Victorian society the female relative, by virtue of her intimate relationship midst hearth and home, held a powerful position for guiding the public man. Is it possible that Trollope was covertly countering the argument held by the radical feminist guard in his century who wanted to eject women from the private home and catapult them into the public world? Was he in fact insinuating that, if the Church was showing signs of moral degeneracy, the solution might lie within the home through the private persuasion of female relatives, at one remove from the institution?

Alford, writing of Trollope's portrayal of the clergy in the mid-1860s, urged the Church to 're-translate...her Scriptures' to overcome its decay.[90] Perhaps Trollope, throughout his novels, 'translate[d]' Alford's feminine metaphor literally. Maybe the solution to the Church's decay lay in women, protected from public contamination and at liberty to pursue radical directions of thought and theology, without fear or favour. The hearth provided both sanctuary and the *real* seat of power.

5
The Church, Politics and Social Reform

Church–state relations were strained during Trollope's era, yet life without this relationship seemed inconceivable. Just as the Church was an integral part of society so, too, was it an integral part of the fabric of the state. No one could escape the partnership of Church and state, which for generations had been represented by the squire and the vicar sitting side by side on the local judicial bench during the week, and the squire's family filling the pew immediately in front of the pulpit, admiring the sermon on Sundays. The Church's power over social life had hitherto been unquestioned by most of the population, but in the nineteenth century even ordinary people came to wish for some redefinition of the boundaries between Church, state and everyday life. The desire for change was, of course, triggered by industrialization and urbanization, with the concomitant packing of a steeply rising population into cities and towns where the old social relations inevitably broke down. By 1890, only in the smaller villages and market towns was 'the unity between Church and State' still 'typified'.[1] The Church had to struggle with the massive social problems of the cities and industrial towns; on its own, it could not cope. But the solutions, which involved state intervention in areas previously the Church's responsibility, were to impinge on the traditional relations between Church and state.

At the same time there seemed to be antithetical impulses. Society wanted the Church to retreat from its garden gate; the state wanted to invade the Church's territory. The push in social reform was for a loosening of ties between the Anglican Church and state; the push in state reform was for a tightening of control over the Anglican Church's governance, revenue and ultimate authority. On the one hand, the Church felt as if society was slipping further and further away from its influence; on the other, it perceived the state to be intruding more and more into its affairs. Moreover, although these issues touched the Church more closely than the general community, Trollope illustrates just how deeply involved ordinary citizens felt about church reforms. In no way were these changes seen to be peripheral. On the contrary, as Trollope showed, people held strong views on all issues involving the Church.

On the issue of these relations, as on so many others, Trollope was equivocal. It may be suggested that the issues in themselves were of less interest to Trollope than the ways in which they were managed. Trollope focused more on people's reactions than on the abstract detail of religion and politics. He was conscious of his own father's self-appointed, hopeless task of explaining the Church as it *had* been in his unfinished *Encyclopaedia Ecclesiastica*, and wished, instead, to explain the Church as it actually *was*.[2] His concern for his Church and nation, lightly expressed in his fiction but more seriously addressed in his non-fiction, was very deeply seated.

In general, Trollope supported the alliance of Church and state, with all the advantages that it brought to the Anglican establishment and to the stability of the state, yet in the particular he approved neither of the Church interfering with secular institutions nor of the state involving itself in areas that traditionally were the responsibility of the Church. But Trollope did approve of the Church exercising its customary moral and legal authority over the community, for he feared that the extension of personal liberty, if gained at the Church's expense through state intervention, might lower people's spiritual horizons.[3] During Trollope's lifetime, however, a number of controversial social and political issues that possessed both spiritual and secular dimensions emerged, the resolution of which inevitably unbalanced the delicate relations between Church and state. Among these were three social issues over which church authorities legitimately thought they should have overriding authority, but which the government, in its desire for reform, attempted to regulate, if necessary at the Church's expense: education, divorce and the disposal of the dead. In addition, three political issues perplexed both Church and state and intrigued Trollope: Roman Catholicism, the disestablishment of the Irish Church, and the question of the disestablishment of the Anglican Church.

The social issues offer an opportunity to examine Trollope's concerns about the growth of government activism in society – leading in effect to an increasingly secular society – at the expense of the Church's social and moral authority. But before Trollope's comments on these specific issues can be analysed, it is necessary to explain both the context of church–state relations in his era and the means whereby he obtained the information on which his opinions were based.

Most of Trollope's adult life was spent under a form of parliamentary government in which two main political parties vied for power: the Conservatives and the Liberals. The Conservatives, otherwise known as Tories, usually comprised the squirearchy and small landowners with their economic dependants, the leaseholders in the country and tradesmen in the local towns. They frequently preferred country pursuits – hunting, shooting and fishing – to parliamentary duty. Trollope loved hunting, yet voted Liberal. The Liberals had grown out of the Whig party, which comprised most of the aristocracy, the upper *échelons* of the landed gentry; they were so powerful that, it was sometimes said, they were not *necessarily* monarchists. Only about a thousand families in 1850 could have justifiably called themselves Whigs of the old school, of whom Trollope's Duke of Omnium was an authentic prototype.[4] Trollope, unlike most writers, Dickens included, did not display resentment towards the Whig aristocracy.[5] Since Trollope's extended family had descended from the Whig aristocracy, he had much more understanding of them than Dickens, of humbler origin. The Liberals themselves were composed of more varied stock than the Conservatives. As well as the old Whig aristocracy, the Liberals comprised large and small business men, industrialists, landlords and labourers. Trollope's way of life and voting preference reflect awareness of his social position, consciousness of his lineage *and* desire for improvement of the human lot.

Trollope's clearest statement of his politics characteristically managed to include the names of both parties: he was, he claimed, 'an advanced, but still conservative Liberal'.[6] Trollope knew what he meant by this; so too would many of his contemporaries – it would have included a respect for tradition, a social conservatism, a commitment to reform of genuine abuses and an acceptance of the broader post-1832 political nation. It has been suggested that, by calling himself a conservative Liberal, Trollope was seeking 'to hold on to what was good while advancing to what might be better'.[7] This, in reality, is as good a definition of traditional conservatism as can be found. The capital 'L' in Liberal is instructive: it denoted allegiance to a particular party. But it was the qualifier which most clearly expressed Trollope's instinctive feeling for moderation in politics and which tempered his loyalty to any strict party line. As an obituary of Trollope concludes, '[o]n some theoretical points his Liberalism was of the most advanced type ... [but] all his instincts and feelings were conservative'.[8]

Trollope would possibly not have felt completely out of place among those in the Conservative party who retained a regard for aristocratic notions of *noblesse oblige*; after all, he did acknowledge the existence of a Tory idealism.[9] But his contempt for both Peel and Disraeli and his admiration for Palmerston and Gladstone played a major role in his choice of party.[10] Ironically, Gladstone's blending of politics and churchmanship derived from his own father's interest in Peel, which persuaded him to override his son's ambition to take holy orders and instead make a statesman out of him under Peel's older wing.[11] Trollope clearly did not see Gladstone as a minion of Peel, for only in the last year of his life did his esteem for Gladstone waver, over an Irish issue when political expediency seemed to have determined Gladstone's policy.[12] In *The Fixed Period* (1882) this change in attitude is mentioned, as is Gladstone's 'effete old age', yet Trollope's naming of the capital of Britannula as Gladstonopolis suggests a lingering respect for the man who was thrice Prime Minister.[13]

Religion was a complicating factor in Victorian politics, if in the longer term its influence declined. Despite the aphorism that the Church of England was the Tory party at prayer, it is difficult to draw exact parallels between denominations, religious groupings and political parties. Anglicans outnumbered any other denomination among the English Parliamentary Liberals, since most MPs were of landed Whig families who worshipped in the Church of England. Although most high church communicants voted Conservative, there were exceptions, the best known being Gladstone, who was high church and Liberal (although, with a deviousness superior to Trollope's, he long called himself a Liberal Conservative).[14] Most Evangelicals voted Liberal, but here too, there were well-known exceptions. Bishop Thorold was Evangelical and Conservative, and so, too, was the Earl of Shaftesbury. Liberal lay support during the nineteenth century came generally from Nonconformists: Protestant Dissenters, Roman Catholics and the small Jewish communities.

The strong links between Church and state were often continued through friendship and consanguinity, as Trollope knew. Politics and religion were thus related both abstractly and concretely. The Church was 'an institution of the realm, an arm of the constitution', partly because its officers were the close relations of the very powerful.[15] The younger sons, brothers, nephews and cousins of magnates and the gentry were encouraged to enter the Church and, consequently, were respected, not so much for their ecclesiastical calling, but for their lineage, a fact of which Trollope was well aware from his own family.

Trollope's political and ecclesiastical connections

Trollope had a multitude of friends among ecclesiastics and politicians who, wittingly or not, acted as source material for his fertile mind. Robert Lowe (1811–92), who had been instrumental in drawing up the Liberal Reform Bill of 1866, had been at Winchester with Trollope and was a close friend.[16] Charles George Merewether QC and Conservative MP for Northampton (1874–80) helped Trollope with political and legal details in his writing.[17] Within Trollope's extended family, Sir John Trollope was the Conservative MP for South Lincolnshire,[18] with whom Trollope at times stayed.

The Lincolnshire connection was possibly the source for some of Trollope's characters. It is known that the Barchester *affaire* was based on two contemporary scandals, that of St Cross Hospital, Winchester and that of the Cathedral Grammar School in Rochester, about both of which Trollope gleaned information from the newspapers. The ramifications of the Rochester scandal, which centred on a dispute between the headmaster of the grammar school and the Dean and Chapter of Rochester Cathedral, have been explored thoroughly. As there are several references to this affair in *The Warden*, the connection has already been made between Rochester and Barchester, but the links between the *dramatis personae* in Rochester and Trollope's Barchester characters are probably not so much due to Trollope's 'instinct for what a bishop, a dean, a prebendary, an archdeacon and a minor canon ought to be like, and how they might be expected to behave',[19] but to his *personal* knowledge. Through his Lincolnshire family connections, Trollope very likely obtained in-house information on the Rochester clergy, at least one of whom, a prebendary, who was not seen in the town for seven years, may have been the prototype for Rev. Vesey Stanhope, the Barchester prebendary who had resided in Italy for twelve years. Trollope's 'mole' in Rochester would have been Walker King, its archdeacon (1827–59). The similarity drawn between Walker King and Archdeacon Grantly for having been appointed to his position in Rochester by his father, Walker King, a former bishop of Rochester (1809–27), is not just coincidental, as has previously been thought.[20] Walker's son was Edward King (1829–1910), intimate friend of Anthony Wilson Thorold, himself a future bishop of Rochester. As shown earlier, there were clear links between the Trollope, Thorold and King families in Lincolnshire. Trollope certainly knew Thorold and would have known of the King family. Through the family grapevine, and possibly over Sir John Trollope's dining table, Trollope could have picked up, from amid the gossip of what had happened at Rochester, information which later he transmuted into fiction.

In addition to relatives and friends, Trollope cultivated friendships with politicians and ecclesiastics through his clubs. Although Trollope did not attend many political *soirées* and might have derived his political information from society newspaper columns,[21] his involvement in clubs gave him easy access to politicians and clergymen, and his gregariousness would have facilitated his acquisition of inside political and ecclesiastical information. He frequented the Alpine Club and the Star and Garter Club and was an actual member of the Cosmopolitan Club, the Garrick Club and the Athenaeum, which was patronized by many bishops. Trollope initially met Sydney Smith at the Sterling Club, where the novelist had been a guest, and the veteran politician Henry Brougham at the Athenaeum.[22] Trollope defended Lord Brougham in 1865 when he was accused of corrupt practices, and helped with his memoirs in 1870. As young men, when they began the *Edinburgh Review*, both Smith and Brougham had been of Whiggish persuasion. Sidney Smith was of the high church, Brougham became an Evangelical. There is mounting evidence, too, that Trollope was a lifelong member of the Freemasons, to which belonged many a politician *and* cleric.[23] Thus, through his club connections, Trollope had many an opportunity to discuss ecclesiastical questions and enlarge his already wide circle of ecclesiastical friends, relatives and acquaintances.

The literary journals were also good sources for Trollope to extend his social network into political and ecclesiastical spheres. Through the *Fortnightly Review*, a Liberal journal, Trollope became friendly with one of its original proprietors, Henry Derby Seymour, MP for Poole, Dorset (1850–68). Through *Saint Pauls Magazine*, begun in Trollope's honour and which James Virtue had wished to bear the writer's name, Trollope shaped 'a vehicle for political articles on the Liberal side'.[24]

Beyond the coteries of clubs and journals, Trollope actively sought the friendship and acquaintance of leading ecclesiastical figures. He invited the Dean of Bristol and his wife to a family dinner when he retired from the Post Office. He was also close friends with Lord Houghton, statesman, and this brought him into contact with the Archbishop of York, William Thomson, in 1868, when he was visiting Beverley close to the election.[25]

The most significant ecclesiastical friendships in Trollope's life, however, were with the leaders of the Oxford Movement, Newman, Manning, Liddon and Pusey, noted earlier. So influential on him was this group that Trollope sent his sons to St Andrew's School, Bradfield, a high church school. Trollope admired the Movement's leaders for their sincerity, learning and vigour. The Oxford men in their turn were so struck by Trollope's ability to explain complex issues and relationships in entertaining narrative that, in modern parlance, they relied on him as a kind of comic spin doctor. Among this group was Frederic William Farrar, Master at Harrow, and, long after Trollope's death, Dean of Canterbury. He contributed to the Liberal *Fortnightly* and corresponded with the novelist. Possibly it was through these Oxford men that Trollope first came to meet Gladstone. Both Trollope and Liddon attended a meeting in St James' Hall, London in 1876, to support Gladstone's stance on the expulsion of the Turks from the Balkans. Furthermore, always keen to have speakers who were influential and interesting, Trollope planned to have Gladstone chair the 1873 Literary Fund Dinner.[26] It would have been from this Oxford group, as well as from his own ecclesiastical kinsmen and friends, that Trollope learnt about the Church's internal workings. His expertise in this area is astonishing; few laymen of his generation would have been so knowledgeable. His understanding of the nuances of the clerical world has therefore made it difficult precisely to assess where he stood personally. He was certainly not a latitudinarian sympathizer, as some commentators have alleged.[27] He was a devout Anglican within a divided communion, with a fondness for the relaxed attitude of the high-and-dry faction towards life's pleasures.[28]

The intermixing of politics and religion

Although both worldly and devout, Trollope did not approve of the Church and politics becoming too deeply entwined. He was not alone in this belief, for it was an unwritten rule for Victorian ecclesiastics to keep the Church away from politics, and Christian laymen usually agreed with this.[29] In one instance close to him, the reform of the Civil Service following the Northcote-Trevelyan report of 1853,[30] Trollope lambasted a prominent university clergyman for interfering in an area outside his province. The cleric in question was Benjamin Jowett (1817–93), tutor of Balliol but subsequently Vice-Chancellor of Oxford.[31] How could Jowett – an 'excellent college tutor we do not doubt' – know, he wondered, 'the desirable requirements in a clerk in the civil service'?[32] The Northcote-Trevelyan report had advocated examinations in the Civil Service, not only for recruitment, but also for promotion. Trollope's anger did not subside, for he satirized Jowett, together with the other two authors of the Northcote-Trevelyan report, as one of 'The Three Kings' in *The Three Clerks* (1858).[33] It would not have been difficult for Trollope's contemporary readers to recognize the target of his satire. Mr Jobbles, as 'a worthy clergyman from Cambridge ... had for many years been examining undergraduates for little goes and great goes' in the second and final year examinations. His ability as a mathematician to divide 'the adult British male world into classes and sub-classes', not to speak of his capacity for getting 'through 5,000 viva voces in every five hours ... with due assistance' made him an 'obvious' choice to fulfil the role of chief examiner for five candidates seeking promotion in Trollope's fictional Civil Service. Trollope recounts with relish the horror of the written papers and viva voce – all occurring in four days – as well as the nerves of most of the applicants, two of whom withdraw after two days. Comparing the process with a horse race, the lottery nature of which results at best in the winner being determined by physical stamina and hyperconfidence, Trollope reveals Alaric Tudor to be the prize winner, his promotion to Chief Clerk now assured.[34] Trollope's indictment of the examinations, the author and agent of which is the clerical Mr Jobbles, can be seen in the cold congratulations of the victor's seniors in the Civil Service and in the young man's later crime of embezzlement. The Church, Trollope believed, should confine itself and its representatives to its own sphere of expertise and not transgress its boundaries into the secular.

The problem was that the boundaries were continually shifting in favour of the secular. Among both clerics and interested laymen, fears for the future of the Church's special role in society stemmed partly from uncertainty as to how politicians would react when matters of concern to the Church were left in their hands, yet conflicted with demands placed on them by lay interest groups. Even Gladstone could be the object of suspicion. Despite him telling Wilberforce, Bishop of Oxford, in 1862 that '[p]art of the Special work of this age ought to be to clear [i.e. clarify] relations between Church and State',[35] the *Quarterly* nevertheless lamented that it was not possible to rely on Gladstone and the Liberals, since ambition and secular politics were more important to him than the concerns of the Church, and that, given the choice, Gladstone would sacrifice Church interests for his own.[36] It was only when there was political controversy involving religious dissent, like Disraeli's Public Worship Regulation Act which 'cut across normal party loyalties', that the Church felt itself free to intervene politically.[37] Even then the *Quarterly* expressed reluctance that the Church should be forced into such confrontations.[38] A number of such issues arose during the nineteenth century, which disturbed Trollope for their propensity to mix religion and politics.

However unavoidable at times the intersections between Church and politics might be, in his fiction Trollope censured too deep an involvement on either side. While Archdeacon Grantly has been termed non-political, simply because he 'resists an increasingly non-Anglican Parliament's control over the church',[39] Trollope's portrayal of the archdeacon does not substantiate this. The archdeacon is shown to be angry with the political process for thwarting his wishes, yet Trollope does not castigate him. His belief that clergymen and politicians had normal drives, ambitions and emotions enabled him to be sympathetic to the desire of clerics for personal advancement, provided that self-promotion did not dominate their activities. His moving treatment in *Barchester Towers* (1857) of Archdeacon Grantly's ambition in conflict with his distress over his father's dying strikes a chord of empathy with the reader,[40] which many critics have already noted. It is not so much Grantly's ambition that Trollope seems to stress; rather it is the son's private shame that his grief should be tempered by his concern that a change in government might rob him of the opportunity to succeed his father. The present Conservative government would choose him; a new Liberal government would certainly favour a low church appointment. A protracted dying would increase the possibility of the archdeacon's disappointment. Bishop Grantly's life lingers sufficiently long for the government to change and the son's hopes are dashed. The reader feels the archdeacon's double blow.

Trollope frequently stresses that Bishop Grantly's successor, Dr Proudie, was appointed because of his capacity for political compromise; he also draws attention to his capacity for hard work. Dr Proudie's appointment closely resembles the kinds of episcopal appointments made by Palmerston. The accusation that Palmerston was a schemer, who weakened the Church by deliberately appointing 'non-activist evangelical bishops',[41] overlooks Palmerston's disquiet at the ageing of the episcopal bench and their intolerable workload. His determination to rejuvenate the Church encouraged him to choose moderate bishops who would appeal to all the community. He also introduced a government bill to allow the bishops of London and Durham to retire on a pension,[42] which had previously not been possible. Trollope was the first to admit that the new kind of bishop was, unlike the high-and-dry churchmen of the earlier age, 'a working man'. Dr Proudie may have been organized by his wife, but was nonetheless an active bishop. As noted in Chapter 3, it was his very activity that alarmed clergymen like Mr Harding, accustomed to taking a leisurely glass of wine with Dr Grantly, the previous bishop. Dr Proudie's facility for political accommodation is merely the crowning insult for the high churchmen.

It is clear that Trollope believes that clergymen should not actively court politics, either for private advantage or for individual persuasion. Archdeacon Grantly's dilemma at least reveals that the son will not *act* in any way to secure his aspirations. The turmoil remains in his head. His haste to notify the Prime Minister by telegram once his father has died is in no way lessened when he learns that the ministry has already changed, even though all hope is lost to him.[43] Thus does Trollope reveal both the man of human frailty and the clergyman of sound principle.

Yet the consequences of church and politics becoming too closely intertwined evidently preyed on Trollope's mind, because he drew attention in his travel writing to the pitfalls arising from such interactions. His life in the late 1850s embraced two long trips overseas, interspersed with a visit to the north of Britain, all on official postal business. Six months after his five-month visit to Egypt and the Holy Land, Trollope left for the West Indies, where he spent seven months. In *The West Indies and the Spanish Main* (1859), Trollope expresses his disapproval of the intermixing of Church and state. His amazement that a Roman Catholic bishop should contemplate forming 'a second party' in Costa Rica is matched by his astonishment that its President can banish a bishop 'by his mere word' *and* that the Church does not appoint another. If priests were needed, they were summoned from Guatemala. He clearly despises the Central American Church's economic strategy in regarding Guatemala as 'any other factory' of priests.[44] Trollope's astonishment is an indicator that Church and politics in his own country had not become so conjoined as they were in Latin America.

Trollope's disapproval of the intermixing of religion and politics is countered, nonetheless, in *The Last Chronicle of Barset* (1867) by his slight wonder over Josiah Crawley's total intractability when religion and politics collide. The bishop's appointment was political. The whole of Barchester knew this, and the warring among the ecclesiastical factions reveals the astuteness of individual clerics in using the political system to score points off each other. The one exception is Crawley, whose principles transcend politics. Trollope admires Crawley's learning and respects his integrity. Yet the comic contrast in the palace scene between Crawley's dishevelment and the bishop's sleekness, between Crawley's unbending pride and the bishop's nervousness, and between Crawley's intransigence and the bishop's tractability implies the novelist's bewilderment. How *could* the clergyman of low rank not understand the political consequences of Dr Proudie's appointment? How *could* the clergyman of high rank not separate his political aspirations from his Christian compassion? Crawley had given sound political advice to Mr Arabin early in his career *not* to take the path to Rome, for he knew that, politically, this would wreck his career. Mr Arabin heeds Crawley's counsel and his career is not only saved, but prospers because of it. The perpetual curate cannot, though, follow his own advice and the reader becomes witness throughout the Barchester series to the man's continued stubbornness in not taking the wider political picture into account when risking his livelihood, as well as the well-being of his family, in order to prove his point. Both government and monarchy now favoured the Evangelical faction of the Church as the serious, steady clerical group most likely to keep English society stable, hardworking and moral. To succeed, a cleric had to tread a careful path between personal conviction and political awareness. Trollope shows Crawley's inability to compromise to be partly responsible for his failure to succeed, and yet at the same time he reserves the right for both himself and the reader to admire the clergyman for his steadfast principles.

Using Crawley's situation as a model, the inability to read political signs in real life has been used to chart the unhappy career of the Rev. Gurney (1763–1848), perpetual curate of St Allen in Cornwall.[45] Gurney, unlike Crawley, did *try* to play the political game to attain preferment among Church and lay patrons, but changed sides too often and failed. Gurney resembled Crawley in his lack of humility but was financially worse off than Crawley and probably more poorly paid than most of his parishioners.[46] This was the kind of situation which the *Quarterly* abhorred, where a state too closely linked to the Church could come to dominate, particularly when religious affiliations within the community were diverse, and the peace of society was, as it claimed, directly under threat.[47]

Trollope himself had occasion to regret clerical interference in politics. His wretched experience as Liberal candidate in the 1868 Beverley elections was all the more disillusioning because he heard the Rev. Canon Birtwhistle, incumbent of Beverley Minster, denounce the Liberals 'as foes of the Protestant Church' at the mayor's breakfast, a gathering where he expected 'all politics would be banished'.[48] Trollope, in his own words, even felt himself '"to be a kind of pariah in the borough"'.[49] Eventually Beverley was disenfranchised on account of Conservative bribery, but the electorate was not improved by the

Church's dignitaries entering the fray, and Trollope was horrified that the clerical meddlers shared his religious inclinations.

Perhaps Trollope actually did take his fictional revenge on the Rev. Canon Birtwhistle in *Ralph the Heir* (1871)[50] at the election of Percycross – a borough in which 'bribery had not been unknown in previous contests... nor petitions consequent upon bribery'. To Sir Thomas Underwood MP, Conservative, the customary Liberal 'treating, and intimidation, and subornation, and fictitious voting' were disgraceful and, should he even suspect his own side of similar practices, would '"throw up the contest in the middle of it, – even if [he] were winning"', a declaration scorned by his party-workers, since bribery was a means of rewarding '"a poor man"' for losing '"his day's wages"' to elect wealthy men to Parliament. Sir Thomas's impatience, then, can well be imagined when the Wesleyan minister Mr Pabsby, having voiced his qualms on being openly pressed for his political views, prevaricates by pointing out that he '"would wish to be guided wholly by duty"' as he owed '"much to the convictions of [his] people"', for he was not a '"private man"' who could '"follow the dictates of – of – of his own heart"'. At the same time, Trollope pointedly refers to Sir Thomas's regret that he has left the respectability of Church attendance for his life in politics, asking himself why he had 'dared to leave that Sunday-keeping, church-going, domestic, decent life'.[51] Unlike the Rev. Canon Birtwhistle in Beverley, the Wesleyan minister acknowledges that his role as public figure precludes him from disclosing his political convictions and, unlike the Beverley election, Trollope's fictional characters still regard the Church as uncontaminated by worldly politics. The rector in *The Duke's Children* (1880), on the other hand, *does* resemble Canon Birtwhistle, for he openly declares Mr Carbottle, the Liberal candidate for Polpenno, to be '"a godless dissenter"'. His judgement influences both the local squire and his wife. Mrs Tregear declares that Polpenno '"should be disenfranchised altogether"' rather than have '"a godless dissenter"' as their Member of Parliament. Mr Tregear regrets that parliamentary candidates can no longer be relied upon to represent the community's religious position or to have any open opinion on this. There had been a time when Polpenno had endeavoured '"to get someone to represent [them] in Parliament, who would agree with [them] on vital subjects, such as the Church of England and the necessity of religion"'. By contrast their son, who is standing as Tory candidate in a bid to show himself worthy to marry the Duke of Omnium's daughter, believes they should '"abstain"' from voicing an opinion about his '"opponent's religion"'.[52] His restraint and the narrator's

The education of the young

Nowhere did the Church traditionally exert its influence more strongly on society than in the field of education. But by the mid-nineteenth century its monopoly of educational provision, even at the higher education level, had disappeared. Where once dissenting interests presented the greatest threat, not just with their academies for children but also with the University of London, now it was the state.

The process, although gradual, hastened the relaxation of ties between Church and state. Secularization within education began with the universities, one area where the Church's writ ran large, but where it was vulnerable to radical demands. 'So intimate is the connexion of the Church and the Universities, so closely are their interests blended and entwined', preached Bishop Monk in 1835, that those who sought the downfall of the Church will begin by 'putting restraint and force upon the Universities'.[53]

Trollope, of course, owing to family circumstances, had had no opportunity to participate in undergraduate life at university. This may have increased his objectivity on the question of reform; on the other hand, his failure to attend university, with all the accompanying social frustrations, made it difficult for him to penetrate the arcane and byzantine carapace the universities displayed to the world, in order to understand how the colleges functioned and what value they gave. Although Trollope confronted the different sides of this issue in his writings, his sympathies lay with reform.

Trollope understood that pressure for reform came from within as well as from without the universities' walls and that opinions among the clerical dons divided along religious factional lines. He stresses in *Barchester Towers* (1857) that Francis Arabin's high church opposition to university reforms, proposed by the Whigs, helps to persuade the master of Lazarus of the younger man's continuing loyalty to the Church of England, Arabin having just resisted Rome's siren call. Arabin shares his dislike of university reform with Tom Staple, tutor of Lazarus, who, Trollope hints, is of the Old School, for he 'always wore a white neckcloth, clean indeed, but not tied with that scrupulous care which now distinguishes some of our younger clergy', and his nose displays the effects of 'a pipe of port' first brought into the college cellars when he was a freshman. Trollope gently derides Staple's reactionary defence of the status quo: university reform was to Staple a matter of 'life and death' and 'any reformation was as bad to him as death'. His expressed willingness to risk martyrdom for the cause appears slightly ridiculous, for 'at the present day, unfortunately, public affairs will admit of no martyrs', nor is he willing to man the barricades, except in his conversations with 'his safe companions'. In any case, 'the *Jupiter* had undertaken to rule the University' and was too powerful for him in single combat.[54] Thus Trollope, in his unstated way, suggests not only that the anti-reform position is doomed to failure, but also that its protagonists know it.

The reforms Trollope is referring to here, as he also does in *Castle Richmond* (1860),[55] are the Oxford University Act of 1854 and the Cambridge Act of 1856, which allowed Nonconformists to take degrees, but this was not the end of the matter or of reforms which reduced the Church's hold on higher education. G. J. Goschen, a friend of Trollope's, was one of the Liberals urging university reform and even tried to pass a bill in 1865. The novelist attended a dinner in 1878 held at the Goschens' for the Princess Royal, Queen Victoria's eldest daughter; long before this he would have learned much from Goschen about the details for reforming the universities. In 1869 Trollope actually proposed to spend an evening with a friend discussing the abolition of the University tests.[56] Their abolition did not occur until 1871. This was welcomed by Liberal scholars, and the Church was now too nervous to express its true opinion, for Nonconformists were confident of getting their own way with Gladstone,[57] having also won the church rate issue in 1868.

The 1871 University Test Act abolished the majority of religious constraints on those wishing to study or teach in universities. Prior to this, anyone wanting to graduate from Cambridge had to subscribe to the Thirty-Nine Articles, and Oxford was even stricter, for no one could become an *under*graduate without subscribing to the Articles. Tait expressed his regret for this Act in 1880, for fewer men were entering holy orders now that, as he noted, free thought had pervaded Oxford and Cambridge, 'exalting the secular over the ecclesiastical'.[58] Two years later, even more secular changes took place in these universities when their headships and fellowships no longer had to be filled by men in holy orders.

Perhaps it was the fact that he had been taught by two great clerical headmasters with a social conscience, Thomas Arnold at Harrow and Longley at both Harrow and Winchester, that made Trollope equally supportive of secular reform in secondary education for all social classes. He even delivered an address on that theme at the Liverpool Institute prize-giving ceremony in 1873. Having unfavourably compared education of the 'labouring and commercial population' in England with that of the United States, Trollope praised the egalitarian nature of Forster's Education Act of 1870, noting that the 'difficulties as to secular and as to denominational education' had now mostly been overcome.[59] Like Trollope, Forster had been the guest speaker at the Annual Prize Distribution at the Liverpool Institute,[60] and as Vice-President of the Committee of Council on Education from 1868, Forster had set out to resolve the problem of the ancient Church schools, many of whose endowments had become anomalous over the years.

The Liverpool Institute had impressed Trollope with its provision of a high level of education for the commercial classes, and because its endowment 'for the more advanced education of scholars' was through 'the munificence of ... friends and townsfolk' rather than through a 'rich founder'. Trollope regretted that the public schools, begun as charity schools to train boys for the Church, were now almost exclusively for the boys of rich parents, mindful that he himself was fortunate, despite his family's financial struggles, to have attended both Winchester and Harrow.[61] Thus Trollope, in his article of the mid-1860s,[62] long before the education bill of 1870 was considered, and again in his election speech at Beverley in 1868, and later still in his address to the Liverpool Institute of 1873, expressed his earnest wish for education to be accessible to all classes, whether or not this entailed a relaxation of control by the Church.

A well-known Anglican and Liberal, he was a supporter both of secular education for the general public *and* of Church educational provision. Athough Trollope supported reform in England, when travelling overseas, he always commented on religion, 'which he saw as closely connected with education'.[63] He particularly commended the education system in Iceland, which was entirely run by priests and empowered the clergy 'to prevent a marriage when the betrothed female is unable to read'.[64] It seems logical to conclude that, in the ideal world, Trollope would have preferred education to have remained within the province of the Church but, knowing that retaining the status quo might delay opening up opportunities for the spread of educational provision, he supported those who wished to secularize educational institutions, from primary to tertiary levels.

The sundering of marital ties

Education takes place beyond the family, so the supremacy of the state over the Church in this area can at least be seen as external to society's most basic institution. The state's increasing grip on marriage, though, was viewed by the Church as deeply damaging. Trollope approached the subject in a variety of ways. In *The Three Clerks* (1858) he presents a cynical viewpoint, speculating on the implications of easier divorce. The editor of the *Daily Delight* suggests to Charley Tudor that he write an article about 'half a dozen married couples all separating, getting rid of their ribs and buckling again, helter-skelter, every man to somebody else's wife; and the parish parson refusing to do the work' in order 'to show the immorality of the thing'.[65] This is an attempt to shock the reader. People were just beginning to come to terms with the possible ramifications of the Divorce and Matrimonial Causes Act of 1857, which was instigated by Palmerston's Liberal government and enabled married couples to divorce by a judicial process, without a special Act of Parliament, and without reference to the Church.[66] The editor's lurid scenarios could not have failed to make readers at least wonder at the wisdom of such an Act.

A few years later Trollope presents a genuinely outraged viewpoint in *The Belton Estate* (1865), focusing on people in the community who object to divorce reform. Mrs Winterfield, a deeply religious woman whom Trollope terms 'affectionate as well as good', alludes to the secularization of divorce more than once. She anxiously tries to find out more of her Conservative nephew's attempt to 'annul that godless Act of Parliament and restore the matrimonial bonds of England to their old rigidity'. Where hitherto the Church had the final say on dissolving marriages and had allowed unhappy couples to separate but not remarry, the state, through its Act, had overridden Church law and allowed couples to divorce in order to remarry. Trollope describes Mrs Winterfield's horror of the state's bypassing of Church authority and has her pressing her nephew, for whom she felt a 'wondrous affection', to tell her 'anything further against that wicked Divorce Act of Parliament'.[67] Her devastation that he has not succeeded acts as a register for devout church-going people. These two reactions thus present a society seemingly polarized into those who would happily regard divorce as a licence for unbridled behaviour and those who would be thoroughly appalled by the absence of church sanctions and control.

A case study later in the narrative of *The Belton Estate* (1865) tests the legitimacy of both extreme reactions. Captain Aylmer, advised by his mother Lady Aylmer, forbids his fiancée Clara Amedroz to continue her friendship with Mrs Askerton because that lady had left her first husband to cohabit with Mr Askerton. Clara's absolute refusal to abandon her friend, either before or after she knows the facts of the case, as well as her defiance of 'the world's rules' to remain friends with the woman 'she had known and loved',[68] regardless of her past adultery, is Trollope's radical way of confronting the reader with an adulterous liaison which is neither permissive nor permissible.

The law itself was trying to accommodate society's changes in attitude to marriage breakdown. Lord Cranworth's Divorce Act of 1857 had been preceded by a Royal Commission of 1850 on marriage law, and its recommended changes were incorporated into the Act. Previously, a marriage could only be dissolved through a private Act of Parliament. The Divorce Act permitted divorce on the grounds of a wife's adultery; a husband's adultery did not provide grounds for divorce until 1923. Trollope draws attention in *The Belton Estate* to the Church's anger over this Act, for many still believed divorce to be wrong and, for twenty years, debate over the Act prolonged the Church's disagreement with the state and disunited the Church. Some bishops believed marriage to be sacrosanct whatever the situation, but others conceded that divorce should be allowed in cases of adultery, citing Christ's 'Mathaean exception'. This refers to 'the single exception endorsed by Christ himself',[69] which allowed a man to divorce his wife if she had committed adultery; a man's adultery was not sufficient reason.[70] Archbishop Sumner accepted the Act because of the Mathaean exception, but was unhappy about the guilty party being allowed to remarry. Bishop Phillpotts was not in favour of the Act, because the Royal Commission of 1850 had not consulted the Church, and the Act enabled the rich to divorce but not the poor. Legal fees and travel to the Divorce Court in London were beyond most people's pockets. Hamilton and Wilberforce, members of the Oxford group, were against the dissolution of marriage on any grounds. Tait, of the broad church, wanted grounds for divorce to be extended beyond adultery.

Extreme though the situation is in *He Knew He Was Right* (1869), because of the husband's monomania, it helped Trollope to show the danger that lay ahead if the Mathaean exception became the accepted ruling by providing the question of the wife's adultery as the central problem. It is one of the very few of Trollope's novels to feature a tiny child; it is his only novel to deal with parental conflict over child custody. Now that divorce was easier, Trollope was evidently urging his readers to consider the Mathaean exception under circumstances where the husband's clarity of judgement was in doubt. Mrs Trevelyan's innocence is never mooted, and the intransigent conviction of Mr Trevelyan of his wife's guilt not only wrecks their marital relations but also threatens the well-being of their child. Both husband and wife are, from the beginning, revealed to be too stubborn to compromise, but the husband's intractability swiftly moves beyond reason. Having forced his wife and sister-in-law to leave the marital home on a maintenance of £800 per year, Louis Trevelyan ponders his next move. As regards his wife, he is determined that 'her conduct would be watched, and that she should be threatened with the Divorce Court', in the vain hope that this would reduce her to contrition. The child's custody becomes one of the key bones of contention, and the child is even abducted at one point at the husband's instigation. The Church, too, comes under critical scrutiny. Mr Outhouse, an East End London clergyman, initially refuses shelter to his wife's niece after her separation, on the grounds that St Paul had said: 'Wives, obey your husbands.' The low church Mr Outhouse is 'very religious, devoted to his work ... but ... strongly-biased'. Nor are the high church followers in the cathedral close of Exeter presented as any less prejudiced in the accused wife's favour. Jemima Stanbury, upright citizen and staunch member of the Church, immediately presumes Emily Trevelyan's guilt, and strongly advises her own sister-in-law and niece to withdraw their protection from the unfortunate woman, while denouncing reform in general as '[m]urder, sacrilege, adultery, treason, atheism'.[71] Jemima later retracts her quick condemnation, but the damage to the innocent wife has already been done. Trollope casts the Anglican community's quick presumption of uxorial guilt as wrong, destructive and counterproductive in situations likely to lead to divorce.

The dichotomy in the Church between those against and those in favour of divorce re-emphasized the links between Church and state. The opponents of divorce believed the 1857 Act to be 'a threat to the union of Church and state, because it opened up a division between the law of the Church and the law of the State'.[72] Yet not every statesman was in favour of the Act, and Gladstone, also high church, was vehemently opposed. The Divorce Act, like the Probate Act also passed in 1857 under Liberal rule and with Palmerston as Prime Minister, transferred much of the work from ecclesiastical courts to civil courts and further eroded the Church's power. High churchmen were particularly dismayed at the state's increasing hold over the Church. Gladstone, caught between his religious beliefs and political affiliations, chose in the 1850s to support the Church and urged Parliament not to meddle in religious affairs. Yet the Church would not be appeased, and the lower house of the Canterbury Convocation rebuked Parliament for not consulting the Church on what it saw as Church doctrine. Gladstone even wrote to Wilberforce in 1857, lamenting that Erastianism was taking hold, and warning that this situation would, 'if uncorrected', become 'thoroughly immoral'.[73]

The problems of divorce and its attendant logistics plagued Church and state throughout the rest of the century. According to the Church, there was no question of the guilty party remarrying, and yet the innocent party had no clear brief either. These practicalities were raised in 1880 during the Church Congress Debate on Marriage and Divorce. Canon Henry Temple, Vicar of St John's, Leeds, expressed concern over the tension between Church and state, yet reiterated the Church's firm position. He even hinted that, if the state insisted on pursuing reform, the Church might have to loosen its ties with the state. In the end the issue died down because the government did nothing.

Trollope's measured portrayal in 1880 of the Peacockes' cohabitation in *Dr Wortle's School* clearly responds to the Church Congress Debate of that year, and allows glimpses of the dilemma faced by ecclesiastical officials. Mr Puddicombe stated that Mr Peacocke had 'behaved very badly'; personally, he would not condone a false marriage under any circumstances. The bishop is no less firm but is more circumspect, noting that they 'cannot alter the ways of the world suddenly', and that setting an example is vital.[74] In this way, Trollope illustrates the Church's dilemma, and shows that not all the Church's representatives were inflexible. Nor is it a coincidence that Mr Peacocke has married in the New World. Trollope knew that his readership would be less offended by this. The choice of America also enabled him to demonstrate the influence of the New World on the Old. Tolerant though Trollope was of unconventionality, he was not one to countenance divorce and remarriage as a general practice. Church vows, for him, were sacrosanct. Friend to George Eliot and George Henry Lewes, Trollope was not at all tolerant of his son Henry's intention to marry a woman of the streets, and he sent him to join his brother Fred in Australia to review his situation. In light of his own conduct, Trollope's fictional exposition of the Church's torment over divorce reveals his ability to view difficult issues from a range of viewpoints in order to explain them.

Trollope returned specifically to the question of divorce in *Kept in the Dark* (1882), written in the year of his death, and 13 years after *He Knew He Was Right* (1869). As in the former work, divorce never actually takes place. Unlike the earlier novel, however, the couple in the later novel resolve their differences. This is thanks largely to the intercedence of the husband's widowed sister, for both husband and wife, as in *He Knew He Was Right*, cling to opposing positions of wounded pride, and the husband's wound gapes the more widely, since he 'seemed to be one who could with difficulty forgive an injury'. How could *he* overlook his wife's neglect to tell him that, 'a month or two before' his own proposal, she 'had been the promised wife' of a man he despised? Why should *she*, whose 'offence' was 'so small', be coerced into 'let[ting herself] down by asking [his] pardon'? Significantly, the Church in this novel does not hover so closely as 'judge and jury' over the unhappy Westerns as it had over the Trevelyans, but retreats instead into the subplot surrounding Francesca Altifiorla, 'noted hater of the other sex', and deemed unmarriageable by both the bishop and the dean. Mr Graham, the lawyer, alludes briefly to the 'one only fault', the wife's adultery, and Mr Western mentions that, although '[t]he law might perhaps demand a third of my income' (in keeping with ecclesiastical court precedent), he will give his wife 'two-thirds if she wishes it'. Fortunately for them and their expected offspring, their reconciliation elicits apologies and forgiveness from both sides of the marital chamber, Mrs Western's forgiveness having given her 'the happy conviction that she had been more sinned against than sinning'! The predominantly secular focus of references to the Divorce and Matrimonial Causes Act,[75] passed a quarter of a century earlier, indicates that the Church had already ceded authority regarding divorce to the secular courts of the realm, however unhappy it was with this situation.

The disposal of the dead

Of all the issues faced by Church and state in the nineteenth century, death and burial had to be the most sensitive; few Victorian families were untouched by premature death, and coping with grief was a common but no less painful experience. The Church would not bury within its walls those of professed Nonconformist views and, since Nonconformism increased during the nineteenth century, the problem continued to grow. The bereaved, in their deepest grieving period, do not forgive a slight directed at the deceased. Criticism of the Church's intransigence became increasingly audible. Yet criticism itself could provoke strong feelings of discomfort.

Trollope had learnt that humour on this topic was unacceptable. His mother had already made that mistake. In 1822, Lord Byron's young illegitimate daughter died in an Italian convent. The poet asked Harrow Church to erect a memorial tablet, but the vestry, including the Rev. Cunningham, an Evangelical master at Harrow, refused, fearing the tribute might set the wrong example. Frances Trollope admired Byron and was angry with Cunningham. She wrote a satirical poem, in which she vented her humour against the clergyman. Trollope copied it out when he was 19, and added a few comments. These notes reveal his disapproval of his mother's lack of taste. He thus makes no direct allusion to this taboo subject, yet his indirect allusions and actions reveal his private views. His mother had infuriated Americans with her forthrightness in *Domestic Manners of the Americans* (1832) and he was determined not to do the same thing in his own country. Even though Fanny Trollope's criticisms may have been justified,[76] Trollope would have learned to be chary of tackling a subject as sensitive as burial. He had experience of several deaths in his own family, having lost his father, two sisters and a brother. His reticence on this matter can best be illustrated by *The Belton Estate* (1865). The death of her father leaves Clara Amedroz 'alone in the world, penniless', but there is no lingering lament over the ceremony: 'Then came the day of the funeral, and after that rite was over ... There was no will to be read.' The funeral is thus quickly glossed over as a 'rite'.[77] Trollope chose rather to dwell on happier times in people's lives, as the lovers' scene in Hadley Churchyard from *The Bertrams* (1859) evinces where, in the very place in which his sister Emily was buried, Trollope uses the engagement of his fictional characters, Sir Henry Harcourt and Caroline Waddington, to recall nostalgically 'those lovers' walks, those loving lovers' rambles'. He could not help, though, in the midst of describing 'the merry marriage-bells' of the couple's wedding, alluding to his sister's burial by admitting he knew 'full well the tone with which' those bells tolled, having 'stood in that green churchyard' when 'the ashes and the dust that were loved so well' were 'laid to earth'. Nor did the worldly couple's marriage turn out well. The bride had loved another and the bridegroom was to commit suicide, once the Hadley bells had 'rung again', 'hardly above their breath', in 'a dirge' for the death of the wealthy miser, old Mr Bertram, whose will had thwarted Sir Henry Harcourt's expectations.[78] There are nonetheless no lengthy funeral scenes in Trollope's fiction; he preferred to glide over this ceremony and dwell on rituals devoted to the living.

He may have regarded burial as too sensitive a subject for his fiction, but Trollope had fairly advanced views on the matter. He joined his friend Millais as one of 16 signatories on the founding document in 1874 of the Cremation Society which was 'under the leadership of the Queen's surgeon, Sir Henry Thompson'. His signing demonstrates that he was forward thinking and far less conservative than most critics allow. He disliked 'extravagant funerals and extended mourning, which celebrated the dead at the cost of the living'.[79] Cremation was in fact made legal in 1884, two years after Trollope's own death, to save space in graveyards and safeguard public health, particularly when death came from contagious disease.

It was not until later that Trollope specifically mentioned cremation in his fiction. *The Fixed Period* (1882), set in 1980 in Britannula, a fictional Australasian country, has its president attempting, unsuccessfully, to introduce euthanasia, known as the 'Fixed Period', to people of 67 and a half years of age, because 'the sufficient sustenance of an old man is more costly than the feeding of a young one'. Such measures – depositing 67 year olds in a college preparing them for death and then finally carrying out the deed six months to a year later – would make its inhabitants 'the richest people on God's earth!' The novel, like several of Trollope's, tackles a taboo subject with irony and offers different perspectives, often leaving the reader wondering as to the writer's own position. The question of cremation, though, is emphasized twice as being quite separate from euthanasia, and as being 'the great work'. Only its logistics seemed to trouble Trollope, for he refers to 'the savour of burnt pork' from experiments conducted on cremating pig carcasses, and to unsightly furnace chimneys, which should not have been built in sight of the preparatory college but more tactfully 'should have been elsewhere', for '[c]remation [was] no part of the Fixed Period'.[80] Cremation itself is seen as a progressive reform. It is not mentioned in conjunction with the Church, so it is possible that Trollope might have believed the Church to be reluctant to condone it.

Euthanasia, but not cremation, is referred to in Oliphant's *Phoebe Junior* (1876) in connection with the College in Carlingford, based on St Cross Hospital, Winchester, and Trollope's Hiram's Hospital. It begins as an angry reaction from the wealthy Mr Copperhead to the expense of maintaining the old, but is taken up seriously by Phoebe, daughter of a Dissenting Minister who adds that euthanasia 'would have to be with the consent of the victims', at which point Mr Copperhead quickly recoils from the idea of active intercession and advocates letting "em die when they ought to die'.[81] Significantly, Oliphant's justification, like Trollope's, is made on economic not compassionate grounds and is made six years earlier than Trollope's.

The subject of euthanasia did not occupy Gaskell's pen, but her fleeting allusion to Dissenters' funerals exemplifies her tolerance, embodies community dissatisfaction and throws light on the Church of England's perceived inadequacies. Her brief aside in *Ruth* (1853) that the Dissenting minister's intention to deliver 'an appropriate funeral sermon' is 'according to Dissenting custom' underscores the attention to individuals,[82] presumably in contrast to the conventions of the Established Church, where the liturgy and prayers are ritualized as formularies and individuals are seen as integral parts of the community rather than separate entities. Since Gaskell does not expand on her remark or explain it, the obliquity and brevity of the comment would have shielded the author from being charged with over-tolerance.

Trollope's own tolerance can be seen in his hint at the end of *The Vicar of Bullhampton* (1870) that Jacob Brattle, the non-believing miller, stern but caring to his family, would meet his imminent death without a qualm.[83] The hint is that, despite the Church's certain prohibition to bury him within its grounds, the miller's fate after death would be no different from any churchman. Trollope's final page would have been understood in its tactful challenge to the Church to change its ways.

The end of life was to be not quite as difficult an issue for the Church as the end of a marriage, but it was still thorny. The question of burials for Dissenters had arisen at about the same time as the question of divorce, and so the 1850s, as Trollope hints, were turbulent times for the Church. Bills to have parish churchyards available for Nonconformist burials and ceremonies appeared frequently in Parliament throughout the 1860s and 1870s. Once again the Church was divided, although the majority were reluctant for change. Gladstone had supported the burials bills as early as 1862 and his new Liberal government ushered in the Burials Act of 1880, permitting non-Anglicans to conduct burial services in churchyards. This Act, then, appropriated Church property as state property and opened up the churchyards to more ecumenical use, but did not extend the same facilities to those of secular persuasion.

Once again, the Liberation Society and Edward Miall had been at the forefront of the demand for change, and Tait, wisely, saw that the last ritual in life should not be seen to be too exclusive, for this would provide the Dissenters with, arguably, a justification for their grievances. Education, divorce and now burial could no longer be used as a means to attack the Established Church, and therefore establishment itself ceased to be an issue. If Nonconformists could pass through the main stages of life without confrontation with the Established Church, then, as far as the majority of people were concerned, there was no necessity to disestablish the Church. On the other hand, although Archbishop Tait's tenure as Archbishop of Canterbury began with the fear of disestablishment in 1868 and ended with the fear totally abated, his victory has been said to be due to indifference.[84] The Church was no longer seen as a great power, having lost much of its hold on the institutions of education and the family. Trollope's acceptance of these social reforms derived from his tolerance, not from any design to weaken the Church. On the contrary, he wanted the Church of England to modernize itself gradually, not weaken itself through intransigence. Above all, he wanted the Church to be sufficiently modern to tolerate other denominations, other views and other systems.

The threat of Roman Catholicism

Without Roman Catholicism the Church of England would never have been born; it owed its very existence to *opposition* to the Italian Church. Since any antagonism can engender anxiety, it was not surprising that state fear of Roman Catholic resurgence in English society prolonged Anglican and community intolerance towards believers in the older faith. From Trollope's perspective, the fear was unnecessary and the intolerance harmful, which is why he returned throughout his writing to this issue. His early adulthood in Ireland had exposed him to seething tensions between Roman Catholicism and Protestantism, and many a critic has lauded his liberal attitude towards Roman Catholics despite his being an Anglican, making the general assumption that his Irish experiences totally shaped his opinion. Both of these judgements oversimplify the situation. Trollope's committed Anglicanism has already been established. He had, however, Roman Catholic antecedents of whom he would have been well aware. He had descended from Roman Catholic Trollopes, one of whom, John Trolop (d. 1611), was prosecuted for recusancy in 1569, and from Roman Catholic Meetkerkes, whose home town of Bruges was 'one of the most deeply Catholic cities left on the earth', to which Trollope and his family had been forced to flee on account of his father's debts.[85] The Meetkerke family branch had held the title and estate which Trollope's father had hoped to inherit and Trollope had maintained a correspondence with Cecilia Meetkerke.[86] He therefore had ample opportunity from the family annals to acquaint himself in a positive way with Roman Catholicism, long before his sojourn in Ireland. Nor does the assumption that Ireland, for Trollope, cast a benign light on Roman Catholicism do justice to the novelist's own understanding of sectarianism and his lifelong urge to place, without bias, his fiction within the contemporary contexts of politics, culture and religion. It is nonetheless true that most of his portraits of Roman Catholics are positive, particularly in his early Irish novels and in *La Vendée*,[87] but there are glimpses in his later work of a darkening attitude towards the Church of Rome.

In the early Irish novels the underlying strain between Roman Catholics and Protestants is not all-consuming. Trollope illustrates that the older generation is less vigorous than the younger generation in guarding sectarian principles and is far less antagonistic towards each other, and that even the younger generation has reservations about violence. Father John McGovery (Roman Catholic) and Captain Ussher (Protestant), of the older generation in *The Macdermots of Ballycloran* (1847), clearly get on well, and the younger Father Cullen, despite the fact that 'he felt towards Keegan [convert to Protestantism] all the abhorrence which a very bigoted and ignorant Roman Catholic could feel towards a Protestant convert . . . would have done anything to prevent his meeting his death by the hands, or with the connivance, of Thady Macdermot', a Roman Catholic.[88] The murder of Captain Ussher is actually motivated more by filial than by sectarian loyalty, even if, understandably, the two become confused in the community's eyes. Significantly authentic is the folklore of Drumsna, now renamed Ballycloran, in which Feemy Macdermot, Catholic, was 'said to be buried in the Protestant churchyard', because 'in those days they buried them all in together'.[89] Tensions in 1840s' Ireland could suddenly flare up if given a reason, but no apartheid at this stage existed between the Church of Rome and the Irish Church, and dissensions were under some kind of control.

As if further to illustrate this control, Trollope, in *The Kellys and the O'Kellys* (1848) and *Castle Richmond* (1860), continues to contrast the positive and negative aspects of Roman Catholic and Protestant characters. In *The Kellys and the O'Kellys* (1848), he compares the tractability of the Rev. Armstrong of the Irish Church with the intransigence of the ultra Protestant Rev. O'Joscelyn. While O'Joscelyn and his wife might sit up 'two nights running, armed to the teeth to protect themselves' from noisy neighbouring Roman Catholics, the Rev. Armstrong would 'sooner by half be a Roman . . . than think so badly of [his] neighbours'. And when O'Joscelyn is horrified by the small size of his colleague's congregation, Armstrong points out that, if he needed a large congregation for a bishop's visit or some other special occasion, the Roman Catholics 'think so well' of him 'that they'd flock in crowds' if he asked them 'and the priest would show them the way'.[90] The famine in *Castle Richmond* (1860) engenders a joint philanthropic enterprise between Roman Catholic and Protestant churches, but private fireside conversations throw light on irrational prejudices. The fact that these prejudices could still be reduced to laughter indicates a sense of proportion. For example, the mild-mannered Protestant Herbert Fitzgerald, educated in England, is able to convince his Aunt Letty of the foolishness of her declaration that she 'would sooner be a Mahommedan than a Papist' and of the aptness of his comment that Mrs Townsend's hatred of 'the sorceries of popery' is akin to a mad 'dog hat[ing] water' and is held 'with the same amount of judgment'.[91] Ireland in the 1840s, Trollope demonstrates, could rely on certain representatives from both Roman Catholic and Protestant communities to maintain a degree of cordiality and reason between the two groups.

Perhaps it was for this reason that in his first English novel, *The Warden* (1855), Trollope mocks the state's suspicion in England of Roman Catholic pretensions and denounces political intrusion into private religious beliefs. By linking the absurd 'Convent Custody Bill', of which there were 137 clauses, with the Irish concern for its poplin *and* its whiskey,[92] Trollope indicates the ludicrousness of state fear that could inspire such a bill. Having just left Ireland, Trollope was confident that there was no cause for concern.

The Catholic Emancipation Act of 1829 had been regretted by many. It is thought that it seriously damaged the Tory party, which split on the issue.[93] In addition, the Papal Aggression of 1850 was still too warm a memory for the state. While sympathetic to community fear, Trollope's love of Ireland and respect for the many Roman Catholics he knew prompted him to regard English measures to curb Roman Catholicism as counterproductive. He even proposed in 1851 that the wisest way of dealing with Papal Aggression was to 'let the whole thing sink by its own weight'.[94]

In contrast to this light-hearted look at fear of Roman Catholicism is Trollope's leaden treatment in *The New Zealander* (1972) in 1855–6. In the midst of a passage waxing heavily on the evils of those denouncing Roman Catholicism, Trollope casts blame on low church ministers like 'Mr Everscreech' who 'will vouchsafe to hold forth against the harlotries of the scarlet woman!' The satire was too sombre for Trollope's contemporary publishers, who decided not to publish the work. Nevertheless, this book gives the modern reader greater insight than his fiction into society's fear of Roman Catholicism and Trollope's genuine concern. Roman Catholic emancipation, a long-running issue reopened by Papal Aggression, had made the Church of England sufficiently fearful to involve itself politically. The non-fiction work was no doubt 'too near the bone' of truth to be marketable. In fact, although Trollope is rather heavy handed, careful reading of his chapter devoted to the

Church uncovers a moving tolerance for a broad range of beliefs, beyond even Roman Catholicism. Emancipation for one religious sector always paves the way for others seeking similar rights. Trollope is pragmatic enough to realize that one could not expect the Church of England to satisfy the religious persuasions of the whole population, and that it really does not matter which dogma a person follows, provided that the basic beliefs are in keeping with Christianity. He therefore beseeches the community to regard the outer signs of religious identification as mere badges of position and to allow divergent opinions as to worshipping styles; he even goes so far as to urge people to include everyone in their Christian fellowship, regardless of creed. Only by doing this, he says, can one be true to oneself: 'Let every one at any rate choose for himself a religion by which he can live.'[95] One wonders if the sentiments expressed in this work might not have been the *real* reason for *The New Zealander* remaining unpublished during his lifetime.[96] Such tolerance might have been seen to be too encouraging of religious choice.

Strong prejudices against Roman Catholicism appear, however briefly, in the work of other novelists. Gaskell describes Squire Hamley's 'dread and abomination' of Roman Catholics as 'something akin to our ancestors' hatred of witchcraft' in *Wives and Daughters* (1866), set in 1832, the year of the Reform Bill and not long after Catholic emancipation.[97] Similar is Squire Wentworth's horror in Oliphant's *The Perpetual Curate* (1864), when ritualism was rife, of his son Gerald's intention to enter the Roman Catholic priesthood, thus abandoning his wife and six children '[f]or . . . damnable Papistical madness'. Gerald's conversion is deemed 'perversion' by his Evangelical aunt, and the family never recovers from Gerald's breaking away 'from the bonds of nature'.[98] The vehemence expressed by these fictional characters matches Trollope's in *The New Zealander*.

A series of events had stirred up anti-Catholic feelings in Britain. There was the flight to Rome of Newman in 1845 which incited others to follow, the Papal Bull of 1850, in which the Pope declared a renewed interest in encouraging Roman Catholicism in Britain, and the 'Papal Aggression' in Britain in the same year. The Liberal Lord Russell shared the nation's fear and ensured the passing of an Ecclesiastical Titles Act, which punished as criminals members of churches other than the Established Church who adopted territorial titles in Britain. Thus the Act forbade Roman Catholic priests from accepting English bishoprics from Rome. Trollope strongly disapproved of this Act.[99] Not surprisingly, Russell's ministry did not last long after this,[100] for the Act was scarcely in accordance with Liberal principles. Trollope's own Liberalism was affronted.

Nor does Trollope's concern with the problems facing Roman Catholics cease once emancipation itself is no longer the contention. Freedom to worship is one thing, but if religious choice precludes the tenure of certain positions in society, the core of resentment continues to seethe. Trollope returns to the new issues confronting practising Roman Catholics in the 1870s in novels published in this decade. In *Phineas Redux* (1874) he remarks that '[s]ome few Protestant spirits regretted' that Phineas Finn, a Roman Catholic Member of Parliament, had been acquitted of murder, 'not even yet allow[ing] themselves to doubt that the whole murder had been arranged by Divine Providence to bring down the scarlet woman'.[101] Contemporary readers would have known that, although at this time there was a Jewish judge, there was no Roman Catholic judge, since state religious tolerance was still less advanced towards those presenting the biggest threat to Anglican supremacy. Trollope's allusions to the Catholic question in *The Prime Minister* (1876) reveal that he was well aware of the catalyst for the Emancipation Act. In July 1828, contrary to the law, Daniel O'Connell, a Roman Catholic, was elected MP for County Clare in Ireland, and the government realized with embarrassment that other seats in Ireland could be 'won' by Roman Catholics, who, even though a majority of the Irish population, were debarred from sitting in Parliament. Wellington, Peel and Lyndhurst wrote a secret memorandum to the King to convince him that now was the time to revoke his decision not to allow Parliament to discuss Catholic emancipation.[102] The King relented, but feeling ran high among the English population and cries of 'No Popery' were legion. Trollope's sympathy to the full acceptance of Roman Catholics is clear in *The Prime Minister* (1876), albeit indirect. While Ferdinand Lopez is an undesirable husband, Trollope has some sympathy towards him for the prejudice meted out to him by Abel Wharton. Abel's professed tolerance for Roman Catholics is undercut by his reluctance to have his daughter marry a member of that Church and, when Lopez assures him that his denomination coincides with the Whartons', Abel declares that it is Lopez's foreign name that concerns him.[103] Although the ensuing narrative justifies Abel Wharton's antipathy to Lopez, the charge of alien religion and origins is shown to be unjust.

Even more covert but no less effective is Trollope's depiction of English fear of Roman Catholicism in *Is He Popenjoy?* (1878), which outlines the possible repercussions of decadent urban living and the dangers awaiting the imprudent and the naive. Lord George Germain utters a stinging rejoinder when his wife admires a painting of Roman Catholic priests, belittles them briefly in his comment that he did not 'care much about old priests' or '[s]acerdotal pictures', and suggests that they go immediately to Swan and Edgar's, a fashionable West End store.[104] The ill temper of Lord Germain, one of the most positive characters in the novel, is a reminder of social prejudice among people who are otherwise both rational and decent.

Trollope's tolerance for other denominations did not prevent him from making critical comparisons. Even *The Fixed Period* (1882), a novel with almost twenty-first century signs of prescience, has Crasweller, who expects to be the first to undergo euthanasia and to whom the reader cannot but be sympathetic, aver that 'I never knew a decent woman who wasn't an Episcopalian'.[105] For all his tolerance this late novel again reveals Trollope's quiet satisfaction in his Church.

His travel writings always include an appraisal of a nation's religion and, while he admires certain qualities in other religious groups, he does not apologize for favouring his own above Roman Catholicism or any other denomination. Having judged in *North America* (1862) that Roman Catholics in Quebec 'do not advance and push ahead . . . as settlers in a new country should', he remarks: 'has it not always been the case with Roman Catholics . . . forced to measure themselves against Protestants?'[106] Here Trollope's pride in his Church cannot help erupting, particularly when making comparisons with the Church of Rome. Similarly, in *Australia and New Zealand* (1873) Trollope notes with satisfaction that, despite South Australia's intention not to have a 'dominant church', the Church of England has been in the ascendant mainly because its members who 'have flocked into the colony have been higher in wealth and intelligence than those of any other creed'.[107] He was a tactful traveller who nonetheless could not help quietly admiring his own Church above all others. Nor could he fail to take advantage of being released from the political sensitivities of his own country to comment more candidly on Roman Catholicism in a much broader context.

More candid about his religious preferences in his travel non-fiction, Trollope was also more open with his criticisms of Roman Catholicism in his fiction set in Europe than in his fiction set in England. Perhaps he was less concerned about inflaming diehard prejudices among his own society; Europe, after all, lay across the English Channel, and he could not be held accountable to the same extent for fanning possibly dangerous flames of anti-Roman passion. Despite the emphasis of both *Linda Tressel* (1868) and *The Golden Lion of Granpère* (1872) weighing more heavily on the narrow-mindedness of European Protestantism, the pivotal point of both novels indicates that Roman Catholicism is not to be seen as the panacea. If Roman Catholicism is less strict than Calvinism, Trollope points out in the earlier novel, it is only because churches become more lenient as time goes by, for in its early days the Church of Rome used 'material ashes... for the personal annoyance of the sinner'. Its greater leniency in forgiving human weakness assumes the shape of laxity in the old servant Tetchen's encouragement of youthful elopement that does not end in marriage. Nor was the Roman Catholic Church necessarily infallible in its means of giving moral guidance. Trollope makes a slight but telling point in *Linda Tressel* through his most sympathetic character, Linda, that the 'somebody' in the Church of Rome who dictates 'what we ought to do and what we ought not to do', might 'possibly be wrong'.[108] Fond of his own comforts, M. le Curé in *The Golden Lion of Granpère* cannot admit defeat in his failure to persuade Marie Bromar to obey him by cajoling and threatening her, for he had 'that strong dislike to yield an inch in practice or in doctrine, which is indicative of his order.'[109] Tolerance of Roman Catholicism, as far as Trollope was concerned, was certainly not tantamount to adherence to its values, and he felt himself freer to offer a frank opinion about this denomination in work set outside his native England.

He was far more cautious in his English novels. It is striking that, in his correspondence, Trollope only once admits to using his personal knowledge of a clergyman to help create one of his fictional clerical characters, and this is a Roman Catholic priest, Father Barham, in *The Way We Live Now* (1875). Father Barham is one of the most sympathetically portrayed characters in this novel fiercely denouncing the decadent greed of 1870s England; incorruptible, he 'was ready to sacrifice anything personal to himself... his time, his health, his money when he had any, and his life'.[110] The recipient of Trollope's confession was Mary Holmes, herself a convert to Roman Catholicism. Having told her that he had drawn Barham as 'a thoroughly good man, anxiously doing his duty according to his lights, at any cost of personal suffering', he then informed her that, when living at Waltham Cross, he had become acquainted with a Roman Catholic priest who 'was a thoroughly conscientious man, an Oxford man, what we call a pervert and you a convert, and a perfect gentleman – so poor that he had not bread to eat'. Trollope, in his kindness, had assisted the priest, at least until he ruined the friendship by 'casting ridicule and opprobrium on my religion, though I would not on any account have hinted a slur upon his'. Trollope admits that he 'was obliged to drop him', for 'he made himself absolutely unbearable'.[111] Trollope's astute knowledge of human nature enabled him to discern when and where he could be candid.

But even his tolerance towards Roman Catholicism – particularly in Ireland – began to show signs of being strained in the final years of his life. Whereas he repeated in *The Macdermots of Ballycloran* (1847) and in *An Eye for An Eye* (1879) the commonplace narrative formula of a young Catholic Irish girl being seduced by an English Protestant (the metaphor of Ireland being raped by England), he stresses in the earlier novel that the Roman Catholic priest tries to discourage the couple and ensure that Feemy does not fall 'immediately into vice'.[112] In the later novel, the role of the Roman Catholic priest is more dubious. Trollope shows Father Marty positively encouraging Kate O'Hara and Fred Neville in their attachment to each other, possibly hinting that the priest was at least partially culpable in causing the tragic outcome; he had even had the young man to dine with him.[113] Still circumspect in this novel, Trollope abandons in his last and unfinished novel, *The Landleaguers* (1883), his sympathy for any Roman Catholic seeking justice by violence. So intent was he to capture the spirit of contemporary Ireland that, in the last six months of his life and beset with ill-health, Trollope visited Ireland twice, accompanied by his niece Florence.[114] The tragic estrangement in *The Landleaguers* (1883) of Protestant Philip Jones from his son Florian, a convert ten-year-old to Roman Catholicism, results in the latter's murder after he has been threatened by a young priest of his new persuasion. The murder is recounted in horrific detail. Trollope is unsparing in the blame he attaches to those pursuing a cause to the point of violence. From the very first page of the novel, Trollope does not recoil from labelling the poor Roman Catholics on Philip Jones' estate as people 'for the most part uneducated', intent though they are on independence. He adds that '[n]ever were a people less fitted to exercise such dominion without control', and attributes their arrogance to teaching from America. Even Trollope's categorizing of Irish Catholic priests into the better educated, who were trained abroad, and the home-nurtured young zealots who knew less 'on general topics', is an indictment of Irish Catholic attitudes of the late 1870s, for politics had superseded religion in their 'feelings and aspirations'.[115] For the law-abiding 70-year old Father Giles, Trollope has respect, but for the zealous young curate, Father Brosnan, Trollope has none. He had lost his sympathy for the Irish Catholic cause, and demonstrates more sympathy for the victimized Protestant Jones family. For him, the end did *not* justify the means. Trollope's early adoption of a balanced stance vis-à-vis Roman Catholicism swiftly turned into rejection once politics became the issue and murder became the means. Once again, he totally disapproved of a church becoming involved in politics.

The example of the disestablishment of the Irish Church

Trollope was the first to admit that he believed change should be gradual, but he was to be a pressing champion of disestablishing the Irish Church. Trollope worshipped in the Irish Church for almost twenty years, and grew weary of hearing the high church of England sharply criticized,[116] simply because the Irish Church saw the high church as being far too close for comfort to Roman Catholicism and in danger of leading the Protestant flock into Roman pastures. This no doubt influenced his eagerness to engage himself in the battle. Not only did he fight the Beverley election by speaking on behalf of Irish Church disestablishment, but he also wrote articles vigorously defending the Liberal position. 'The Irish Church Debate' (1868), appearing just before the election, stressed the inevitability of disestablishment.[117] Each parish in the Irish Church often contained only two or three Protestants, so establishment could hardly be justified. Trollope, well aware of this, provides a pitiful picture in *The Kellys and the O'Kellys* (1848) of the Rev. Armstrong, whose sole parishioners are 'one old lady and her daughters', and of his neighbouring parson, whose congregation consists of the policeman and two spinsters.[118] Trollope urged, therefore, that the Maynooth Grant and the *Regium Donum* be continued and added 'to the entire property of Establishment' so that the total could be equally divided among the three main churches of Ireland: the Roman Catholic, the Presbyterian and the Irish Churches.[119]

The Maynooth Grant had been established during the French wars to fund the main Irish seminary, and its modest grant of about £10,000 a year had still not been changed by the 1840s. Peel's decision in 1845 to augment the grant had been extremely unpopular, for it looked as if the Conservative government wished to appease Irish Catholics and, at an annual increase to £26,000 as well as an immediate grant of £30,000 for building the college, it was thought that the appeasement was not only excessive but dangerous.[120] Roman Catholics in Britain generally might think that the Established Church had grown weak, particularly since this was the year in which Newman converted to Roman Catholicism and took many others with him. Trollope thought otherwise.

This first article of Trollope's in fact develops some of the arguments of John Herbert Stack who, under Trollope's editorship of *Saint Pauls Magazine*, had already shown the problems faced by the state in 1868 in disestablishing the Irish Church. While Stack urged the state to hasten its decision, he pointed out the difficulties in Ireland between religion, politics and education. The Roman Catholics of Ireland, he said, were 'a political as well as a religious party' and, in addition to the Maynooth Grant for training priests, were demanding an endowment for the Catholic University in Stephen's Green. He advised against complete withdrawal of state aid to the Catholic and Protestant Churches; voluntary aid would ensue, and the Roman Catholic Church would be supported by the poor, while the Irish Church would be helped by landed proprietors. He suggested equal endowments to Catholic and Protestant churches, so that the Catholic Church had a semblance of autonomy. A plan was needed to 'satisfy Peter without totally despoiling Paul', and Stack urged disestablishment.[121]

Trollope himself had referred to the Maynooth Grant in his fiction. Nor did he always staunchly defend Roman Catholics who benefited from the grant. He emphasizes the point in *The Macdermots of Ballycloran* (1847) that, unlike the older, cultured priests such as Father John McGrath, who were educated in France, the younger priests, like Father Cullen, were educated at Maynooth and were often illiterate farmers' sons, adding that, despite Catholic emancipation, Cullen held grievances against Protestants. In the unrevised text prior to 1860, Trollope waxes much more vehemently about the 'errors' of the Romanists whom he calls 'political fanatics and bigots', at the same time as insisting that more, not less, should be done 'for the priests of the next generation', in order that they will be 'less likely to be imbued with the crimes which are now attributed to their predecessors'.[122] Trollope was always a great believer in the power of education as a means of expunging dangerous prejudices, which is why he argued for the continuation of Maynooth. Ten years later in *Barchester Towers* (1857), he significantly attributes to Dr Proudie support for the maintenance of both Maynooth and *Regium Donum*.[123] Bishop Proudie is normally seen as a target for Trollope's comic indictment of the Evangelicals, yet his agreement with the continuation of the Maynooth Grant to the Roman Catholic Church and the *Regium Donum* to the Presbyterians was totally in keeping with the novelist's advocacy of unbiased help for the Irish.

This lack of bias can also be seen in Trollope's uncomfortable account in *Castle Richmond* (1860) of the dispatching of the Rev. Carter to Ireland to help relieve the suffering of the Protestant poor. Trollope refers to an inquiry 'into a charge made against a seemingly respectable man ... purporting that he had appropriated to his own use a sum of twelve pounds sent to him for the relief of the poor of his parish'. In brief, the case for the defence reveals that, because the money of the Misses Walker had been sent to alleviate the want of the Protestant poor of the parish of Kilcoutymorrow and because Mr Hobbs was the only Protestant in the parish, he was perfectly entitled to these funds. Trollope's comment pointedly laments that 'that Protestant should have learned so little from his religion'.[124] It was long past time, Trollope believed, to disestablish the Irish Church.

His second article, 'The Irish Church Bill in the Lords' (1869), while condoning the steady brakes imposed by the House of Lords on the passing of the bill, confidently expected disestablishment to take place, and noted the Lords' ultimate acceptance of other contentious legislation like the Reform Bills (of 1832 and 1867), the emancipation of Roman Catholics, the repeal of the Corn Laws and the abolition of Church Rates. He was angry with the Bishop of Peterborough for speaking against the bill, and refers to the 'common fault' of clergymen speaking in public as if they had 'the security of the pulpit', calling this a 'sense of irresponsibility'. Trollope regretted the Lords' disinclination to be seen to favour Roman Catholics by continuing the Maynooth Grant, but defended their right to do so.[125] In fact, the bishops in the House of Lords preferred to be generous to all denominations in Ireland, and Bishop Wilberforce saw no problem in a disestablished church continuing to be endowed. Their amendments, though, were squashed by the Lower House, and Nonconformists hoped that English disestablishment would follow.

Even after his defeat at Beverley, Trollope continued to advocate a division of revenues among the three churches and wrote an article, 'The New Cabinet, and What It Will Do for Us' (1869), to this effect.[126] In the end, the Act of March 1868, instigated by Gladstone, terminated the Maynooth Grant to the Roman Catholics and the *Regium Donum* to the Presbyterians, and disestablished the Irish Church. Trollope has Mr Griffenbottom in *Ralph the Heir* (1871) seek voters' support in 1868 for his disaffection with Gladstone, 'who was one thing one day and another thing another day', for Gladstone had, in 1845, resigned over an increase to the Maynooth Grant and his 1868 Act was seen by many as hypocrisy on his part.[127]

Trollope's strong support for Ireland was soon to change. Demand in Ireland at the end of 1869 for the release of Fenian prisoners, the forerunners of the Irish Republican Army, infuriated him. That Irish clerics were involved in this movement stung him deeply. In 'What Does Ireland Want?' (1869), he regrets Ireland's absence of gratitude for England's 'great and noble concession' of disestablishing the Irish

Church, and remarks that 'the Irishman is as loud as to his wants as ever'.[128] Instead of ameliorating relations between Roman Catholics and Protestants, disestablishment and disendowment of the Irish Church, Trollope observed, appeared to prompt Roman Catholics to seek greater and greater liberties, culminating in an urgent push for Home Rule, which he was to oppose[129] but which Gladstone and the Liberals subsequently pursued. *The Landleaguers* (1883) is an indictment of this cause, the impetus for which, the novelist alleges, came originally not from the Irish but from the Americans, who used the younger generation of zealous priests like Father Brosnan to follow it through to completion,[130] even if murder was used to achieve their goal. Trollope felt betrayed: fanaticism and violence were anathema to him and *his* Church, and he could never condone such extremes. For him, this was worse than secularism.

Trollope's change of heart towards Roman Catholicism may account for his admission in *Phineas Finn* (1869) that Roman Catholic bishops are still very well off, or 'very warm men',[131] for he was well aware that the upper ranks of Irish Roman Catholicism had never suffered. Nor does Trollope forget to stress Episcopalian partisanship in the Church of England since, in *Ralph the Heir* (1871), he notes that '[t]he bishops came out very strong last night' against the bill for disestablishment.[132] Moreover, Trollope may scorn the Irish Church as an institution in his articles, particularly in its failure to attract converts,[133] but he was at pains to redress any wrongs imputed to its particular officers in an earlier article, 'The Irish Beneficed Clergyman' (1866). Public opinion may inform the Irish clergyman of his unjust position among the Irish, but Trollope reminded his readership that he was a sincere man on a pittance, for he 'knows that he and his are barely able to subsist', and yet 'they tell him that he is robbing the public'.[134] In his call for reform, Trollope called also for understanding on behalf of the beleaguered representatives of this anachronistic institution.

Not all Liberals favoured disestablishing the Irish Church. Lord Stanley and Sir James Graham were against disestablishment, and Stanley believed that the Irish Church could be maintained if they appealed to the anti-popery beliefs of England and Scotland.[135] Both ministers resigned over the issue. Lord Stanley was the Conservative Lord Derby's son. The bishops, too, realized that their Church's future could be shaky, so few supported Gladstone in his quest for disestablishment, disendowment and the secularization of surplus ecclesiastical funds in Ireland, even though several, like Tait, were Liberals. It was an awkward time for ecclesiastical conscience, and this was why Trollope extended the situation in *Phineas Redux* (1874) to focus on a Conservative plan to disestablish the English Church. He wanted readers to reflect on the possible offshoots of reform, even though he had personally favoured Irish disestablishment.

His failure to become an MP did not prevent Trollope from following the progress of Irish disestablishment. Just four days before the Act received Royal Assent in 1869, Trollope figuratively wagged his finger at the English clergy, urging them to press for a voluntary system paying proper salaries according to the work performed, rather than continuing to allow ancient endowments to acknowledge consanguinity and contiguity instead of merit. If the clergy do not change their mode of payment, Trollope warned, the endowments would not be sufficient to provide a 'crust'.[136] He believed Irish Church disestablishment to be right, and became impatient with the Church of England's inability to reform itself. He wanted the Church to change in order to survive.

The threat of disestablishment of the Church of England

Several critics have explored Trollope's treatment of disestablishment of the Church as the hottest election issue in *Phineas Redux* (1874), and his reversing of party political roles in its enactment through Parliament, as well as its fictional extension to Britain as a whole.[137] One critic even claims that Trollope thought disestablishment of the Church of England to be inevitable.[138]

Inevitable or not, Trollope was not in favour of disestablishing the Church of England,[139] and his treatment of its possible occurrence may have been shock tactics to jolt his readers, particularly those with Nonconformist tendencies, into drawing back from further assaults on the Church. His extension suggests that those who had voted against disestablishing the Irish Church were fearful of the link between Church and state being severed in England. Dissenters were increasing and, if the Established Church had to prove its majority to retain state privileges, disestablishment might prove as inevitable in England as it did in Ireland.

Disestablishment as a possibility in England had begun in the 1840s among Dissenters disgruntled with three measures of Peel's: the educational clauses of the 1843 Factory Bill, making Anglican education compulsory; the Dissenters' Chapels Act of 1844, giving religious freedom to Unitarians but not to Evangelical sects, and the increase in the Maynooth Grant of 1845.[140] Gladstone, like Trollope, had pressed the need to disestablish the Irish Church in the 1860s, but insisted that this would not lead to English disestablishment. At the same time he argued that majority support was necessary for the maintenance of an Established Church. The fear, then, was that increased Nonconformism would risk the demise of the Established Church if it were seen to be dependent on popular opinion,[141] and therefore on majority support.

Trollope, throughout his writing career, referred to Church reforms possibly leading to its disestablishment. He urged some changes and regretted others. *The Warden* (1855) has been exhaustively discussed for its treatment of church abuse.[142] Trollope himself was equivocal about certain reforms, and stressed the problems liable to arise from libertarian causes pursued too closely. In *The Warden* (1855) he actually mentions the notorious Lord Guilford,[143] warden of the St Cross Hospital in Winchester, on which Hiram's Hospital is said to be modelled. Yet the entire story demonstrates that Mr Harding has neither the social standing nor the vices of his real-life counterpart. Mr Harding is a kindly old man who may lack the vision of his reforming future son-in-law, but his old bedesmen ultimately lament his removal from their hospital. In the quest for financial supplement, Trollope seems to hint, other considerations can be overlooked. As mentioned earlier, Mr Quiverful's appointment as warden in *Barchester Towers* (1857) is more an act of politically motivated philanthropy by the Liberal Evangelicals than an act of justice to the bedesmen.[144] The latter may have more pocket money, but they also have a warden visibly burdened by his 15 dependants. On the surface, Mr Quiverful seems a worthier choice, since he is in greater need of a substantial income. Yet would he be a better warden for the bedesmen? On which side of the hospital wall should common morality lie? Should the philanthropic deed help the warden or the bedesmen? Mr Harding, in contrast to Mr Quiverful, was an old man himself, who not only had the leisure to spend with his charges, but positively relished it. He was as happy as the bedesmen to reminisce. Through the storylines of the early Barchester novels, therefore, Trollope draws attention to the illusory nature of certain reforms imposed on the Church by the state.

Trollope's discomfort in *The Warden* (1855) over the state's zeal in imposing standards on the Church is a reminder that Nonconformists were not the only ones expecting the English Church to disestablish. There has been speculation that, if the government of 1832 had proposed disestablishment with their Reform Bill, it would probably have been carried out without much opposition.[145] Although, however, Trollope thought that the Church of England should remain established, he believed that Church and state should observe their demarcation lines.

While the Liberation Society was strongly instrumental in augmenting the rumblings of English disestablishment, the Society itself was symptomatic of the changes in religious faith of the English population. By 1870 the Church of England could no longer declare itself to be the nation's Church; it was merely *one* of the denominations and, therefore, the issue of disestablishment was regarded in some quarters as inevitable.[146] There were other reasons, too, for the Church's attenuating supremacy. As Trollope intimated again and again, the Church's disinclination to reform its stipendiary system weakened its position. As early as 1811, Lord Sidmouth warned that the Established Church in England was under threat because its system of remuneration caused clerical poverty to be so severe that it resulted in social alienation, leaving Nonconformism to develop within this vacuum.[147] Trollope's insistence on changes would therefore seem to be in accordance with his wishes to save the Church. He comments disapprovingly in *North America* (1862) that religion is not a concern of 'the central government at Washington' and that Americans probably 'reverence' the Constitution more 'than they reverence their Bible'.[148] He did not want a secular state.

The threat of disestablishment, then, was attributed to pragmatic causes, and Trollope was all too aware of this. The view that Trollope was too much of a Victorian to imagine a world without the Church[149] is certainly not borne out in the novelist's writing. Trollope was very conscious of increasing secularism in the community, and that circumstances could conspire to damage the Church beyond repair. While he had been in favour of disestablishing the Irish Church he was firmly against the same measures being taken in the Church of England, but was fearful that Church and state would be rent asunder. In *North America* (1862), he admitted that his belief in the Established Church was based on emotion rather than reason: 'I love the name of State and Church, and believe that much of our English well-being has depended on it ... Nevertheless I am not prepared to argue the matter. One does not always carry one's proofs at one's finger-ends.'[150]

Trollope's wish for church reform took account of his fears of both fanaticism in Ireland and secularism in England. Yet he was a realist. For wealthy Church officials, he knew that Church reform did not present much of a threat, even though the state was encroaching more and more on religious matters, especially through such bodies as the Ecclesiastical Commission, which gave laymen majority control of Church property. Dr Grantly's wish for his father's bishopric in *Barchester Towers* (1857), despite its reduced remuneration effected by the Ecclesiastical Commission, is not lessened by this knowledge.[151] Thus Trollope reminds the reader that pecuniary advantage is never the sum total of human ambition, and Church officers are no different from other mortals. Archdeacon Grantly even resumes his ambition for a bishopric in *Framley Parsonage* (1861)[152] when the Liberal Lord Brock, based on Lord Palmerston, brings in a bill to increase the number of bishoprics.[153] That Archdeacon Grantly aspires a second time, and on this occasion from a more strenuous position, emphasizes his desire for active industry rather than material recompense. Not all clergymen, Trollope implies, are guided solely by Mammon. He has already given sufficient evidence of Grantly's wealth, and there is the suggestion that human beings, having acquired a comfortable amount of capital, seek social advancement. And yet the bishopric sought on this second occasion is not a sinecure. Nor is it to be Grantly's, and he is again disappointed.

A *caveat* generally about reform is sounded in The *Last Chronicle of Barset* (1867) in its reference to the Second Reform Bill of 1867.[154] Archdeacon Grantly recalls for Mr Harding that the First Reform Bill of 1832 made a Liberal Prime Minister in the form of Lord Brock who, in his turn, made their shared enemy, Dr Proudie, a bishop. Grantly then bids Mr Harding drink the last glass of his 1820 port, implying that there will be no more.[155] The pleasure derived by these men from their worldly, but innocent, indulgences indicates the downside of the effects of reform, for Trollope knew that the hedonist was always more appealing than the slave to duty.

Ecclesiastical reform is similarly queried in *Rachel Ray* (1863). Dr Harford's liberal tendencies are shown to transform themselves into 'violent Tory[ism]' when the Ecclesiastical Commissioners, whose work began in 1835, 'separated off from him a district of his own town'.[156] In this instance, Trollope stresses that it was the clergyman's pique at losing his parishioners to someone less experienced, and thirty years had not dimmed his antipathy towards the Dissenters who had won the booty. Church reform in the 1820s had received considerable Conservative backing and the Tory *Quarterly* had remained positive towards the proposed ecclesiastical changes.[157] Trollope is thus drawing attention to the consequences of change and the discomfort it can wreak, even when the principles seem worthy.

Some of these consequences considerably reduced the Church's stature. Revealing his knowledge of the workings of Church and state in 'The Archdeacon' (1866), Trollope acknowledges the weakening political powers of Convocation, the Church's governing body, which he now terms a 'clerical toy, a mere debating society'. Only the bishops know how powerless Convocation now is, he notes, and claims that the archdeacon, fresh from the country, still clings to the vain hope that, when promoted to bishop, most of his reward will derive from sitting in Convocation. Although the archbishop is 'secure from murder', unlike Thomas à Becket, Trollope stresses that the state has more power over the Church than the latter has over the former.[158] Alford emphatically disagreed. He accused Trollope of being ignorant of the constitution even to imagine that the Ecclesiastical Commission, or any commission of the state, could possibly have the authority 'to preserve, or not to preserve, an ecclesiastical corporation'.[159] This sounds more like wishful thinking, however. No one else, then or now, seems to have agreed with Alford.

Trollope's reference to Convocation as a 'clerical toy' was particularly apt. The weakening political role of the bishops in the second half of the nineteenth century was owing to the deepening division between the two political parties and to the 'bipartisan nature of most sorts of social reform', both of which polarized questions into 'political' or 'moral'. Consequently, it became the custom for bishops only to attend Parliament when debates concerned the Church's interests.[160]

Trollope judged the situation rather earlier than most, since he was well informed on these matters. The Oxford group and the ecclesiastical members of his own family had probably apprised him of the facts of Convocation. Yet it was not until 1884 that Gladstone was candid enough to remark to Lord Hartington that 'the political function is, properly on the whole, sacrificed to diocesan duty'. In fact the Church's expanded ministration at this time was bound to limit 'other public duties', for diocesan work was only slightly reduced by the new suffragan bishops.[161] Trollope's cousin, Edward Trollope, was to become a suffragan bishop in Nottingham in 1877, rewarded for his hard work, and his relative by marriage, Anthony Wilson Thorold, was to become Bishop of Rochester in the same year, rewarded for his work in London's slums. This is possibly one of the reasons why the novelist stresses in *Clergymen of the Church of England* (1866) that the bishop is now a 'working man'.[162] He would, for many years, have seen his relatives and other ecclesiastics actively engaged in their diocesan duties, at the expense of their wider political role.

The Church's accelerated loss of power after the mid-nineteenth century has been attributed to three literary works in the period from 1859 to 1862: *Origin of Species* (1859) by Charles Darwin, *Essays and Reviews* (1860) by F. D. Maurice, Rowland Williams, C. W. Goodwin and

Benjamin Jowett, and *Pentateuch* (1862) by Colenso. The greatest damage perpetrated to the Church's position was not by Darwin's secular work, but by the works of the active Church members, Maurice, Williams, Goodwin, Jowett and Colenso.[163] Liddon's correspondence with Hamilton between 1862 and 1865 reveals their concern about the effect of Colenso's teaching, based as it was on controversial scholarship. Above all, their magnanimity is apparent, despite Colenso's ultimate excommunication. Trollope, incidentally, in his plan to spend an evening in 1869 discussing politics and the Church, mentioned Dr Temple, whose recent nomination to the see of Exeter had been debated because of his contribution to *Essays and Reviews*.[164] The Liberal Temple had been deliberately nominated by Gladstone, with Tait's support, to replace the high church Philpotts as Bishop of Exeter, and his appointment caused a stir. Temple later became Bishop of London and Archbishop of Canterbury.[165] Trollope shared the concern of leading high churchmen that too many libertarian moves by the Church could diminish community respect; at the same time, Trollope believed that too few reforms by the Church could try the patience of a community seeking greater freedom of choice in conduct and belief.

Just what was Trollope's personal motive in his treatment of the disestablishment question, and what was his actual position? Perhaps, as has been argued, Trollope's novels did help to control damage through his advocacy of slow change and his admission that he was an advanced conservative-liberal.[166] It is possible also to extend this argument to assert that Trollope's balanced comic treatment of religious issues and ecclesiastical personnel of various persuasions threw the readership off the scent of Trollope's own persuasions and moderated community demand for reform.

Victorian Liberalism was really quite conservative,[167] and Trollope's Liberalism stemmed from a moderate stance rather than a radically progressive one,[168] yet, for most of his life, Trollope was utterly contemptuous of the Tories.[169] His young life was surrounded by radicals and liberals, entertained at home by both parents who nurtured in their children a sense of scorn for Conservatives, and Rose, his wife, was the daughter of a Unitarian.[170] Trollope's Liberalism, does not, therefore, seem so strange. Moreover, beyond straightforward party *politics*, Trollope genuinely wanted better conditions for society, even if he wanted change to be slow and peaceful.

Furthermore, if Trollope's novels were ambiguous so, too, were his throwaway lines. Trollope once informed a correspondent that 'taking holy orders was crippling to man's mentality',[171] and, because of this, perhaps, Trollope has been seen to be more interested in moral law and common morality than in religion.[172] For the minority acknowledging Trollope's Christianity to be central to his work, the novelist's underlying 'doctrine' of his work is stated in *Barchester Towers* (1857): 'Till we can become divine, we must be content to be human, lest in our hurry for a change we sink to something lower.'[173] Trollope's religion was very important to him, but he preferred to wear it lightly. Perhaps the clearest indication of his depth of belief was his insistence, when the *Fortnightly* was founded, that 'nothing should be written in it to challenge the divinity of Christ'.[174] The *Fortnightly* was a Liberal journal, edited by the *secular* George Henry Lewes, in which Trollope and its other contributors encouraged social reform. Trollope's insistence on the journal's retention of Christian principles reveals that his genuine belief in social reform did not involve abandoning Christianity, even if he was sufficiently tolerant to encourage the Church to give way to secularism on issues like education. It is easy to dismiss Trollope's tolerance for lack of interest. Although attention has been drawn to Trollope's assertion in his *Life of Cicero* that '[t]he divine birth and the doctrine of the Trinity and the Lord's Supper are not necessary to teach a man to live with his brother',[175] the fact that Trollope, in this same work, devotes his final chapter to Cicero's religion has escaped notice. Here Trollope argues that, had Cicero lived at another time, he would have been a devout Christian. In his acknowledgement of the strangeness of writing about the religion of a pagan, Trollope insists that, from his study of Cicero, he has found that he was 'not dealing with a pagan's mind'.[176] Clearly, Trollope used self-deprecating understatement to soften public opinion towards the Church and its position within society.

The spectre of disestablishment loomed throughout Trollope's mature years. His travelling revealed that Church and state did not have to be joined at the hip, for the Colonies had never considered this option, a fact frequently paraded by Nonconformists. The pressures on the Church grew intense. Leaders of the Church found it easier with their 'upper-class liberalism' to adapt to parliamentary measures to appease Nonconformists than did parish clergymen, who were closer to grassroot pressures. Archbishop Sumner, for example, had no qualms about granting the proposal in 1858 to eliminate State Prayers from the Prayer Book, for they '"savoured of politics as much as religion"'.[177]

The treatment of disestablishment in *Phineas Redux* (1874) betrays Trollope's worst fears. The Church to be disestablished is the Church of England. The party bringing about disestablishment in the novel is the Conservative Party, unlike the actual agents of change in 1868, although

Trollope adds an extra literary flourish by having the Liberals agitating for reform and the Conservatives ultimately carrying them through. This twist reminded contemporary readership of political events in 1867 when the Conservative Disraeli carried through a Reform Act which the Liberals had been urgently pushing, thus, as Trollope puts it, 'running away with his clothes' on finding the latter bathing.[178] The twist also reminded readers that it was often the Conservatives who enacted reforms, despite Liberal urging;[179] many a landowning Whig, despite his Liberalism, was actually fearful of rising democracy.

Nonetheless, in the year in which *Phineas Redux* (1874) was published, the Liberals lost power to the Conservatives because of the persistent demands of the Liberationists, who had revelled in the disestablishment of the Irish Church and shown hostility to the inclusion of religion in state education.[180] People had become nervous of too many changes affecting the Church's relationship with the state.

Several Church leaders, like Tait and Wordsworth, stressed the importance of establishment in maintaining a sense of nationhood, Christian morality and loyalty, and feared disestablishment. Dean Stanley, of the broad church, believed that establishment forced the clergy to adhere to the laws of the land. Moreover, it was popularly held that establishment helped to keep the Church out of party politics, and Lord Selborne speculated that disestablishment would lead to the Church being politicized and to the political importuning of laypeople by clergymen eager to exert a wider influence. On the other hand, high church leadership did not favour Stanley's push for maintaining establishment, for it feared that the state would hold too great a power over the Church.[181]

And yet, while demanding a greater gulf between state and Church, Nonconformists wanted a strong link between the law and Christian morality, with particular reference to sexual conduct.[182] They wanted the government to uphold Christian morality and few intellectuals wanted a *completely* secular state. The community's scrutiny in *The Vicar of Bullhampton* (1870) of the Rev. Fenwick's interest in helping Carry Brattle is perhaps indicative of Trollope's awareness of this trend. His mocking of community opinion reflects his scorn for people who want to have 'their cake and eat it'.

Yet, even with all the manoeuvrings of the Liberation Society and its demands for the Church to relinquish its hold on everyday matters, the state's support of the Church by the end of the century remained very strong indeed. The Church had lost none of its actual endowments, ecclesiastical or educational, or its property, and its clerical officers had retained their senior positions in institutional chaplaincies. Despite efforts to dismiss the bishops from the House of Lords, they remained, their infrequent attendance perhaps having saved their seats, for they were no longer perceived to be a threat. At the parochial level, the clergy maintained their secular functions and, although the Parish Councils Act of 1894 secularized the parish, the Church's influence was still felt, if only in the village halls built by the Church. Even the high church clergy by this time were content to keep the Church established, for they had contrived mechanisms to protect its autonomy, and the power of the Liberation Society had declined. But this was long after Trollope's death, and his mature years were dominated by the Church's power waning in inverse proportion to the state's crescent dominion.

As far as the state and the Church were concerned, Trollope believed it was the duty of the individual to take into account not only loyalty to the larger group but also examination of one's own conscience in the conduct of life. Likewise, he urged, whether seriously in his non-fiction or by default in his comic fiction, that institutions not overwhelm the individual. He was not alone in this conviction. Lowe, with whom Trollope went to school, wrote *Duty* in 1880, and his exhortation sounds remarkably like his old school friend's: 'Men cannot be raised in masses, as the mountains were in the early geological states of the world. They must be dealt with as units; for it is only by the elevation of individuals that the elevation of the masses can be effectively secured.'[183]

By the same token, Trollope felt deeply that Church and state should be wary of invading the private sphere of the individual in their common areas of responsibility. Once again, Trollope has not been the sole voice to express this creed. Lord Denning, as recently as 1989, sought fit to quote from William Temple, the son of Trollope's ecclesiastical contemporary Frederick Temple,[184] as well as from St Paul, to stress this very principle: 'The primary principle of Christian ethics and Christian politics must be respect for every person simply as a person ... The person is primary, not the society: the State exists for the citizen, not the citizen for the State.' Lest the state be otherwise deluded, Denning adds:

> The Christian Church has always insisted that the State has no ultimate and omnipotent authority of its own but derives its authority from God. St Paul in his Epistle to the Romans (13.1) made this clear. 'There is no power but of God: the powers that be are ordained by God.' This has been the shield under which our forefathers resisted oppression. St Paul: – the Ruler of the State was the 'Minister of God for good,' and so long as he fulfilled his high trust, it was not right

to resist him: but if he forsook it and sought absolute power, then resistance was justified.[185]

Denning's quotation from St Paul even sounds a quiet revolutionary note should the institutions of Church and state not heed the call of the individual voice. Trollope's genius lies in the fact that he himself, despite his social conservatism, was a quiet revolutionary in resisting the mammoth powers of both institutions, and he subtly encouraged others to do the same.

Conclusion

It would be less than just to dismiss, as Trollope did, the fact that his living creations just happened to be clerical. His very dismissal bears its own significance. Trollope believed and reiterated more than once that '[t]he object of a novel should be to instruct in morals while it amuses'.[1] Trollope's serious purpose did not just involve an engagement with the social and political issues of his time, an aim of his long recognized. He had a further intention. While wishing to entertain his readers, he was trying to inveigle the Victorian reading public, grown weary of sombre sermonizing and ecclesiastical wrangling, into a reappraisal of the complexities and function of the Church of England and its unique brand of Christianity. The 97 clerical characters of Trollope's fiction were not incidental; they were integral to his serious purpose.[2]

The Church's benign influence over Trollope's fictional characters labouring under extreme circumstances is especially striking, whether or not clergymen are involved, whether or not the fictional personae are responsible for their predicament. For much of *Ralph the Heir* (1871), the lot of the Rev. Gregory Newton seems dismal. A decent man, he seems unable to convince Clarissa Underwood to marry him. In despair over his brother and his own gloomy future, he is palpably helped by walking through his own churchyard where, 'within this hallowed enclosure', he could feel the presence of God and 'after a fashion, be happy, in spite of the misfortunes of himself and his family'. Even his awareness of 'unbelief, and of the professors of unbelief, both within and without the great Church' fails to trouble him, for in his own church 'there were more worshippers now than there had ever been before'.[3] Trollope thus presents the Church as a source of strength and comfort to those in dire distress.

The Church is equally beneficial for characters far less deserving of sympathy than Newton. Both Lady Mason in *Orley Farm* (1862) and Henry Jones in *Cousin Henry* (1879) are increasingly checked in their acts of guilt and helped to partial redemption by their memories of biblical passages of the kind read aloud in the Victorian Church. While the Old Testament story of Rebekah is twice cited as having possibly encouraged the well-respected and beautiful Lady Mason to commit forgery – her single deed of guilt – enabling her infant son to inherit Orley Farm instead of his older half-brother, her awareness of Christian compassion and its requisite 'cleansing' for 'men' who had 'sinned as she had sinned' prevent her from further acts of betrayal. Her confession of guilt to Sir Peregrine Orme frees him from his marriage proposal and attracts his sympathy in equal measure to his horror, for '[l]et her be ever so guilty, and her guilt had been very terrible, she had behaved very nobly to him'. And, when her guilt is publicly exposed, there are several references to the knowledge 'that God does temper the wind to the shorn lamb',[4] one of Trollope's favourite biblical allusions. Despite Henry Jones being a far less attractive character than Lady Mason and despite the fact that he is not religious, the many references to the power of the Lord's Prayer, and the power of God, mentioned six times in only twice as many lines, are shown to exercise a restraint on Henry's conscience to the extent that he finally confesses his guilt. His awareness of his uncle's most recent will depriving him of Llanfeare brings 'drops of sweat' to stand 'thick upon his forehead'. So leaden was 'that weight upon his heart, that incubus on his bosom, that nightmare which robbed him of all his slumbers', that 'he lived in the one room', 'rarely left the house' and was entirely 'without occupation'. His chance discovery of the will among Jeremy Taylor's sermons leads him to agonizing vacillations: 'No sooner had he resolved to destroy the will than he was unable to destroy it. No sooner had he felt his inability than again he longed to do the deed.' Paralysed by fear, Henry 'even repeated the Lord's Prayer to himself', and petitioned God, for 'God would know that he had not meant to steal the property! God would know that he did not wish to steal it now!' The reader has already been reminded that '[w]e are too apt to forget when we think of the sins and faults of men how keen may be their conscience in spite of their sins'.[5] Trollope could never bring himself to abandon anyone, either in his fiction or in real life, and always invoked the Church and its creed to anyone in need of them. The agnostic John Morley, on being interviewed for the editorship of a journal, was completely taken aback by Trollope loudly demanding a reply to his question: ' "Do you believe in the divinity of our blessed Lord and Saviour Jesus Christ?" '[6] The Church, as far as

Trollope was concerned, could and should be criticized, but it should not be ignored or sidelined.

It cannot be a coincidence that *The Bertrams* (1859), published in the same year as *Origin of Species*, has its main character 'come full circle' in his commitment to the Church, after a period of quandary in which he wrote books expressing his uncertainty 'that all Scripture statements' could 'be taken as true to the letter'. While Trollope seems to censure George Bertram for flagrantly flaunting his possible apostasy, he reasons that '[m]en may be firm believers and yet doubt some Bible statements – doubt the letter of such statements'. The religious sites of Syria and the Mount of Olives convince George Bertram that 'he would be a clergyman' and he 'thanked his God that he had brought him there to this spot'. Bertram had already oscillated between the Church and the law, and his subsequent abandonment of the former, 'his high and holy purpose', after falling in love with a young woman challenging him to be more ambitious, does not surprise the reader. And yet, even though he does not take holy orders, his challenger admits that, despite her own ambitions, there was always the possibility of her one day 'marrying a clergyman'. The brilliant promise of his double-first brings him neither success nor satisfaction and, although his love for Caroline does not wane, Bertram was ultimately to regret that 'he had exchanged the aspirations of his soul for the pressure of a soft white hand'.[7] Nor is the reference to the Mount of Olives as a place for confirming Christian faith an isolated one. The secondary character of 'A Ride Across Palestine' (1861), a young girl disguised as a youth, deprecates the holy sites of Palestine because of their commercialism. But the narrator stolidly affirms their holiness, for although '[m]an may undo what man did', 'here we have God's handiwork and his own evidences'.[8] Trollope's own experience of Palestine in 1858 had clearly left its mark.

Nor can it be a coincidence that Bertram in *The Bertrams* writes a book, *Romance of Scripture*, in which he analyses the New Testament stories as myths, at the same time as his barrister friend is studying the corn-law question. Bertram's method of theological inquiry and its timing suggest that Trollope is alluding to George Eliot's translation of Strauss's *Das Leben Jesu* (*The Life of Jesus*) in 1846 when the Corn Laws were repealed. Bertram's second book, dealing with the Old Testament, even dares to call 'the whole story of Creation a myth' and results in his losing his Oxford fellowship. Having abandoned the Church and 'given up all idea of practising as a barrister', Bertram contemplates life as an author of secular works. It is only in the novel's final line – after Bertram has become a barrister – that Trollope hints that Bertram, now confident of

Caroline's love, might just *possibly* return to his 'aspirations ... as he sat upon the Mount of Olives',[9] and renew his commitment to the Church by becoming a clergyman. Not only did Trollope manage to encapsulate in Bertram the turmoil of many an intellectual at the end of the 1850s, but he also made a point of showing his readers how his doubting intellectual *reconverts* into a committed Anglican without losing the woman he loves. The implication by Trollope seems to be that religious doubt is the concomitant of youth, while religious commitment is the choice of mature reflection. The novel conveys a heady mixture of the rebellious energies of youth together with romantic and religious fulfilment, all within the Church of England.

Trollope's examination of the vacillations of religious belief in *The Bertrams* perhaps had resonance for his friend George Eliot, for she had also translated Feuerbach's *The Essence of Christianity* (1854), another work questioning Christian orthodoxy. Trollope's exposition indicates how well he understood the keen interrogation of her translated work and its power over readers. Darwin's theories on evolution were already well known and social problems had encouraged the pursuit of pragmatism like that of Smiles, whose *Self-Help* shared *The Bertrams'* year of publication. Trollope's religious tolerance, even at this early date, is surely evident in this novel. Yet its denouement and 'A Ride Across Palestine' leave no doubt of his belief in the importance of the Church of England for society and his own commitment. Both works present a subtle, yet potent, challenge to the fashionable inquiries of Victorian intellectuals.

Trollope's criticisms of the Church as an institution increased as he grew older but his belief in the Church's beneficent power did not disappear. *The Fixed Period*'s (1882) treatment of euthanasia in a supposed republic is full of biblical references. Some are specific: '"If reason of strength they be fourscore years, yet is their strength labour and sorrow"'; others are vague: 'flocks and herds'. Trollope cannot conceive of any country not having a church for someone to practise 'the old habit of saying his prayers in a special place on a special day'. The president himself, about to be removed from office, thinks immediately of God when dreaming of 'the evening of my day'.[10] Furthermore, it is significant that Trollope's last completed work of fiction, 'Not If I Know It' (1882), stresses the Church as a positive force. The story comically illustrates a minor altercation about to escalate between two brothers-in-law. Dr Burnaby's brief 15-minute sermon, followed by the Sacrament, 'more powerful with its thoughts than its words',[11] is the catalyst enabling the pair to heal their rift. In his laconic treatment of the

Church, Trollope often surprised his readers, inured to religious didacticism, into accepting as given its essential beneficence.

Evidence from fictional sources as to a writer's beliefs can be dubious, but Trollope's non-fiction, too, provides testimony to his strong belief in Christianity. Having, in *The West Indies and the Spanish Main* (1859), discussed the slavery question in Cuba with his usual fair-mindedness, Trollope stresses that '[t]he point which most shocks an Englishman is the absence of all religion, the ignoring of the black man's soul'. The fact that 'the white men here ignore their own souls also' and that 'Roman Catholic worship seems to be at a lower ebb in Cuba than almost any country in which I have seen it' is no excuse; it is Trollope's condemnation.[12] He is similarly forthright with the northern part of that continent, because he attributes the 'evil in the structure of American politics' in *North America* (1862) and its 'social evil' to 'the absence of any national religion'. Even if people 'say their prayers', he observes, their 'rowdiness' actually 'robs religion of that reverence which is . . . its chief protection'.[13] From this statement alone, it is easy to imagine Trollope comparing American church services unfavourably with those of the Church of England.

Nor could events, whether past or current, or people, whether deceased or living, escape Trollope's Christian appraisal. His review of Harriet Parr's *The Life and Death of Jeanne d'Arc* (1866) includes his avowal that 'a man does not do a good day's work without a voice from God'.[14] His estimation of Cicero's treatises, *De Naturâ Deorum, De Divinatione* and *De Fato* (1877), underscores that Cicero's paganism 'had advanced far beyond negative disbelief', to 'believe in one great and good God who made all things'.[15] Trollope's imagination could in no way encompass a civilization without a Christian God. And he could not possibly contemplate a discussion on sovereignty (1867) without the Old Testament being his initial reference point, '[f]or it seems to be thus and thus only that we can read the lesson taught us in the early history of the children of Abraham'. He bids Americans who see the throne of England as 'the source of political power and action' to divert their gaze to the great tower and spire of Salisbury Cathedral, to explain that power lies in symbolism, not essence.[16] For Trollope, the monarch's position as Head of the Established Church was indivisible from his strong belief in this institution.

Nor did travelling curb his every effort to attend church. His catalogued attendance at church services is at all points on his journey in *How the 'Mastiffs' Went to Iceland* (1878). In Campbeltown one service was in Gaelic; in St Kilda the bibles were in Gaelic; in the Faroes he visits the Danish Church past midnight and at Reykjavik he is one of the few to call on the Bishop *and* the Governor.[17] Mindful that Trollope's travel writings are 'the index to the man and his concerns',[18] it can safely be assumed that no tired churchgoer would have troubled himself to make such gratuitous assertions in non-fiction. Trollope's faith remained firm, but he was wise enough not to assume that his views were shared by everyone. As he said in 'Novel-Reading' (1879), sermons are as old as the Greek Chorus and they are needed so that 'the violence of the active may be controlled by the prudence of the inactive, and the thoughtlessness of the young by the thoughtfulness of the old', but a sermon 'does not catch a hold of the imagination as it used to do'.[19] His fiction thus took public opinion into account.

He achieved, perhaps, what few clerics, with tract, sermon or lecture, managed to attain for such a long time: the attention of the middle classes. Often driven by self-advancement and material accumulation, the Victorian middle classes actually stopped for a while to read about the Church. While they did indeed read many writers on the subject of religion, they gained a more human view of the Church from Trollope. He eschewed the abstract in the form of doctrine, and concentrated instead on the human enactment of ecclesiastical policies and positions. Sermons were not acceptable in literature and, while he acknowledged Mrs Sewell's laudable intention in *The Rose of Cheriton*, he stressed that 'small pietistic books' were written 'without much regard either to literary excellence or to truth of argument'.[20] Comedy, by contrast, was acceptable. Nothing can seem more absurd than causes pursued relentlessly by men and women taking themselves too seriously and losing sight of their main goal: a better life for humankind, in body and spirit. Through Trollope's laughter at the fictional officials of the Church, puffed up with pride over the arbitrary importance of creed and faction, Victorian readers were able to see that the institution sometimes overwhelmed an individual's ability to act sensibly, rightly *and* spiritually.

If Trollope seems more pessimistic in his later novels, it is because he saw the increase in institutions as a threat to individual endeavour and valour. It is no accident that his novels began by focusing on the Church and then widened out to include comic appraisals of other powerful institutions like government, the law and the Civil Service. He often disliked what he saw, and he saw so much in his 67 years, both on a global scale through his overseas travels and on a local scale through his horseback rides of the postal routes of Britain. It was on a horseback ride of a postal route that he first conceived his idea for the Barchester series.

Trollope was a strong advocate of universal education, regardless of gender, class or race, even if the ecclesiastical had to give way to the secular. He believed strongly that human beings had spiritual as well as physical duties at the same time as they had spiritual and physical needs. His wish for a balance to be reached between duty and need is paramount throughout his work. He provided readers with the opportunity to laugh at those who discharge duty too bleakly, but he also exposed as odious those who demanded fulfilment of their needs unmindful of others. Even the delicate question of race drew from Trollope a radical response for any era. He advised intermarriage between races in *The West Indies and the Spanish Main* (1859), since this would produce a 'good and efficient punch', and the progeny of such unions should not ponder on the 'dark subject' of their grandmothers, but on their grandchildren, 'the most interesting side from whence to view the family'.[21] From his first written word to his last, Trollope's human thesis was paramount. His Christianity was inherent, not ostentatious.

His own striving in no way made him oblivious to the needs of others. Perhaps it was the changes in his own fortunes which enabled him to be sensitive to the varying conditions of human life and the misery caused through deprivation of physical or emotional comfort. He was aware that changed circumstances are part of the human lot, and took care to understate his own achievements for he knew that, if he took himself too seriously, he might end up like his father – a horror to himself and his family. He lived during a period when people feared turbulence in politics, were excited by, but nervous of technological advances, and sought changes to the social structure which could accommodate the new world opening to them. Many solutions were circulated to help alleviate social ills. The Church tried to continue its role in every sphere but, as an old institution, it was seen to be in the greatest need of change, and it therefore attracted the fiercest loyalty and the loudest opposition. As this book has illustrated, Trollope, in his realization that the Church's pervasion of every facet of social life was now under question, sought to make people aware of its strengths as well as its weaknesses.

Trollope reminded readers that clerics were only human. Although tolerant of Roman Catholicism, he did not believe in the infallibility of any human being. He thought that the community should excuse the human failings of clerics, but they should also not be too trusting of dogmatic assertions. The corporatization of human labour and aspiration he accepted as inevitable, but he warned of the dangers of ossifying beliefs and procedures into doctrine and regulations. Whether he was making people laugh at representatives of new professions and institutions or at old ones, he returned readers again and again to the dangers of ignoring the Christian tenets. He was fearful that either the Church would not transform itself sufficiently to withstand open rebellion, or that it would accommodate change so much that its basic Christian principles would disappear.

Trollope was so quietly progressive that many readers, both during his lifetime and after, have fallen into the trap, which he deliberately laid, of assuming that he was the model of a conventional man. Superficial readers, then and now, have confused his loyalty with complicity. If his works are examined on a deeper level there are distinct glimpses of the man who dared make everyone question the received opinion and the corporate action of the time. It is no wonder that individuals, politicians, clerics, lawyers, civil servants and many other professionals, caught up in the maelstrom of institutional life have and will continue to delight in Trollope's literary antidote to institutional dominion. And beneath all the fun of his fiction abides Trollope's unwavering Anglican adherence.

Notes

Introduction

1. A. Trollope, *An Autobiography* ([1883] Oxford, 1980), p. 169.
2. Ibid., p. 93.
3. R. Mullen with J. Munson (eds) *The Penguin Companion to Trollope* (London, 1996), p. 78.
4. Calculations from E. Trollope, *The Family of Trollope* (Lincoln, 1875); all genealogical references are from this book; M. N. Trollope, *A Memoir of the Family of Trollope* (London, 1897); H. Trollope (1994), personal correspondence. For further details, see J. Durey, 'In the Spirit of Truth: Anthony Trollope's Ecclesiastical Ancestors and Relatives', *Family History*, XVII, no. 143 (1995), 259–94; and 'Church and Family', *Genealogists' Magazine*, XXV, no. 11 (1997), 441–50.
5. Calculations from N. J. Hall (ed.) *The Letters of Anthony Trollope* (Stanford, 1983), 2 vols.
6. Thomas Adolphus Trollope, the eldest of AT's brothers, took three exhibitions from Winchester. Henry, the second brother, died young, having gone to Cambridge. AT, *Autobiography*, pp. 6–7, 17.
7. V. Glendinning, *Trollope* (London, 1993), p. 12.
8. Trollope wrote: 'my novels, whether bad or good, have been as good as I could make them', *Autobiography*, p. 122.
9. Ibid., pp. 93, 146, 222.
10. AT, *The Warden* (Oxford, 1980), p. 9.
11. AT, *The Last Chronicle of Barset* (Oxford, 1981), p. 864.
12. AT, *Warden*, pp. 10, 65, 58.
13. AT, *Barchester Towers* (Oxford, 1991), I, p. 45.
14. Ibid., I, pp. 68, 90. Dr Vesey Stanhope holds four positions in *The Warden* as Rector of Crabtree Canonicorum, Eiderdown and Stogpingum and Prebendary of Goosegorge – from all which he is usually absent. AT, *Warden*, p. 176. In *Framley Parsonage* (1861) Peter Edwards explains Trollope's satirical, 'O Doddington! and O Stanhope!' and his reference to the disparity in bishops' incomes. Stanhope is named after Stanhope in Durham, one of the richest livings in England at £4000 a year, and Doddington had an absentee rector, whose £8000 a year 'was the highest of any parish priest in England'. Contemporary readership would have known that Henry Philpotts, newly appointed as Bishop of Exeter, had wanted to retain Stanhope 'to boost his relatively meagre episcopal stipend [£3500 a year]'. AT, *Framley Parsonage* (Oxford, 1980), pp. 169–70, 584–5n. Doddington and Stanhope, however, were *personally* significant to Trollope. Doddington, a 'magnificent seat', lay in Lincolnshire, close to the Trollope family estate. In the 1850s George K. Jarvis, Esquire, owned Doddington and was patron of its rectory. His son, the Rev. Charles Edwin Jarvis, rector of Hatton, married Ann Elizabeth Trollope, whose brother, the Rev. Andrew Trollope,

was also a pluralist – but a poor one. Ann Elizabeth Trollope and the Rev. Andrew Trollope were the grandchildren of Sir John Trollope (1766–1820) and his wife, Anne *née* Thorold. Trollope must have known them, for the Thorolds had intermarried with the Trollopes more than once and their lands abutted each other. Doddington thus reminded Trollope of both rich and poor clerics. The name Stanhope also had close associations for him, for the Stanhopes were well known in Lincolnshire. Edward Stanhope, the Assistant Commissioner on Employment of Children, Young Persons and Women in the 1860s, pronounced Doddington to be neglected. R. W. Ambler, 'Social Change and Religious Experience: Aspects of Rural Society in South Lincolnshire with Specific Reference to Primitive Methodism, 1815–1875', Unpublished PhD, University of Hull (1984), pp. 51, 82. Stanhope's relative, Lord Philip Henry Stanhope, helped elect Trollope to the Athenaeum in 1864 and presented him at court in 1868. Doddington and Stanhope were ingenious puns, then, associated with current events, yet bearing a private allusion.

15. Dr Stanhope, a prebendary, may have been based on Dr George F. Nott, a prebendary of Winchester (1810–41) and of Salisbury (1814–41). Nott had presided over Trollope's parents' marriage and later gave religious instruction to their children. A pluralist, he neglected his parish: 'This gentleman has been for a long time missing; should this meet his eye, we beg to inform him, that the parishioners of Woodchurch are very desirous of seeing him, and they wish to know where he may be found; they have been served with notices for the payment of tithes by the solicitor of the reverend pluralist, who has only been once in the parish during the whole of last reign, and that for a day only.' J. le Neve, *Fasti Ecclesiae Anglicanae 1541–1857* (London, 1974), III, p. 106; VI, p. 79; J. Wade, *The Extraordinary Black Book: An exposition of abuses in church and state* ([1832] New York, 1970), p. 117.
16. AT, *Barset*, p. 885.
17. AT, *Towers*, I, pp. 147, 201, 202.
18. AT, *Autobiography*.
19. AT, *Towers*, I, pp. 21, 36.
20. Ibid., I, p. 206, II, p. 271.
21. AT, *Autobiography*, p. 355.
22. Trollope saw England with fresh eyes on his return from Australia and resolved to write *The Way We Live Now* (1875). He was '[i]nstigated ... by some such reflexions': 'If dishonesty can live in a gorgeous palace with pictures on all its walls, and gems in all its cupboards, with marble and ivory in all its corners, and can give Apican dinners, and get into Parliament, and deal in millions, then dishonesty is not disgraceful, and the man dishonest after such a fashion is not a low scoundrel.' Ibid., p. 355.
23. J. Keane, 'The Limits of Secularism: Does the Marginalizing of Religion Impose a New Intolerance?', *Times Literary Supplement*, 4945 (9 January 1998), p. 12.
24. I. Collins, *Jane Austen and the Clergy* (London, 1993).
25. P. Hodgson, *Theology in the Fiction of George Eliot* (London, 2001). See also M. Thormahlen, *The Brontës and Religion* (Cambridge, 1999).
26. AT, *Towers*, I, p. 16.

Chapter 1 Divisions in the Church: Trollope's Decline into Pessimism

1. AT, *Towers*, I, p. 188.
2. A. Pollard, 'Trollope and the Evangelicals', *Nineteenth-Century Literature*, XXXVII (1982), pp. 329–39.
3. J. P. Hennessy, *Anthony Trollope* (London, 1971), p. 368.
4. Doctor Thorne's mother was 'a Thorold', and '[t]here was no better blood to be had in England'. AT, *Doctor Thorne* (Oxford, 1991), p. 28.
5. Charles Longley became Archbishop of York (1860–2) and of Canterbury (1862–8).
6. R. Mullen, *Anthony Trollope: A Victorian and his World* (Clwyd, 1990), pp. 28, 35; Hennessy, *Trollope* p. 280; R. ap Roberts, *Trollope Artist and Moralist* (London, 1971), p. 16.
7. AT, *Warden*, pp. 62, 61, 60.
8. AT, *Towers*, I, p. 46.
9. Not long before his death, Trollope thanked Newman, a Roman Catholic convert with whom he had long corresponded, for prescribing medication for his asthma, thrilled that he enjoyed his novels. Cardinal Manning thanked Trollope for a book. Hall, *Letters AT*, II, pp. 991, 831.
10. Ambler, 'Social Change and Religious Experience', p. 24.
11. AT, *Towers*, I, p. 188.
12. K. Hylson-Smith, *High Churchmanship in the Church of England: from the sixteenth century to the twentieth century* (Edinburgh, 1993), p. 36.
13. I. Ker, *John Henry Newman: A Biography* (Oxford, 1990), p. 197.
14. N. Yates, *The Oxford Movement and Anglican Ritualism* (London, 1983), p. 19.
15. AT, *Towers*, I, p. 190.
16. HAM 6/18/21, 3 July 1845.
17. HAM 6/95/85, 23 October 1866.
18. HAM 6/95/67, 19 November 1865.
19. AT, *The Three Clerks* (Oxford, 1989), p. 214. Cardinal Wiseman (1802–65) had become Roman Catholic. Handley records (p. xvi) that, for the single-volume edition, Trollope removed a passage describing the unattractive Harry Norman's ritualist practices.
20. Ibid., p. 211.
21. AT, *The Kellys and the O'Kellys* (Oxford, 1992), p. 490. According to Mullen, Mr O'Joscelyn's name was a joke, since Lord Jocelyn 'was a leading fanatic who spent his time uncovering new horrors perpetrated by the "Scarlet Woman"'. Mullen, *Trollope*, p. 214.
22. AT, *Castle Richmond* (Oxford, 1992), p. 53.
23. apRoberts, *Trollope Artist and Moralist*, p. 92.
24. AT, *Towers*, I, pp. 188–9.
25. E. Jay, *The Evangelical and Oxford Movements* (Cambridge, 1983), p. 11.
26. HAM 6/3/47, 1846.
27. AT, *Towers*, I, p. 190.
28. Hansard, CCI, p. 80.
29. AT, *Thorne*, pp. 85, 418–24, 541, 583, 419.
30. AT, *The Bertrams* (Oxford, 1991), p. 10.

31. AT, *North America* (Gloucester, 1987), I, p. 430.
32. O. Chadwick, *The Mind of the Oxford Movement* (London, 1960), p. 55.
33. P. B. Nockles, *The Oxford Movement in Context: Anglican High Churchmanship 1760–1857* (Cambridge, 1994), p. 217.
34. AT, *Miss Mackenzie* (Oxford, 1992), p. 155.
35. Neale's wife queried Mrs Dale's purchase of silk in *The Small House at Allington* (1864). Both she and her husband wished Archdeacon Grantly to be granted a bishopric, which Trollope ignored. Hall, *Letters AT*, I, pp. 252–3.
36. P. T. Marsh, *The Victorian Church in Decline* (Pittsburgh, 1969), p. 229.
37. AT, *He Knew He Was Right* (Oxford, 1992), p. 55.
38. Marsh, *Victorian Church in Decline*, p. 117.
39. According to Hylson-Smith, the low churchmen and the Evangelicals were quite separate, but Nockles says this was only before the 1840s, which I mention later in the chapter. K. Hylson-Smith, *The Evangelicals in the Church of England 1734–1984* (Edinburgh, 1988), p. 115n; Nockles, *The Oxford Movement in Context*, p. 32.
40. B. Booth, *Anthony Trollope: Aspects of his Life and Work* (London, 1958), p. 31; A. O. J. Cockshut, *Anthony Trollope: A Critical Study* (London, 1955), p. 70.
41. Mullen, *Trollope*, p. 257; R. Mullen with J. Munson, *The Penguin Companion to Trollope* (Harmondsworth, 1996), p. 159.
42. Mullen, *Trollope*, p. 444.
43. AT, *Clerks*, p. 17.
44. D. Skilton, *Anthony Trollope and his Contemporaries* (New York, 1972), p. 81.
45. F. Trollope, *The Vicar of Wrexhill* (New York, 1975), p. 343.
46. O. Chadwick, *The Victorian Church Part 1: 1829–1859* (London, 1971), p. 449.
47. AT, *Barset*, p. 675.
48. Hylson-Smith, *Evangelicals in the Church*, p. 165.
49. AT, *Towers*, I, p. 18.
50. G. Eliot, 'The Sad Fortunes of the Rev. Amos Barton', *Scenes of Clerical Life* (Harmondsworth, 1975), p. 59.
51. AT, *Rachel Ray* (Oxford, 1990), pp. 13, 15.
52. AT, *Mackenzie*, p. 19.
53. AT, 'About Hunting', in N. J. Hall (ed.), *Writings for Saint Paul's Magazine* (New York, 1981), p. 218; 'About Hunting' Part II, p. 677.
54. AT, *Is He Popenjoy?* (Oxford, 1991), I, pp. 91–2.
55. AT, *An Old Man's Love* (Oxford, 1992), pp. 94, 140, 183.
56. Hylson-Smith, *Evangelicals in the Church*, p. 50.
57. E. Gaskell, *Cranford/Cousin Phillis* (Harmondsworth, 1976), p. 264.
58. E. Gaskell, *North and South* (Harmondsworth, 1970), p. 474.
59. E. Gaskell, 'A Parson's Holiday', five pieces in *Pall Mall Gazette* (1865), 17 and 21 August.
60. I. Bradley, *The Call to Seriousness* (London, 1976), pp. 17, 36.
61. AT, *Towers*, I, p. 84.
62. AT, *Framley*, p. 74.
63. AT, *Thorne*, p. 210.
64. Belton was a village on a Lincolnshire estate, contiguous with those of the Welbys and Trollopes. The Welbys, Thorolds and Trollopes were interlinked

by marriage. There are 'marriages and intermarriages between the Winterfields and the Folliots and the Belton-Amedroz families', and Will Belton has a clerical uncle 'not far off' in Lincolnshire. Ambler, 'Social Change and Religious Experience', p. 40; AT, *The Belton Estate* (Oxford, 1991), pp. 7, 37.
65. Ibid., pp. 119, 165.
66. No critic has accommodated, within Trollope's alleged anti-Evangelicalism, his friendship with Dr Norman Macleod (1812–72), Queen Victoria's Scottish Presbyterian Chaplain. Macleod, undeterred by Trollope's mockery of Evangelicals in the Barchester novels, asked him to write a novel for Alexander Strahan's Presbyterian journal, *Good Words*. The novel, *Rachel Ray* (1863), was rejected for its mocking references to low church disapproval of community pastimes. Macleod's tact, Strahan's £500 compensation and the encouragement to publish elsewhere appeased Trollope. Trollope's loyalty was later demonstrated when hecklers shouted their disapproval during Macleod's dinner speech marking the 201st anniversary of London's Scottish Hospital. He even defended Macleod's condemnation of Scottish sabbatarianism. Their friendship nullifies criticism of Trollope's imputed *personal* bias against Evangelicals. Hall, *Letters AT*, I, pp. 177–8, 222–4; *Fortnightly Review* (1866), pp. 529–38.
67. AT, 'The Fourth Commandment', *Fortnightly*, III [1866], 15 January, in M. Y. Mason (ed.), *Trollope Miscellaneous Essays and Reviews* (New York, 1981), p. 538.
68. AT, 'Mr Anthony Trollope and the "Saturday Review"', *Pall Mall Gazette*, V February (1866), p. 395.
69. AT, *Towers*, I, pp. 49–50.
70. AT, *Clerks*, p. 57.
71. AT, *Ray*, pp. 51, 53, 7, 345.
72. AT, *Framley*, pp. 105, 164.
73. Chadwick, *Victorian Church* Part 1, p. 70.
74. D. Rosman, *Evangelicals and Culture* (London, 1984), pp. 34, 88.
75. Nockles, *Oxford Movement in Context*, p. 32.
76. AT, *Popenjoy?*, I, p. 93.
77. Charles James Blomfield (1787–1857) was Bishop of London 1828–56. Henry Philpotts (1778–1860) was Bishop of Exeter 1830–69, and Samuel Wilberforce (1805–73) was Bishop of Oxford 1845–69. AT, *Warden*, pp. 98, 287n.
78. AT, *Towers*, I, p. 28.
79. Hylson-Smith, *Evangelicals in the Church*, p. 125.
80. Handley in AT, *Clerks* (Oxford, 1989), p. xvi.
81. M. A. Crowther, *Church Embattled* (Newton Abbot, 1970), p. 22.
82. AT, *Towers*, I, p. 20.
83. Hall wrongly assumes that Bertram in *The Bertrams* (1859) is Trollope's alter ego: '[t]hat segment of the Church of England informally denominated "broad" suited Trollope nicely.' N. J. Hall, *Trollope: A Biography* (Oxford, 1991), p. 184.
84. G. Landow, *Victorian Types Victorian Shadows* (London, 1980), pp. 20–1.
85. Chadwick, *Mind of the Oxford Movement*, p. 15.
86. HAM 6/95/92, 15 November 1866.

87. B. M. G. Reardon, *Religious Thought in the Victorian Age* (London, 1995), p. 134.
88. O. Chadwick, *The Victorian Church Part 2: 1860–1901* (London, 1972), p. 95.
89. AT, *Clergymen of the Church of England* (London, 1998), pp. 119, 127–8.
90. *Essays and Reviews* (1860) was the idea of Benjamin Jowett (1817–93) and Frederick Temple (1821–1902), and was a collection of essays by seven clergymen, querying Anglican doctrine and a literal reading of the Bible. It was still controversial years after its publication.
91. AT, *Clergymen*, pp. 122–3, 126, 129, 128.
92. AT, *Belton*, pp. 215–16.
93. Reardon, *Religious Thought*, p. 255.
94. AT, *Right*, p. 65.
95. AT, *South Africa* (London, 1968), I, p. 259.
96. Colenso enjoyed Trollope's novels. Mullen, *Trollope*, p. 306.
97. AT, *South Africa*, I, pp. 258–9, 284.
98. AT, 'The Heroines of Plumplington', in J. Thompson (ed.), *Anthony Trollope: The Collected Shorter Fiction* (London, 1992), p. 926.
99. AT, *Clergymen*, p. 124.
100. AT, *Framley*, p. 561.
101. Marsh, *Victorian Church in Decline*, p. 281.
102. AT, *Towers*, I, pp. 18–19.
103. HAM 6/95/131, 23 April 1868.
104. AT, *Bertrams*, p. 11. The Sewell family, William (1804–74), Elizabeth née Missing (1815–1906), the novelist (and author of 'The Rose of Cheriton', referred to in the Conclusion), and William's two brothers were all high church – one became premier of New Zealand and the other Warden of New College, Oxford. Keble's assize sermon in 1833, referred to earlier, led to the founding of the Oxford Movement and William Faber (1824–63) became a Roman Catholic in 1845 (*Bertrams*, p. 583n), along with Newman.
105. Mullen, *Trollope*, pp. 262–3.
106. AT, *Framley*, pp. 486–8, 44, 481–2.
107. 632/143, F. Atkins (low church clergyman) to W. A. K. Hamilton, high church Bishop of Salisbury. The letter relates to doctrinal differences: Real Presence and auricular confession, between 1861 and 1864.
108. 632/145, Rev. H. H. Wood, Rector of Holwell, Dorset, to Hamilton, 14 December 1864.
109. AT, *Ray*, pp. 403, 51.
110. AT, *Mackenzie*, pp. 155, 33.
111. Unbound Liddon Papers, Pusey House, 9 November, year unknown, Anonymous letter, 'The Ritualist'.
112. AT, *Clergymen*, pp. 13, 26–7.
113. AT, *The Claverings* (Oxford, 1991), pp. 16, 20, 434.
114. HAM 6/95/90, 10 November 1866.
115. AT, *The Vicar of Bullhampton* (Oxford, 1990), pp. 306, 188–9, 527, 329, 493.
116. HAM 6/95/113, 15 August 1867.
117. AT, *The Eustace Diamonds* (Oxford, 1992), I, p. 101; II, p. 239.
118. Stephen Boatright ignores *Nina Balatka* (1867), and oscillates between

whether Trollope is anti-Semitic or 'trying to get his audience to see how unjust and illiberal the accepted anti-Semitism of Victorian society was'. S. Boatright, 'Anti-Semitism in the "Pallisers"', *Trollopiana* (November 1999), pp. 4–12; *The Penguin Companion to Trollope* is non-committal, but gives Trollope the benefit of the doubt. Mullen with Munson, *Penguin Companion to Trollope*, pp. 243–4; *Oxford Reader's Companion to Trollope* presumes Trollope was 'warmly sympathetic to Judaism and the Jews', since [h]is friends included the Rothschild banking family'. R. C. Terry (ed.), *Oxford Reader's Companion to Trollope* (Oxford, 1999), p. 283.
119. Their marriage dramatically disintegrates in *Phineas Redux* ([1874] Oxford, 1992), II, p. 41.
120. AT, *The Way We Live Now* (Oxford, 1992), I, pp. 148–9.
121. AT, *Popenjoy?*, II, pp. 45, 287, 213; I, p. 9.
122. AT, *John Caldigate* (Oxford, 1993), pp. 302, 211, 161, 2, 172, 539, 615.
123. AT, *Dr Wortle's School* (Oxford, 1984), pp. 191, 158, 98, 96.
124. AT, *Marion Fay* (Oxford, 1992), pp. 301, 323, 196, 394.
125. R. C. Terry (ed.), *Trollope: Interviews and Recollections* (London: 1987), p. 217.

Chapter 2   Patronage versus Philanthropy

1. W. L. Bowles, *The Patronage of the English Bishops* (Bristol, 1836), p. 6.
2. AT, *Clergymen*, pp. 97–8.
3. AT, *Barset*, p. 32.
4. H. Alford, 'Mr Anthony Trollope and the English Clergy', *Contemporary Review*, June (1866), pp. 240, 246.
5. AT, *Clergymen*, p. 77.
6. AT, 'Curates' Incomes', *Pall Mall* (1866), pp. 251–2.
7. 'The Charities and the Poor of London', *Quarterly*, XCVII (1855), p. 414.
8. AT, *Framley*, p. 174.
9. T. H. S. Escott, *England: Its People, Polity, and Pursuits* (London, 1890), p. 14.
10. Harrison, 'Philanthropy and the Victorians', *Victorian Studies*, IX (1966), p. 370.
11. AT, *Barset*, p. 527.
12. Gaskell, *North and South*, p. 65.
13. AT, *Kellys*, p. 329. The cheque and rector's new black coat re-echo in *Barset* (1867) as the cheque allegedly stolen by Mr Crawley and new black coat donated by Mrs Arabin.
14. AT, *Clerks*, p. 382.
15. AT, *Warden*, p. 173.
16. B. K. Gray, *A History of English Philanthropy: From the Dissolution of the Monasteries to the Taking of the First Census* ([1905] London, 1967), p. vii.
17. F. Gladstone, *Charity, Law and Social Justice* (London, 1982), p. 46.
18. H. G. Carter and F. M. Crawshaw, *Tudor on Charities: A Practical Treatise on the Law Relating to Gifts and Trusts for Charitable Purposes* (London, 1929), p. 8.
19. Gladstone, *Charity, Law*, p. 46.

20. AT, *Warden*, pp. 106–7.
21. The most detailed study of stipend holders taking advantage of the profits from Victorian charities grown rich is: R. B. Martin, *Enter Rumour: Four Early Victorian Scandals* (London, 1962).
22. G. Jones, *History of the Law of Charity 1532–1827* (Cambridge, 1969), p. 5.
23. Gray, *English Philanthropy*, p. 115.
24. Ibid., p. 264.
25. Trollope may have based Carry Brattle on Rebecca Jarrett, a fallen woman who became a brothel visitor under Catherine Booth and Josephine Butler's guidance. Rachel O'Mahoney's life as actress in *The Landleaguers* (1883) prompts Trollope to refer to women's rights – the suffrage societies of the 1860s and Josephine Butler's pamphlet, *The Education and Employment of Women* (1868), which campaigned for the repeal of the Contagious Diseases Acts of the 1860s, under which women, 'identified as prostitutes', could be given 'regular internal examinations'. Prochaska, *Women and Philanthropy*, pp. 161, 202. AT, *The Landleaguers* (Oxford, 1993), p. 426n.
26. AT, *Bullhampton*, pp. 329, 186.
27. AT, *Wortle*, pp. 154, 144.
28. J. Petersen, *Family, Love and Work in the Lives of Victorian Gentlewomen* (Bloomington, IN, 1989), p. 136.
29. D. Roberts, *Paternalism in Early Victorian England* (London, 1979), p. 157.
30. AT, *Mackenzie*, pp. 354–5.
31. Gray, *English Philanthropy*, p. 269.
32. AT, 'Bazaars for Charity', *Pall Mall*, XXI (1866), p. 12.
33. Anonymous, 'Our Charities', *Pall Mall* (1867), p. 11.
34. AT, *Right*, pp. 463, 834, 106, 136, 154. Sutherland mistakenly identifies Miss Fanny Bent (d. 1860), with whom Trollope used to stay in Devon and whom Aunt Stanbury resembles, as a friend. She was the daughter of Trollope's maternal grandfather's sister, Mary Bent née Milton. Trollope's two great-aunts – his maternal grandmother's sister and his maternal grandfather's sister – lived in Crediton and became the wives of two clerical brothers Bent, the Revs. John and George. The two Misses French hunt 'unmarried clergymen in couples', but compete over Mr Gibson. AT, *Right*, pp. 934n, 141; Hall, *Letters AT*, I, p. 143n.
35. AT, *Richmond*, pp. 65, 103, 206, 205, 83.
36. Five kinds of ecclesiastical patronage appear in D. McClatchey, *Oxfordshire Clergy 1777–1869: A Study of the Established Church and of the Role of Its Clergy in Local Society* (Oxford, 1960), p. 2.
37. AT, 'Christmas Day at Kirkby Cottage', in *Trollope: Collected Shorter Fiction*, p. 659.
38. J. M. Bourne, *Patronage and Society in Nineteenth-Century England* (London, 1986), p. 5.
39. M. J. D. Roberts, 'Private Patronage and the Church of England 1800–1900', *Journal of Ecclesiastical History*, April (1981), pp. 205, 203–4.
40. AT, 'Kirkby Cottage', p. 659.
41. AT, 'The Lady of Launay', in *Trollope: Collected Shorter Fiction*, p. 794.
42. AT, *Old*, pp. 94, 158, 160, 163, 186, 143.
43. Frank Wentworth in *The Perpetual Curate* (1864) is denied *two* family livings, because his aunts disapprove of his ecclesiastical practices and his father

believes gossip. Denied patronage and the fortuitous final appointment indict the system. M. Oliphant, *The Perpetual Curate* (New York, 1975), III, p. 275.
44. Marsh, *Victorian Church in Decline*, p. 208.
45. AT, *The American Senator* (Oxford, 1986), pp. 86–7, 354, 542.
46. George Trollope (1802–64), chief clerk of Christ's Hospital and son of its Headmaster, married into the Welbys, wealthy pluralists; West Allington was one of their rural deaneries. Sir John Trollope (1800–74), Conservative MP for south Lincolnshire from 1868 to 1884, succeeded William Earle Welby (1829–98), Tory MP for Grantham from 1857 to 1868. Like many other private livings, the West Allington living soared between 1710 and 1830, from £80 to £685 a year, despite the fact that the Queen Anne's bounty had been established to rectify church abuses. *The Small House at Allington* (1864) possibly describes scenes of life among Trollope's forebears. P. Virgin, *The Church in an Age of Negligence: Ecclesiastical structure and problems of church reform 1700–1840* (Cambridge, 1989), pp. 73, 69.
47. AT, *The Small House at Allington* (Oxford, 1986), pp. 3, 4.
48. AT, *Bullhampton*, p. 396.
49. Similarly, the Rev. Cecil St John's precarious position in *The Curate in Charge* as curate for 20 years in a college living bestowed on a non-resident rector is exacerbated when the college, on the rector's death and unaware of St John's existence despite his being an alumnus, gives the living to someone else. The curate's acceptance of a curacy in Liverpool with 'people very degraded' and premature death are bleaker depictions of the collegiate patronage system than Trollope's. M. Oliphant, *The Curate in Charge* ([1876] New York, 1987), p. 167.
50. AT, *Clergymen*, p. 28.
51. A. Haig, *The Victorian Clergy* (London, 1984), pp. 267–8.
52. C. Dewey, *The Passing of Barchester* (London, 1991), p. 28.
53. W. D. Rubinstein, 'The End of 'Old Corruption' in Britain 1780–1860', *Past and Present*, CI (1983), p. 73.
54. In N. C. Smith (ed.), *The Letters of Sydney Smith* (Oxford, 1953), pp. 585–6.
55. P. Virgin, *Sydney Smith* (London, 1994), p. ix.
56. In Smith, *Letters Sydney Smith*, p. 618.
57. AT, *Warden*, p. 121.
58. Gaskell, *North and South*, pp. 49, 179.
59. AT, *Clergymen*, p. 21.
60. AT, *Towers*, I, p. 19.
61. D. W. R. Bahlman, 'The Queen, Mr Gladstone and Church Patronage', *Victorian Studies*, II (1960), pp. 349–80; W. T. Gibson, 'Disraeli's Church Patronage: 1868–1990', *Anglican Episcopal History*, LXI (1992), pp. 197–210.
62. AT, *Towers*, II, p. 260.
63. Roberts, *Paternalism in Early Victorian England*, p. 42.
64. E. Burke, *Reflections on the Revolution in France* (London, 1964), pp. 30–1, 75–6.
65. AT, *Towers*, II, p. 184.
66. E. Gaskell, *Sylvia's Lovers* (London, 1996), pp. 418, 455.
67. M. Oliphant, *Phoebe Junior* (London, 1989), pp. 63, 136, 124.

68. W. T. Warren, *St Cross Hospital: near Winchester: Its History and Buildings* (Winchester, 1899), *passim*.
69. AT, *Framley*, p. 64.
70. E. M. Sigsworth (ed.), *In Search of Victorian Values: Aspects of Nineteenth-Century Thought and Society* (Manchester, 1988), pp. 165–6.
71. AT, *South Africa* (London, 1968), II, pp. 186, 188.
72. AT, *Mackenzie*, pp. 366, 369.
73. Sigsworth, *In Search of Victorian Values*, p. 64.
74. W. O'Hanlon, 'Our Medical Charities and their Abuses', *Transactions of the Manchester Statistical Society*, III, 12 February (1872–3), p. 41.
75. 'Scientific versus Amateur Administration', *Quarterly*, CXXVII (1869), p. 52.
76. D. Roberts, *Victorian Origins of the British Welfare State* (New York, 1969), p. 86.
77. R. Humphreys, *Sin, Organised Charity and the Poor Law* (London, 1995), p. 170.
78. Gray, *English Philanthropy*, p. 247.
79. In AT, *Clergymen of the Church of England* (Leicester, 1974), appendix, pp. ⟨57⟩–⟨60⟩.
80. 'The Charities and the Poor of London', *Quarterly*, XCVII (1855), p. 443.
81. 'Church Extensions', *Quarterly*, CIII (1857), p. 168.
82. C. I. Foster, *An Errand of Mercy: The Evangelical United Front 1790–1837* (Chapel Hill, NC, 1960), p. 70.
83. Owen, *English Philanthropy 1660–1960* (Cambridge, MA, 1964), p. 113.
84. R. Hole, *Pulpits, Politics and Public Order in England 1760–1832* (Cambridge, 1989), pp. 91–2.
85. AT, *Ray*, pp. 67, 156, 66, 119.
86. D. M. Valenze, *Prophet Sons and Daughters: Female Preaching and Popular Religion in Industrial England* (Princeton, NJ, 1985), p. 93.
87. These societies were named after the biblical Dorcas of Joppa, who was known for making clothes for the poor and other good works; Dorcas even became a brand of needle. F. K. Prochaska, *Women and Philanthropy in Nineteenth-Century England* (Oxford, 1980), pp. 16, 64.
88. AT, *Towers*, II, p. 181.
89. AT, *Ray*, p. 229.
90. Gray, *English Philanthropy*, p. 236.
91. AT, *Thorne*, pp. 44–5, 27, 44, 176, 410, 611.
92. Edith Tilley was taken into Trollope's household in 1849, Florence Bland in 1863 and Beatrice Trollope in 1865.
93. AT, *Ralph the Heir* (Oxford, 1991), p. 84.
94. Mullen, *Trollope*, p. 646.
95. 'The Queen in the Islands and Highlands', *Quarterly*, CXXIV (1868), pp. 74–5.
96. Petersen, *Family, Love and Work in the Lives of Victorian Gentlewomen*, p. 133.
97. Owen, *English Philanthropy*, p. 139.
98. Mullen, *Trollope*, p. 636.
99. AT, *Lady Anna* (Oxford, 1991), pp. 134, 138.
100. Foster, *Errand of Mercy*, pp. 98, 93.
101. G. Kitson Clark, *Churchmen and the Condition of England 1832–85* (London, 1973), p. 144.

102. AT, *Mackenzie*, pp. 20, 66, 152–3.
103. AT, *Towers*, I, p. 128.
104. AT, *Thorne*, p. 621.
105. AT, *Barset*, p. 328.
106. AT, *Ayala's Angel* (Oxford, 1992), p. 503.
107. AT, *Old*, pp. 127, 139.
108. AT, *Anna*, pp. 134, 140, 147, 202, 494.
109. AT, 'The Relics of General Chassé', in *Trollope: Collected Shorter Fiction*, pp. 2, 5–6, 10.
110. AT, *Framley*, p. 249.
111. Virgin, *Church in an Age of Negligence*, p. 62.
112. W. L. Mathiesen, *English Church Reform 1815–40* ([1856] London, 1923), p. 147.
113. Virgin, *Church in an Age of Negligence*, pp. 145, 258.
114. AT, *Senator*, p. 29.
115. D. Verey (ed.), *The Diary of a Cotswold Parson* (Gloucester, 1978), pp. 157, 10.
116. E. Trollope, *Family of Trollope*, p. 23.
117. AT, *Warden*, p. 37.
118. AT, *Towers*, II, p. 259.
119. AT, *Claverings*, pp. 507, 463.
120. The preferment – an annual cask of cider. E. Trollope, *Family of Trollope*, p. 29.
121. AT, *Bullhampton*, p. 86.
122. AT, *Ralph*, pp. 127, 23.
123. AT, *Clergymen*, p. 96.
124. Mathiesen, *English Church Reform*, pp. 113–14.
125. D. Newsome, *The Parting of Friends: A Study of the Wilberforces and Henry Newsome* (London, 1966), pp. 124, 130, 155.
126. Hylson-Smith, *Evangelicals in the Church*, p. 34.
127. Bradley, *Call to Seriousness*, p. 60.
128. Hylson-Smith, *Evangelicals in the Church*, p. 75.
129. R. J. Olney, *Lincolnshire Politics 1832–1885* (London, 1973), pp. 155, 29.
130. AT, *Clergymen*, pp. 76–7.
131. Gray, *English Philanthropy*, p. 117.
132. Roberts, *Paternalism in Early Victorian England*, p. 88.
133. T. Ransom, *Fanny Trollope: A Remarkable Life* (Stroud, 1995), p. 152.
134. Flaubert: 'As to making known my own opinion about the characters I produce, no, no, a thousand times no!' Gustave Flaubert to Georges Sand, 6 February 1876, in M. Allott, *Novelists on the Novel* (Columbia, OH, 1966), p. 33.
135. Martin, *Enter Rumour*, pp. 137–184.
136. *Quarterly*, XCVII (1855), pp. 420, 446.
137. R. Tompson, *The Charity Commission and the Age of Reform* (London, 1979), p. 29.
138. E. Trollope, *Family of Trollope*, p. 14.
139. AT, *Wortle*, p. 2.
140. Owen, *English Philanthropy*, pp. 286, 298.

141. N. McCord, 'The Poor Law and Philanthropy' (1976), in D. Fraser (ed.), *The New Poor Law in the Nineteenth Century* (London, 1976), p. 92.
142. Gladstone, *Charity, Law*, p. 43.
143. AT, *Warden*, p. 197.
144. C. Dickens, *Martin Chuzzlewit* (Liverpool n.d.), p. 60.
145. C. Dickens, *Bleak House* (London, 1996), p. 52.
146. AT, *The Macdermots of Ballycloran* (Oxford, 1991), p. 128. Lord Birmingham, notes Robert Tracy, may have been based on Viscount Clements (1805–39), although he 'lived in Ireland for part of each year, and actively encouraged local agriculture' (p. 682n).
147. AT, *North America*, II, p. 171.
148. AT, 'Public Schools', *Fortnightly Review* (1865), p. 481.
149. 'The Functions of Charity', *Quarterly*, XCIII (1853), p. 215.
150. Gladstone, *Charity, Law*, pp. 61–2.
151. In an interview with me on 14 January 1994, the Rev. Outhwaite, current Master of St Cross, confirmed the close links between Winchester Cathedral, Winchester College and St Cross Hospital. St Cross's beneficiaries were often former Winchester schoolmasters or Cathedral clergymen and the boys at Winchester College visit St Cross on a regular basis, as Trollope himself would have done. The three institutions are linked by a pathway running through the Water Meadows behind the Cathedral.
152. R. Gilmour, 'The Challenge of Barchester Towers', in H. Bloom (ed.), *Modern Critical Interpretations: Anthony Trollope's Barchester Towers and The Warden* (New York, 1988), p. 142; Christopher Herbert, 'Barchester Towers and the Charms of Imperfection', ibid., p. 158.
153. AT, *Warden*, pp. 15, 197.
154. AT, *Barset*, p. 99.
155. Since his appointment as dean, 'he must have become a doctor'. AT, *Towers*, II, p. 270.
156. AT, *Barset*, p. 7.
157. AT, *Framley*, p. 257.
158. Bahlman, 'The Queen, Mr Gladstone and Church Patronage', p. 351.
159. Bourne, *Patronage and Society*, p. 6.
160. AT, *Towers*, I, p. 128, 127.
161. Hylson-Smith, *Evangelicals in the Church*, p. 124.
162. Gibson, 'Disraeli's Church Patronage: 1868–1990', p. 197.
163. Marsh, *The Victorian Church in Decline*, p. 286. Disraeli's unawareness of Christopher Wordsworth's ritualism, before promoting him to the see of Lincoln, fuelled even more dissension within the Church in light of the Public Worship Act. Nonetheless, the varied appointments across the political and ecclesiastical spectrum tended to work out. Gibson, 'Disraeli's Church Patronage: 1868–1990', pp. 198, 201.
164. AT, *Fay*, p. 100.
165. HAM 6/95/82, 29 July 1866.
166. Bourne, *Patronage and Society*, p. 23.
167. Chadwick, *Victorian Church*, I, p. 137.
168. Dewey, *Passing of Barchester*, p. 146.
169. Roberts, 'Private Patronage', pp. 199–223.

170. AT, 'The Civil Service as a Profession', *Cornhill Magazine*, February, in M. Y. Mason, *Trollope Miscellaneous Essays*, p. 214.
171. W. E. Chadwick, *The Church, the State, and the Poor: A Series of Historical Sketches* (London, 1914), p. 63.
172. Trollope knew that philanthropy could not help during the famine: 'Much abuse ... was thrown upon the government ... in my opinion the measures ... were prompt, wise, and beneficent.' AT, *Richmond*, p. 69.
173. Ibid., pp. 189, 192, 190, 191.
174. There was no Poor Law in Ireland at the time in which Trollope was writing.
175. AT, *Claverings*, p. 102.
176. P. Barrett, *Barchester: English Cathedral Life in the Nineteenth Century* (London, 1993), p. 4.
177. Trollope would have known *Self-Help* (1856). S. Smiles, *Self-Help* (Harmondsworth, [1856] 1986).
178. T. Noel, 'Rhymes and Roundelays: the pauper's drive', in Sigsworth, *In Search of Victorian Values*, p. 56.
179. H. Massingberd, 'All Flats, Fogs and Fens', *Spectator* (1994), 6 August, pp. 20–1.
180. D. Prince, 'The Truth about the Loss of Royalties', *Spectator* (1996), 27 July, p. 9.
181. The law, refined in 1891, listed the following charitable uses of money: 'relief of poverty, advancement of education, advancement of religion and other purposes beneficial to the community'. But 'what a religion is, or what a charity is, or what it means to be religious in a charitable sense' has still not been established. J. King, 'Watch Out, There's A Charity About', *Spectator* (2000), 28 October, p. 30.
182. AT, *Mackenzie*, p. 197.

Chapter 3 Gentlemen Clergymen

1. N. Annan, *The Dons: Mentors, Eccentrics and Geniuses* (London, 1999), p. 12.
2. S. R. Letwin, *The Gentleman in Trollope: Individuality and Moral Conduct* (London, 1982), pp. 3, 7–8, 15.
3. R. Tracy, *Trollope's Later Novels* (Berkeley, 1978), p. 73.
4. A. O. J. Cockshut, *Anthony Trollope: A Critical Study* (London, 1955), p. 149.
5. C. Lansbury, *The Reasonable Man: Trollope's Legal Fiction* (Princeton, 1981), pp. 22–3, 109.
6. J. W. Clark, *The Language and Style of Anthony Trollope* (London, 1975), p. 61.
7. AT, *Towers*, I, pp. 29–30.
8. In Verey, *Diary of Cotswold Parson*, p. 90.
9. AT, *Towers*, I, pp. 31, 126.
10. B. Heeney, *A Different Kind of Gentleman: Parish Clergy as Professional Men in Early and Mid-Victorian England* (Ohio, 1976), p. 6.
11. AT, *Towers*, II, pp. 231, 260.
12. Hall, *Letters AT*, I, p. 46.

13. AT, *Thorne*, pp. 403, 100.
14. A. Pollard, 'Trollope's Idea of the Gentleman', in J. Halperin (ed.), *Trollope, Centenary Essays* (London, 1982), p. 87.
15. AT, *Framley*, pp. 146, 435.
16. Oliphant in E. Jay, *Margaret Oliphant: A Fiction to Herself* (Oxford, 1995), p. 234.
17. M. Oliphant, *Phoebe Junior* (London, 1989), p. 67.
18. M. Oliphant, *A Son of the Soil* (London, 1883), p. 354.
19. AT, *Allington*, pp. 300, 10, 662.
20. AT, *Ray*, pp. 2, 31, 53, 52, 78.
21. Heeney, *Different Kind of Gentleman*, pp. 23, 41.
22. Rosman, *Evangelicals*, p. 205.
23. C. R. Sumner, *Charge to the Diocese of Winchester: 9th Visitation* (London, 1862), p. 27.
24. AT, *Ray*, p. 79.
25. HAM 6/95/147, 16 August 1868.
26. AT, *Ray*, pp. 119, 117 (italics mine), 139.
27. AT, *Mackenzie*, pp. 56, 112, 118, 132, 138.
28. Ibid., p. 139.
29. AT, 'Public Schools', *Fortnightly Review* (1865), pp. 486, 477.
30. Ibid., pp. 486–7.
31. AT, *Orley Farm* (Oxford, 1991), I, pp. 269–70.
32. AT, 'The Sisterhood Question in the High Church', *Pall Mall* (1865), p. 363.
33. AT, *Clergymen*, pp. 2, 24–5.
34. AT, *Thorne*, p. 215.
35. AT, *Clergymen*, p. 26.
36. Ibid., pp. 37, 42, 44–5, 49, 87, 90.
37. Ibid., p. 59.
38. W. G. Jervis, *The Poor Condition of the Clergy* (London, 1856), pp. 28–9.
39. AT, *Clergymen*, pp. 59–61, 68.
40. AT, *Dark*, p. 7.
41. D. Macleane, 'The Church as a Profession', *The National Review*, VI (1899), p. 952.
42. AT, *Clergymen*, pp. 68–9.
43. AT, *Right*, p. 458–9.
44. AT, *Clergymen*, pp. 103–4.
45. Jervis, *Poor Condition of Clergy*, p. 6.
46. AT, *Clergymen*, p. 104.
47. W. J. Conybeare, 'The Church of England in the Mountains', in Heeney, *Different Kind of Gentleman*, p. 24.
48. AT, *Barset*, p. 76.
49. Macleane, 'Church as Profession', pp. 948, 951.
50. AT, *Barset*, p. 90.
51. Jervis, *Poor Condition of Clergy*, p. 14.
52. AT, *Barset*, pp. 99, 176–80, 675.
53. G. Eliot, *Middlemarch* (New York and London, 1977), pp. 21, 33. Casaubon's *Key to All Mythologies* resembled the *Encyclopedia Ecclesiastica* of Thomas Anthony Trollope, Trollope's father. Glendinning, *Trollope*, p. 44n.
54. AT, *Barset*, p. 220.

55. AT, *Right*, p. 330.
56. R. J. Merrett, 'Port and Claret: The Politics of Wine in Trollope's Barsetshire Novels', *Mozaic*, XXIV (1991), p. 113.
57. AT, *Barset*, pp. 881–2.
58. AT, *Senator*, p. 173; AT, *Ayala's*, pp. 631, 630.
59. AT, *Claverings*, pp. 510, 236, 276, 356–7.
60. Ibid., pp. 346, 508, 510–11.
61. AT, *Right*, p. 842.
62. Sutherland explains Trollope's joke, for 'outhouse' implies the reality of working among the poor. William Rogers (1819–96), rector of St Botolph's, in London from 1863, prebendary of St Pancras from 1862 and Chaplain in Ordinary to Queen Victoria from 1857, in Trollope's words, was 'a very dear friend of mine'. Trollope shifted 'd's' to 'b's' and 'd's' to 't's' to protect the borough's inhabitants. Blomfield (Rogers' patron and Bishop of London) was Evangelical, Queen Victoria had Evangelical leanings and Rogers' philanthropy suggests Trollope's friend was Evangelical. AT, *Right*, p. 942n; Hall, *Letters AT*, II, p. 697n.
63. AT, *Right*, pp. 131, 271, 304, 574, 58, 330, 65.
64. AT, *Bullhampton*, pp. 6, 116, 164–5, 240, 302–3.
65. AT, *Eustace*, I, p. 33.
66. Ibid., I, p. 325.
67. Ibid., II, pp. 52, 372.
68. AT, *Popenjoy?*, I, p. 131, II, p. 33, I, pp. 185, 227, II, pp. 90, 119, 118.
69. AT, *Wortle*, pp. 12, 5.
70. R. Wells (ed.), *Victorian Village: The Diaries of the Reverend John Coker Egerton of Burwash 1857–1888* (Gloucester, 1992), p. 31.
71. AT, *Wortle*, pp. 155, 142, 251.
72. AT, 'The Two Heroines of Plumplington', in *Trollope: Collected Shorter Fiction*, p. 916.
73. Verey, *Diary of Cotswold Parson*, p. 137.
74. AT, *Fay*, pp. 134, 137.

Chapter 4 Women and the Church

1. A. Owen, *The Darkened Room: Women, Power and Spiritualism in Late Nineteenth-Century England* (London, 1989); G. Malmgren, *Religion in the Lives of English Women, 1760–1930* (London, 1986); A. Summers, 'Pride and Prejudice: Ladies and Nurses in the Crimean War', *History Workshop: Journal of Socialist and Feminist Historians*, XVI (1983), pp. 33–55; J. Hoch-Smith and A. Spring (eds), *Women in Ritual and Symbolic Roles* (New York and London, 1978); L. Holcombe, *Victorian Ladies at Work: Middle-Class Women in England and Wales 1850–1914* (Newton Abbot, 1873); A. M. Allchin, *The Silent Rebellion: Anglican Religious Communities 1845–1900* (London, 1958).
2. J. Perkin, *Women and Marriage in Nineteenth-Century England* (London, 1989), p. 258.
3. L. Davidoff and C. Hall, *Family Fortunes: Men and Women of the English Middle Class, 1780–1850* (Chicago, 1987), p. 114.

4. D. Mermin, *Godiva's Ride: Women of Letters in England 1830–1880* (Bloomington and Indianapolis, 1993), pp. 108, 114.
5. R. D. McMaster, 'Women in *The Way We Live Now*', *English Studies in Canada*, VII (1981), pp. 68–80; J. Nardin, *He Knew She Was Right: The Independent Woman in the Novels of Anthony Trollope* (Carbondale, 1989); M. Markwick, *Trollope and Women* (London, 1997).
6. P. D. Edwards, *Anthony Trollope: His Art and Scope* (Queensland, 1977), p. 22.
7. In G. F. A. Best, *Temporal Pillars: Queen Anne's Bounty, the Ecclesiastical Commissioners, and the Church of England* (Cambridge, 1964), p. 263.
8. M. Hill, *The Religious Order: A Study of Virtuoso Religion and its Legitimation in the Nineteenth-Century Church of England* (London, 1973), p. 277.
9. A. Jameson, *Sisters of Charity, Catholic and Protestant, Abroad and at Home* (London, 1855), p. 116.
10. AT, *Autobiography*, p. 291.
11. W. L. Burn, 'Anthony Trollope's Politics', *Nineteenth Century and After* (1948), p. 165; J. Kincaid, 'Barchester Towers and the Nature of Conservative Comedy', *English Literary History*, XXXVII (1970), pp. 595–612; A. O. J. Cockshut, 'Trollope's Liberalism', in T. Bareham (ed.), *Anthony Trollope* (London, 1980), pp. 163–4; J. Halperin, *Trollope and Politics: A Study of the Pallisers and Others* (London, 1977), pp. 56–78; J. Nardin, 'The Social Critic in Anthony Trollope's Novels', *Studies in English Literature*, V (1990), pp. 679–96; P. Neville-Sington, *Fanny Trollope: The Life and Adventures of a Clever Woman* (London, 1998).
12. Glendinning calls it 'a painful document to read'. Glendinning, *Trollope*, p. 328.
13. J. McMaster, *Trollope's Palliser Novels: Theme and Pattern* (New York, 1978), p. 162.
14. AT, 'Higher Education of Women', in M. L. Parrish (ed.), *Four Lectures* (London, 1938), pp. 79–80, 83, 88.
15. AT, 'Merivale's History of the Romans', Review of, *Dublin University Magazine*, III, IV, V (1856), in Mason, *Trollope: Miscellaneous Essays*, p. 43.
16. Hall, *Letters AT*, I, pp. 17, 25, 29.
17. R. Rathburn and M. Steinman Jr (eds), *From Jane Austen to Joseph Conrad: Essays Collected in Memory of James T. Hillhouse* (Minneapolis, 1958), p. 172.
18. J. Hawthorne, 'Shapes the Pass: Memories of Old Days' [1928], in Terry, *Trollope: Interviews*, p. 147.
19. Hall, *Letters AT*, II, p. 651.
20. AT, *Towers*, I, p. 45.
21. AT, *Framley*, pp. 206.
22. AT, *Warden*, pp. 20–2.
23. Hall, *Letters AT*, II, p. 953.
24. Owen, *Darkened Room*, p. 15.
25. AT, *Towers*, I, p. 24.
26. Ibid., I, p. 23.
27. Heeney, *Different Kind of Gentleman*, pp. 20–1.
28. AT, *Popenjoy?* II, pp. 237, 242.
29. AT, *Towers*, I, p. 239.
30. S. Smith [1838], in Best, *Temporal Pillars*, p. 263.

31. M. Edgeworth, *Patronage* ([1813] London, 1986), pp. 424–500.
32. Dewey, *Passing of Barchester*, p. 94.
33. Hall, *Letters AT*, I, pp. 61–2.
34. AT, *Towers*, I, p. 159.
35. AT, *Barset*, pp. 42, 812.
36. AT, *Right*, pp. 459–60.
37. Stephen Gill outlines this thirteenth-century legend of a female pope disguised as a man, who left after childbirth two years later. AT, *Barset*, p. 680, 896n.
38. T. J. Williams and A. W. Campbell, *The Park Village Sisterhood* (London, 1965), p. 2.
39. W. Arnstein, in Malmgren, *Lives of English Women*, p. 99.
40. AT, *Barset*, p. 680.
41. AT, *Claverings*, pp. 14, 428.
42. Verey, *Diary of Cotswold Parson*, p. 174.
43. Macleane, 'Church as Profession', p. 949.
44. Hylson-Smith, *High Churchmanship*, p. 142.
45. AT, *Framley*, p. 132.
46. Ibid., pp. 207, 481–2.
47. AT, 'Alice Dugdale', in *Trollope: Collected Shorter Fiction*, pp. 840, 842, 838, 843, 855, 865, 859.
48. Hall, *Letters AT*, II, p. 920.
49. A. Summers, 'Pride and Prejudice: Ladies and Nurses in the Crimean War', *History Workshop: Journal of Socialist and Feminist Historians*, XVI (1983), pp. 35, 42.
50. Glendinning, *Trollope*, p. 457n.
51. AT, *Framley*, p. 474.
52. AT, *Allington*, pp. 604, 608–9.
53. AT, *Barset*, pp. 27, 614, 418.
54. AT, *Popenjoy?* I, p. 150, II, p. 308.
55. Glendinning, *Trollope*, pp. 159, 96–7.
56. C. Tilley, *Chollerton* (London, 1846), pp. 380–1.
57. AT, 'Higher Education for Women'.
58. McMaster, *Trollope's Palliser Novels*, p. 162.
59. Allchin, *Silent Rebellion*, pp. 116–18.
60. Sir Harry Hotspur is prepared to do anything for his daughter in *Sir Harry Hotspur of Humblethwaite* (1870), once he realizes that her life is ebbing away. Having introduced her to the Pope, he enables her to visit the poor. Had she lived, she would have become a conventual sister, such was her power over her father. AT, *Sir Harry Hotspur of Humblethwaite* (Oxford, 1991), pp. 242–3.
61. Allchin, *Silent Rebellion*, pp. 39, 116.
62. Hill, *Religious Order*, p. 296.
63. AT, *Orley*, II, pp. 179–80.
64. S. P. Casteras, 'Virgin Vows: The Early Victorian Portrayal of Nuns and Novices', in Malmgren, *Lives of English Women*, p. 133.
65. Hill, *Religious Order*, pp. 277, 272.
66. C. H. Simpkinson, *The Life and Work of Bishop Thorold* (London, 1896), p. 171.

67. AT, 'The Sisterhood Question in the High Church', *Pall Mall* (1865), p. 363.
68. In Williams and Campbell, *Park Village Sisterhood*, pp. 32, 38.
69. AT, *La Vendée* (London, 1993), III, p. 965.
70. AT, *Right*, p. 392.
71. AT, *South Africa*, II, p. 269.
72. Anonymous, 'Mr Trollope's Novels', *National Review*, VII, p. 422.
73. AT, *Clergymen*, pp. 60, 77, 95–104.
74. W. G. Jervis, *The Poor Condition of the Clergy and the Causes Considered with Suggestions for Remedying the Same* (London, 1856), pp. 20–1, 54–7.
75. AT, *Bertrams*, pp. 318–19, 35, 213, 336, 517.
76. Oliphant, *Curate in Charge*, p. 127.
77. M. Oliphant, *The Rector and the Doctor's Family* (London, 1986), p. 15.
78. W. T. Gibson, 'Disraeli's Church Patronage: 1868–1880', *Anglican Episcopal History*, LXI (1992), pp. 204, 209.
79. Arnstein agrees with Chadwick on this in Malmgren, *Lives of English Women*, p. 103.
80. AT, *Framley*, pp. 3, 13.
81. Heeney, *Different Kind of Gentleman*, p. 87.
82. Anonymous, '*Rachel Ray*', *Saturday Review* (1863), pp. 554–5.
83. AT, *Ray*, pp. 7, 123, 305, 7, 328.
84. Rosman, *Evangelicals*, p. 86.
85. Oliphant, *Rector and The Doctor's Family*, pp. 144, 6; *Perpetual Curate*, passim.
86. AT, *Warden*, p. 94.
87. AT, *Mackenzie*, p. 200.
88. AT, *Bullhampton*, p. 266.
89. C. Dickens, *Bleak House* (London, 1996), p. 123.
90. H. Alford, 'Mr Anthony Trollope and the English Clergy', *Contemporary Review* (1866), p. 262.

Chapter 5 The Church, Politics and Social Reform

1. T. H. S. Escott, *England: Its People*, p. 9.
2. R. Polhemus, *The Changing World of Anthony Trollope* (London, 1968), p. 124.
3. According to Kincaid, Trollope's clergymen were intended as 'a spiritual guide'. J. Kincaid, *The Novels of Anthony Trollope* (Oxford, 1977), p. 96.
4. D. Southgate, *The Passing of the Whigs 1832–1886* (London, 1962), pp. 77–8.
5. W. L. Burn, 'Anthony Trollope's Politics', *Nineteenth Century and After*, CXLIII (1948), p. 163.
6. AT, *Autobiography*, p. 291.
7. Mullen, *Trollope*, p. 477.
8. In Mullen with Munson, *Penguin Companion to Trollope*, p. 402.
9. G. Butte, 'Trollope and Politics', in Terry, *Oxford Reader's Companion to Trollope*, p. 436.
10. Mullen with Munson, *Penguin Companion to Trollope*, p. 402; Butte, 'Trollope and Politics', p. 435.

11. Both Peel and Gladstone attended Christ Church, Oxford, but Peel detested the Oxford Movement and advised Gladstone that his career would be wrecked by pursuing strong high church interests. *DNB*, XXII Supplement (1973), p. 707.
12. P. D. Edwards, 'Trollope to Gladstone: An Unpublished Letter', *Notes and Queries* (1968), May, pp. 184–5.
13. Skilton assumes that Gladstonopolis is named after the intended state capital of Queensland, Gladstone, visited by Trollope on his 1871 Australian trip. AT, *The Fixed Period* (Oxford, 1993), pp. 10, 183n.
14. Mullen, *Trollope*, p. 477.
15. Southgate, *Passing of the Whigs*, p. 88.
16. T. H. S. Escott, *Anthony Trollope: His Work, Associates and Literary Originals* (London, 1913), p. 291.
17. R. D. McMaster, *Trollope and the Law* (New York, 1986), p. 10.
18. Olney, *Lincolnshire Politics*, p. 22n.
19. R. Arnold, *The Whiston Matter* (London, 1961), p. 9.
20. Ibid., p. 31.
21. Halperin, *Trollope and Politics*, p. 220.
22. Escott, *Trollope: His Work*, p. 143.
23. D. Hawes, 'Was Trollope a Freemason?', *Trollopiana* (1999), pp. 14–22. For Hawes, this is evidence of Trollope's radicalism. Handley also alludes to Trollope's radicalism. G. Handley, *Anthony Trollope* (Stroud, 1999), p. 91.
24. Hall, *Letters AT*, I, p. 394.
25. Ibid., I, pp. 396–7, 453.
26. Ibid., I, p. 447, II, p. 587.
27. F. F. Jillson, 'The 'Professional' Clergyman in Some Novels by Anthony Trollope', *Hartford Studies in Literature*, I (1969–70), p. 194; D. J. Kenney, 'Anthony Trollope's Theology', *American Notes and Queries*, IX (1970–1), pp. 51–4.
28. D. Cecil, *Early Victorian Novelists* ([1934] London, 1963), p. 253.
29. E. R. Norman, *Church and Society in England 1770–1970: A Historical Study* (Oxford, 1976), p. 167.
30. Sir Charles Trevelyan, Sir Stafford Northcote and the Rev. Benjamin Jowett wrote the report.
31. For Jowett, see Annan, *Dons*, pp. 61–78.
32. AT, 'The Civil Service', *Dublin University Magazine* [October 1855], in Mason, *Trollope: Miscellaneous*, p. 410.
33. Trollope depicted Northcote as Sir Warwick Westend, Trevelyan as Sir Gregory Hardlines, and Jowett as Mr Jobbles. Mullen with Munson, *Penguin Companion to Trollope*, p. 491.
34. AT, *Clerks*, pp. 125, 129–31.
35. G. I. T. Machin, *Politics and the Churches in Great Britain 1832 to 1868* (Oxford, 1977), title page.
36. 'The Church and Her Relations to Political Parties', *Quarterly*, CXVIII (1865), p. 213.
37. Norman, *Church and Society*, p. 167.
38. 'The Church and Her Relations to Political Parties', p. 193.
39. J. Kucich, 'Transgression in Trollope: Dishonesty and the Antibourgeois Elite', *ELH*, LVI (1989), p. 599.

40. AT, *Towers*, I, p. 10.
41. Kucich, 'Transgression', p. 600.
42. F. E. Robbins, 'Chronology and History in Trollope's Barset and Parliamentary Novels', *Nineteenth-Century Fiction* (1951), pp. 310–11.
43. AT, *Towers*, I, p. 7.
44. AT, *The West Indies and the Spanish Main* (London, 1860), p. 282.
45. E. Jaggard, 'A Meddlesome Man: The Reverend Thomas Peter Gurney of St Allen, 1763–1848', *Social Science Forum*, IV (1988), pp. 17–27.
46. Ibid., p. 26.
47. 'The Church and Her Curates', *Quarterly*, XXIII (1867), p. 124.
48. *Beverley Recorder*, 14 November 1868, in L. O. Tingay, 'Trollope and the Beverley Election', *Nineteenth-Century Fiction*, V (1950–1), p. 28.
49. *Beverley Recorder*, 14 November 1868, in Halperin, *Trollope and Politics*, p. 116.
50. Tingay, 'Trollope and Beverley Election', p. 28.
51. AT, *Ralph*, I, pp. 234, 239–40, 244, 247, II, p. 286.
52. AT, *The Duke's Children* (Oxford, 1992), p. 437.
53. Cambridge Sermon, in Norman, *Church and Society*, p. 117.
54. AT, *Towers*, I, p. 191, II, pp. 78–9.
55. AT, *Richmond*, p. 395.
56. Hall, *Letters AT*, II, p. 778, I, p. 491.
57. Norman, *Church and Society*, p. 217.
58. In Norman, *Church and Society*, p. 217.
59. F. G. Blair, 'Trollope on Education: An Unpublished Address' [1873], in *The Trollopian*, I (1947), pp. 1–9, 6.
60. Blair, 'Trollope on Education', p. 3.
61. AT, in 'Trollope on Education', pp. 8–9, 7.
62. AT, 'Public Schools', in *Fortnightly* (1865), pp. 476–87.
63. Mullen, *Trollope*, p. 542.
64. AT, *How the 'Mastiffs' Went to Iceland* ([1878] New York, 1981), p. 22.
65. AT, *Clerks*, p. 534.
66. Halperin, in AT, *Belton*, p. 436n; Handley, in AT, *Clerks*, p. 611n.
67. AT, *Belton*, pp. 98, 92, 100.
68. Mr Askerton ultimately married Clara's friend. AT, *Belton*, pp. 209–10, 234.
69. Norman, *Church and Society*, p. 211.
70. St Matthew's Gospel, V, v. 31–2.
71. AT, *Right*, pp. 257, 132, 131, 208–9.
72. Norman, *Church and Society*, p. 211.
73. In Machin, *Politics and the Churches*, p. 288.
74. AT, *Wortle's*, pp. 98, 116.
75. AT, *Dark*, pp. 57, 111, 117, 23, 179–80, 126, 143, 216, 219–20.
76. Neville-Sington, *Fanny Trollope*, passim.
77. AT, *Belton*, p. 285.
78. AT, *Bertrams*, pp. 357, 382–3, 557.
79. Skilton, in AT, *The Fixed Period* (Oxford, 1993), p. xii.
80. *Fixed* was written two years before it was published. AT, *Fixed*, pp. 5, 7–9, 86, 184n, 164, 153.
81. Oliphant, *Phoebe Junior*, pp. 263–4.
82. E. Gaskell, *Ruth* (London, 1997), p. 372.

83. AT, *Bullhampton*, p. 527.
84. Marsh, *Victorian Church*, p. 281.
85. Mullen, *Trollope*, p. 77.
86. Hall, *Letters AT*, I, pp. 212, 399 and *passim*.
87. For Mullen, *La Vendée* (1850) demonstrates Trollope's sympathy towards Roman Catholicism, but this conflates Trollope's support for the monarchy with respect for French monarchists, who were mainly Roman Catholic. Trollope's faith was too strong to favour non-Christians over Christians. Mullen, *Trollope*, p. 218; AT, *Vendée*, I, pp. 210–15, III, p. 967.
88. AT, *The Macdermots of Ballycloran* ([1847] Oxford, 1989) (Intro. R. Tracy), pp. 199, 246.
89. R. Tracy, *Macdermots* (Oxford, 1989), pp. xvii–xviii.
90. AT, *Kellys*, pp. 494, 488.
91. AT, *Richmond*, p. 129.
92. AT, *Warden*, p. 94.
93. Chadwick, *Victorian Church*, I, p. 24.
94. Hall, *Letters AT*, I, p. 25.
95. AT, *The New Zealander* (London, 1995), pp. 90, 97, 104.
96. Its delayed publication in the twentieth century was perhaps because it was regarded as obscure.
97. E. Gaskell, *Wives and Daughters* (London, 1996), p. 304.
98. Oliphant, *Perpetual Curate*, I, p. 275, II, p. 181, I, p. 260.
99. Hall, *Trollope*, p. 119.
100. McCord, *British History*, p. 172.
101. AT, *Redux* II, p. 281. The murderer was in fact an Anglican clergyman of Jewish birth.
102. M. Bentley, *Politics Without Democracy* (Oxford, 1984), p. 67.
103. AT, *The Prime Minister* (Oxford, 1991), I, p. 30.
104. AT, *Popenjoy?*, I, p. 111.
105. AT, *Fixed*, p. 37.
106. AT, *North America* (Gloucester, 1987), I, p. 74.
107. AT, *Australia* (Gloucester, 1987), II, p. 109.
108. AT, *Linda Tressel* (Oxford, 1991), pp. 354, 381.
109. AT, *The Golden Lion of Granpère* (Oxford, 1993), pp. 193, 198, 245.
110. AT, *Live Now*, II, p. 52.
111. Hall, *Letters AT*, II, p. 645.
112. AT, *Macdermots*, p. 241.
113. AT, *An Eye for An Eye* (Oxford, 1992).
114. M. Hamer, in AT, *Landleaguers* (Oxford, 1993), p. xi.
115. Ibid., pp. 3, 23.
116. Mullen, *Trollope*, pp. 264–5.
117. AT, 'The Irish Church Debate', *Saint Pauls Magazine* (1868), p. 159.
118. AT, *Kellys*, pp. 265, 443.
119. AT, 'Irish Church Debate', p. 160.
120. McCord, *British History*, p. 164.
121. J. H. Stack, 'The Irish Church', *Saint Pauls Magazine* (1868), pp. 568–9, 575.
122. AT, *Macdermots*, pp. 40, 44, 680n, 643 (appendix).
123. AT, *Towers*, I, p. 19.
124. AT, *Richmond*, pp. 413–15.

125. AT, 'The Irish Church Bill in the Lords', *Saint Pauls Magazine* (1869), pp. 542, 545, 553–4.
126. AT, 'The New Cabinet, and What It will Do for Us' (1869), in Hall, *Writings for Saint Paul's*, p. 541.
127. AT, *Ralph*, I, p. 301, II, p. 378n.
128. AT, 'What Does Ireland Want?' (1869), in Hall, *Writings for Saint Paul's*, pp. 289–90.
129. AT, in Escott, *Trollope: His Work*, p. 250.
130. AT, *Landleaguers*, pp. 24–5.
131. AT, *Phineas Finn* (Oxford, 1991), I, p. 1.
132. AT, *Ralph*, I, p. 57.
133. AT, 'Irish Church Debate', p. 156.
134. AT, 'The Irish Beneficed Clergyman', *Pall Mall* (1866), and *Clergymen*, pp. 105–18, 117–18.
135. Southgate, *Passing of the Whigs*, p. 49.
136. Hall, *Letters AT*, I, p. 476.
137. Tingay, 'Trollope and Beverley Election', pp. 23–37; A. Pollard, *Trollope's Political Novels* (Hull, 1968); Halperin, *Trollope and Politics*.
138. apRoberts, *Trollope Artist and Moralist*, p. 98.
139. Burn, 'Trollope's Politics', p. 167.
140. J. Parry, *The Rise and Fall of the Liberal Government in Victorian Britain* (New Haven, 1993), p. 160.
141. Norman, *Church and Society*, p. 197; G. F. A. Best, 'The Whigs and the Church Establishment in the Age of Grey and Holland', *History*, XLV (1960), p. 112.
142. Arnold, *Whiston Matter*; Best, 'The Road to Hiram's Hospital', *Victorian Studies*, V (1961), pp. 136–47; Martin, *Early Victorian Scandals*; Jerome Meckier, 'The Cant of Reform: Trollope Rewrites Dickens in *The Warden*', *Studies in the Novel*, XV (1983), pp. 202–23.
143. Trollope misspells his name as Guildford, *Warden*, p. 11.
144. AT, *Towers*, II, p. 176.
145. Dewey, *Passing of Barchester*, p. 1.
146. F. Knight, *The Nineteenth-Century Church and English Society* (Cambridge, 1995), p. 201.
147. D. W. Lovegrove, *Established Church, Sectarian People: Itinerancy and the Transformation of English Dissent, 1780–1830* (Cambridge, 1988), p. 13.
148. AT, *North America*, II, pp. 195–6, 189.
149. A. Wright, *Anthony Trollope: Dream and Art* (Chicago, 1983), p. 35.
150. AT, *North America*, I, p. 427.
151. AT, *Towers*, I, p. 10.
152. AT, *Framley*, pp. 273–5.
153. R. W. Chapman, 'Personal Names in Trollope's Political Novels', in G. Cumberlege (ed.), *Essays Mainly on the Nineteenth Century: Presented to Sir Humphrey Milford* (London, 1948), p. 75.
154. S. Gill, in AT, *Barset*, p. 894n.
155. Ibid., p. 220.
156. AT, *Ray*, p. 235.
157. Best, *Temporal Pillars*, p. 242.
158. AT, *Clergymen*, pp. 51, 7.

159. H. Alford, 'Trollope and the English Clergy', p. 245.
160. Norman, *Church and Society*, p. 189.
161. Ibid.
162. AT, *Clergymen*, p. 24.
163. B. Willey, 'Darwin and Clerical Orthodoxy', in P. Appleman, W. A. Madden and M. Wolf (eds), *Entering an Age of Crisis* (Bloomington, 1959), p. 60.
164. Hall, *Letters AT*, I, p. 491.
165. Temple was Bishop of Exeter (1869–85), Bishop of London (1885–96), and Archbishop of Canterbury (1896–1902).
166. C. A. Craig, 'Victims and Spokesmen: The Image of Society in the Novel', in Appleman, Madden and Wolf, *Entering an Age*, pp. 231–2.
167. J. Halperin, 'Trollope's Conservatism', *South Atlantic Quarterly*, LXXXII (1983), pp. 56–78.
168. Escott, *Trollope: His Work*, p. 177.
169. Burn, 'Trollope's Politics', p. 165.
170. Mullen, *Trollope*, pp. 11, 131.
171. P. A. Welsby, 'Anthony Trollope and the Church of England', *Church Quarterly Review*, CLXIII (1962), p. 218.
172. Cockshut, *Trollope: Critical Study*, p. 90; Nardin, *Trollope and Moral Philosophy*, pp. 1–16.
173. Kincaid, *Novels of Anthony Trollope*, pp. 96–7.
174. AT, *Autobiography*, pp. 189–90.
175. Welsby, 'Trollope and the Church of England', p. 218.
176. AT, *Life of Cicero* (London, 1880), II, pp. 392–404, 392.
177. Norman, *Church and Society*, p. 218.
178. AT, *Lord Palmerston* (London, 1882), p. 83.
179. Halperin, *Trollope and Politics*, p. 168.
180. J. R. Vincent, *The Formation of the British Liberal Party 1857–1868* (Sussex, 1976), p. 125.
181. HAM 6/95/131, 23 April 1868.
182. Norman, *Church and Society*, p. 219.
183. R. Lowe, in A. Briggs, 'Trollope, Bagehot and the English Constitution', *Cambridge Journal*, V (1951–2), p. 332n.
184. Father and son both became Archbishop of Canterbury.
185. Lord Denning, *The Influence of Religion on Law* (London, 1989), pp. 27–8.

Conclusion

1. AT, *Thackeray* ([1879] London, 1997), p. 109.
2. Mullen with Munson, *Penguin Companion to Trollope*, pp. 89–90.
3. AT, *Ralph*, I, pp. 175–6.
4. AT, *Orley*, II, pp. 203–4, 355–6, 233, 304, 405.
5. AT, *Cousin Henry* ([1879] Oxford, 1987), pp. 69, 148, 144, 174, 229, 232, 197.
6. Mullen, *Trollope*, p. 253.
7. AT, *Bertrams*, pp. 222, 220, 81, 140, 123, 329.
8. AT, 'A Ride Across Palestine', in *Trollope: Collected Shorter Fiction*, p. 169.
9. AT, *Bertrams*, pp. 218–22, 233, 235, 581.

Notes

10. AT, *Fixed*, pp. 6 (Psalm 90, v. 10), 38 (*passim*, Old Testament), 19, 129.
11. AT, 'Not If I Know It', in *Trollope: Collected Shorter Fiction*, p. 957.
12. AT, *West Indies*, p. 135.
13. AT, *North America*, I, p. 427.
14. AT, 'Harriet Parr's *The Life and Death of Jeanne D'Arc*, Review, in *Fortnightly*, 15 June (1866), in Mason, *Trollope: Miscellaneous*, n. p.
15. AT, 'Cicero as a Man of Letters', in *Fortnightly* (1877), in Mason, *Trollope: Miscellaneous*, p. 419.
16. AT, 'On Sovereignty', in Hall, *Writings for Saint Pauls Magazine*, pp. 76, 87.
17. AT, *'Mastiffs'*, pp. 2, 9, 16, 19.
18. G. Handley, *Trollope the Traveller: Selections from Anthony Trollope's Travel Writings* (London, 1993), p. xxxiii.
19. AT, 'Novel-Reading', *Nineteenth-Century*, V, January (1879), p. 25.
20. AT, 'Mrs Sewell's *The Rose of Cheriton*', Review, in *Fortnightly*, June 1 (1867), p. 253.
21. AT, *West Indies*, pp. 77, 86.

Bibliography

Primary sources

Pusey House, Oxford:
HAM6: Henry Parry Liddon Correspondence, 1840–1868
Wiltshire County Record Office, Trowbridge:
632/143–145: W. K. Hamilton Correspondence, 1861–1864
1900/267: Sermon by Rev. Peter Hall, 1833
D1/27/5/1: Bishop Denison's Correspondence, 1837
Personal correspondence:
1994 Personal correspondence with Hugh Trollope

Printed primary sources

Hansard

Journals
Pall Mall Gazette, 1866–1867
Quarterly Review, 1853–1872

Letters, diaries, personal journals

Ayres, J. (ed.) *Paupers and Pig Killers: The Diary of William Holland A Somerset Parson 1799–1818* (Gloucester: Alan Sutton, 1984).
Harris, M. and Johnston, J. (eds) *The Journals of George Eliot* (Cambridge: Cambridge University Press, 1998).
Smith, C. N. (ed.) *The Letters of Sydney Smith*, Vol. 1 (Oxford: Clarendon Press, 1953).
Verey, D. (ed.) *The Diary of a Cotswold Parson* (Gloucester: Alan Sutton, 1978).
Wells, R. (ed.) *Victorian Village: The Diaries of the Reverend John Coker Egerton of Burwash 1857–1888* (Gloucester: Alan Sutton, 1992).

Collected writings of Anthony Trollope

Hall, N. J. (ed.) *Writings for Saint Paul's Magazine* (New York: Arno Press, 1981).
——. *The Letters of Anthony Trollope*, 2 vols (Stanford, CA: Stanford University Press, 1983).
Handley, G. (ed.) *Trollope the Traveller: Selections from Anthony Trollope's Travel Writing* (London: William Pickering, 1993).
Mason, M. Y. (ed.) *Trollope Miscellaneous Essays and Reviews* (New York: Arno Press, 1981).
Terry, R. C. (ed.) *Trollope: Interviews and Recollections* (London: Macmillan Press, 1987).
Thompson, J. (ed.) *Anthony Trollope The Collected Shorter Fiction* (London: Robinson Publishing, 1992).

Other contemporary sources

Alford, H. 'Mr Anthony Trollope and the English Clergy', *Contemporary Review*, June (1866) 240–62.
Anonymous. 'Mr Trollope's Novels', *National Review*, VII (1858) 422.
Anonymous. '*Rachel Ray*', *Saturday Review*, 24 October (1863) 554–5.
Blair, F. G. 'Trollope on Education: An Unpublished Address', *The Trollopian*, I, no. 4 ([1873] 1947) 1–9.
Bowles, W. L. *The Patronage of the English Bishops* (Bristol: Gutch & Martin, 1836).
Burke, E. *Reflections on the Revolution in France* (London: Dent, [1790, 1792] 1964).
Collins, W. L. 'Autobiography of Anthony Trollope', *Blackwood's Magazine*, 134 (1883) 577–90.
Grimthorpe, Lord. 'Church Patronage', *Quarterly Review*, no. 164 (1887) 167–92.
Hutton, R. H. *Essays, Theological and Literary* I (London: Strahan & Co., 1871).
Jameson, A. *Sisters of Charity, Catholic and Protestant, Abroad and at Home* (London: Ongman, Brown, Green & Longmans, 1855).
Jervis, W. G. *The Poor Condition of the Clergy and the Causes Considered with Suggestions for Remedying the Same* (London: Thomas Hatchard, 1856).
Maclean, D. 'The Church as a Profession', *The National Review*, VI, no. 33, August (1899) 945–55.
Noel, T. 'Rhymes and Roundelays: the pauper's drive', in E. M. Sigsworth (ed.) ([1841] 1988) 56.
O'Hanlon, W. 'Our Medical Charities and their Abuses', *Transactions of the Manchester Statistical Society*, III, 12 February (1872–3) 41–69.
Phelps, L. R. 'The Use and Abuse of Endowed Charities', *Economic Review*, II (1892) 88–104.
Smiles, S. *Self-Help* (Harmondsworth: Penguin Books, [1856] 1986).
Stack, J. H. 'The Irish Church', *Saint Pauls Magazine*, February (1868) 564–77.
Stanley, M. *Hospitals and Sisterhoods* (London, 1854).
Stoughton, J. *Religion in England from 1800 to 1850*, 2 vols (London: Hodder & Stoughton, 1884).
Sumner, C. R. *Charge to the Diocese of Winchester: 9th Visitation* (London: Hatchard, 1862).
Trollope, E. *The Family of Trollope* (Lincoln: James Williamson, 1875).
Trollope, M. N. *A Memoir of the Family of Trollope* (London: Spottiswoode & Co., 1897).
Wade, J. *The Extraordinary Black Book: An exposition of abuses in church and state* (New York: Augustus M. Kelly, [1832] 1970).

Trollope's writings

The Macdermots of Ballycloran ([1847] Oxford: Oxford University Press, 1989) Intro. R. Tracy.
The Kellys and the O'Kellys ([1848] Oxford: Oxford University Press, 1992).
La Vendée ([1850] London: Penguin, 1993).
'Merivale's History of the Romans', Review of Charles Merivale's *The History of the Romans under the Empire*, I and II, *Dublin University Magazine*, May, in Mason (ed.) ([1851] 1981) 611–24.

The Warden ([1855] Oxford: Oxford University Press, 1980).
'The Civil Service', *Dublin University Magazine*, October, in Mason (ed.) ([1855] 1981) 409–23.
'Merivale's History of the Romans', Review of III, IV and V, *Dublin University Magazine*, July, in Mason (ed.) ([1856] 1981) 30–47.
Barchester Towers ([1857] Oxford: Oxford University Press, 1991).
The Three Clerks ([1858] Oxford: Oxford University Press, 1989).
Doctor Thorne ([1858] Oxford: Oxford University Press, 1991).
The Bertrams ([1859] Oxford: Oxford University Press, 1991).
The West Indies and the Spanish Main ([1859] London: Frank Cass, 1968).
Castle Richmond ([1860] Oxford: Oxford University Press, 1992).
Framley Parsonage ([1861] Oxford: Oxford University Press, 1980) (Intro. P. D. Edwards).
Framley Parsonage ([1861] Oxford: Oxford University Press, 1991).
'The Civil Service as a Profession', *Cornhill Magazine*, February, in Mason (ed.) ([1861] 1981) 214–28.
Orley Farm ([1862] Oxford Oxford University Press, 1985).
North America, I ([1862] Gloucester: Alan Sutton, 1987).
North America, II ([1862] London: Granville Publishing, 1986).
Rachel Ray ([1863] Oxford: Oxford University Press, 1990).
The Small House at Allington ([1864] Oxford: Oxford University Press, 1991).
'The Sisterhood Question in the High Church', *Pall Mall Gazette*, 11 September (1865) 363.
'Public Schools', *Fortnightly Review*, II, 1 October (1865) 476–87.
'The Zulu in London', *Pall Mall Gazette*, 10 May (1865) 3–4.
Miss Mackenzie ([1865] Oxford: Oxford University Press, 1991).
Hunting Sketches ([1865] London: Trollope Society, 1996).
The Belton Estate ([1865] Oxford: Oxford University Press, 1991).
'The Fourth Commandment', *Fortnightly Review*, no. 3, 15 January (1866), in Mason (ed.) (1981) 529–38.
'Mr Anthony Trollope and the "Saturday Review"', *Pall Mall Gazette*, 5 February (1866) 395.
Clergymen of the Church of England ([1866] Leicester: Leicester University Press, 1974) (Intro. R. apRoberts).
Clergymen of the Church of England ([1866] London: Trollope Society, n. d.).
'Bazaars for Charity', *Pall Mall Gazette*, no. 21, April (1866) 12.
'Curates' Incomes', *Pall Mall Gazette*, 24 July (1866) 251–2.
'Harriet Parr's *The Life and Death of Jeanne D'Arc*', Review, *Fortnightly Review*, 15 October, in Mason (ed.) ([1866] 1981) no page nos.
Nina Balatka and Linda Tressel ([1867] [1868] Oxford: Oxford University Press, 1991).
The Claverings ([1867] Oxford: Oxford University Press, 1991).
The Last Chronicle of Barset ([1867] Oxford: Oxford University Press, 1991).
'Mrs Sewell's *The Rose of Cheriton*', Review, *Fortnightly Review*, 1 February, in Mason (ed.) ([1867] 1981) no page nos.
'On Sovereignty', October, in Hall (ed.) ([1867] 1981) 76–91.
'About Hunting', November in Hall (ed.) ([1867] 1981) 206–19.
'Whom Shall We Make Leader of the New House of Commons?', February, in Hall (ed.) ([1868] 1981) 531–45.

'About Hunting', Part 2, March, in Hall (ed.) ([1868] 1981) 675–90.
'The Irish Church Debate', *Saint Pauls Magazine*, 2 May (1868) 147–60.
'Higher Education of Women', in M. L. Parrish (ed.) *Four Lectures* ([1868] London: Constable & Co., 1938) 65–88.
'The New Cabinet, and What It Will Do For Us', February, in Hall (ed.) ([1869] 1981) 538–51.
'The Irish Church Bill in the Lords', *Saint Pauls Magazine*, 4 August (1869) 540–4.
Phineas Finn ([1869] Oxford: Oxford University Press, 1991).
He Knew He Was Right ([1869] Oxford: Oxford University Press, 1992).
'What Does Ireland Want?', December, in Hall (ed.) ([1869] 1981) 286–301.
Review of *Phineas Finn*, *Saturday Review*, 27 March, in D. Skilton (ed.) ([1869] 1972) 431–2.
The Vicar of Bullhampton ([1870] Oxford: Oxford University Press, 1990).
Sir Harry Hotspur of Humblethwaite ([1871] Oxford: Oxford University Press, 1991).
Ralph the Heir ([1871] Oxford: Oxford University Press, 1990).
The Golden Lion of Granpère ([1872] Oxford: Oxford University Press, 1993).
The Eustace Diamonds ([1873] Oxford: Oxford University Press, 1992).
Australia and New Zealand, 2 vols ([1873] London: Dawsons of Pall Mall, 1968).
Australia, 2 vols ([1873] Gloucester: Alan Sutton, 1987).
Phineas Redux ([1874] Oxford: Oxford University Press, 1992).
Lady Anna ([1874] Oxford: Oxford University Press, 1991).
The Way We Live Now ([1875] Oxford: Oxford University Press, 1992).
The Prime Minister ([1876] Oxford: Oxford University Press, 1991).
'Cicero as a Man of Letters', *Fortnightly Review*, 1 September, in Mason (ed.) ([1877] 1981) 401–22.
The American Senator ([1877] Oxford: Oxford University Press, 1986).
South Africa, 2 vols ([1878] London: Dawsons of Pall Mall, 1968).
Is He Popenjoy? ([1878] Oxford: Oxford University Press, 1991).
How the 'Mastiffs' Went to Iceland ([1878] New York: Arno Press, 1981).
'Iceland', *Fortnightly Review*, XXIV, 1 August, in Mason (ed.) ([1878] 1981) 175–90.
An Eye for An Eye ([1879] Oxford: Oxford University Press, 1992).
Thackeray ([1879] London: Trollope Society, 1997).
John Caldigate ([1879] Oxford: Oxford University Press, 1993).
Cousin Henry ([1879] Oxford: Oxford University Press, 1987).
'Novel-Reading', *Nineteenth-Century*, V (1879) 24–43.
The Duke's Children ([1880] Oxford: Oxford University Press, 1992).
Life of Cicero, 2 vols (London: Chapman & Hall, 1880).
Dr Wortle's School ([1880] Oxford: Oxford University Press, 1991).
Ayala's Angel ([1881] Oxford: Oxford University Press, 1992).
The Fixed Period ([1882] Oxford: Oxford University Press, 1993).
Marion Fay ([1882] Oxford: Oxford University Press, 1992).
Lord Palmerston (London: Isbister Ltd, 1882).
Kept in the Dark ([1882] Oxford: Oxford University Press, 1992).
Mr Scarborough's Family ([1883] Oxford: Oxford University Press, 1991).
The Landleaguers ([1883] Oxford: Oxford University Press, 1993).
An Autobiography ([1883] Oxford: Oxford University Press, 1980).
An Old Man's Love ([1884] Oxford: Oxford University Press, 1992).
The New Zealander ([1972] London: Trollope Society, 1995).

Other contemporary novels

Dickens, C. *Martin Chuzzlewit* ([1844] Liverpool: Bunneys Ltd, n. d.).
——. *Bleak House* ([1853] London: Penguin, 1996).
Edgeworth, M. *Patronage* ([1813] London: Pandora Press and Routledge & Kegan Paul, 1986).
Eliot, G. *Scenes of Clerical Life* ([1858] Harmondsworth: Penguin, 1973).
——. *Adam Bede* ([1859] New York: Airmont Publishing, 1966).
——. *Middlemarch* ([1872] New York & London: W. W. Norton, 1977).
Gaskell, E. *Ruth* ([1853] London: Penguin, 1997).
——. *North and South* ([1854-5] London: Penguin, 1970).
——. *Sylvia's Lovers* ([1863] London: Penguin, 1996).
——. *Cranford/Cousin Phillis* ([1863-4] London: Penguin, 1976).
——. *Wives and Daughters* ([1864-6] London: Penguin, 1996).
——. 'A Parson's Holiday', Five Pieces in *Pall Mall Gazette*, 11, 17, 21 August, 5 September (1865) 12.
Oliphant, M. *The Rector and the Doctor's Family* ([1863] London: Virago Press, 1986).
——. *The Perpetual Curate*, 3 vols ([1864] New York & London: Garland, 1975).
——. *The Curate in Charge* ([1876] Gloucester: Alan Sutton, 1987).
——. *Phoebe Junior* ([1876] London: Virago Press, 1989).
——. *A Son of the Soil* (London: Macmillan, 1883).
Tilley, C. *Chollerton: A Tale of Our Own Times* By A Lady (London: John Ollivier, 1846).
Trollope, F. *The Vicar of Wrexhill* ([1837] New York: Garland, 1975).

Reference works

Burke's Peerage and Baronetage (1965).
Crockfords (London: Horace Cox, 1858-1882).
Debrett's Illustrated Baronetage (1939).
Debrett's Illustrated Baronetage (1990).
Dictionary of National Biography.
Fasti Ecclesiae Anglicanae 1541-1857, J. le Neve, III-VII (London: Athlone Press, 1971).
Novum Repertorium Ecclesiasticum Parochiale LONDINENSE or London Diocesan Clergy Succession From the Earliest Time to the Year 1898, Comp. Rev. George Hennessy (London: Swan Sonnenschein & Co., 1898).

Secondary sources

Allchin, A. M. *The Silent Rebellion: Anglican Religious Communities 1845-1900* (London: SCM Press, 1958).
Allott, M. *Novelists on the Novel* (Columbia: Columbia University Press, 1966).
Annan, N. *The Dons: Mentors, Eccentrics and Genuises* (London: HarperCollins, 1999).
Appleman, P., Madden, W. A. and Wolf, M. (eds) *Entering An Age of Crisis* (Bloomington: Indiana University Press, 1959).

apRoberts, R. *Trollope Artist and Moralist* (London: Chatto & Windus, 1971).
Arnold, R. *The Whiston Matter* (London: Rupert Hart-Davis, 1961).
Arnstein, W. 'Queen Victoria', in Malmgren (1986) 88–128.
Bahlman, D. W. R. 'The Queen, Mr Gladstone and Church Patronage', *Victorian Studies*, III (1960) 349–81.
Baker, J. E. *The Novel and the Oxford Movement* (Princeton, NJ: Princeton University Press, 1932).
Bareham, T. (ed.) *Anthony Trollope* (London: Vision, 1980).
Barrett, P. *Barchester: English Cathedral Life in the Nineteenth Century* (London: SPCK, 1993).
Bentley, M. *Politics Without Democracy* (Oxford: Basil Blackwell, 1984).
Best, G. F. A. 'The Whigs and the Church Establishment in the Age of Grey and Holland', *History*, XLV (1960) 103–18.
——. 'The Road to Hiram's Hospital', *Victorian Studies*, V (1961) 136–47.
——. *Temporal Pillars: Queen Anne's Bounty, the Ecclestiastical Commissioners, and the Church of England* (Cambridge: Cambridge University Press, 1964).
Bloom, H. (ed.) *Modern Critical Interpretations: Anthony Trollope's Barchester Towers and The Warden* (New York: Chelsea House, 1988).
Booth, B. *Anthony Trollope: Aspects of his Life and Work* (London: Edward Hutton, 1958).
Bourne, J. M. *Patronage and Society in Nineteenth-Century England* (London: Edward Arnold, 1986).
Bradley, I. *The Call to Seriousness* (London: Jonathan Cape, 1976).
Briggs, A. 'Trollope, Bagehot and the English Constitution', *Cambridge Journal*, V (1951–2) 327–38.
Burn, W. L. 'Anthony Trollope's Politics', *Nineteenth Century and After*, no. 143 (1948) 161–71.
Carter, H. G. and Crawshaw, F. M. *Tudor on Charities: A Practical Treatise on the Law Relating to Gifts and Trusts for Charitable Purposes*, 5th edn (London: Sweet & Maxwell, 1929).
Casteras, S. P. 'Virgin Vows: The Early Victorian Portrayal of Nuns and Novices', in Malmgren (1986) 129–60.
Cecil, Lord D. *Early Victorian Novelists* ([1934] London: Constable, 1963).
Chadwick, O. *The Mind of the Oxford Movement* (London: Adam & Charles Black, 1960).
——. *The Victorian Church Part 1: 1829–1859* (London: SCM Press, 1971).
——. *The Victorian Church Part 2: 1860–1901* (London: SCM Press Ltd, 1972).
Chadwick, W. E. *The Church, the State, and the Poor: A Series of Historical Sketches* (London: Robert Scott, 1914).
Chandler, A. 'Faith in the Nation? The Church of England in the 20th Century', *History Today*, XLVII, no. 5 (1997) 9–15.
Chapman, R. W. 'Personal Names in Trollope's Political Novels', in G. Cumberlege (ed.), *Essays Mainly on the Nineteenth Century: Presented to Sir Humphrey Milford* (London: Oxford University Press, 1948) 72–81.
Clark, J. W. *The Language and Style of Anthony Trollope* (London: André Deutsch, 1975).
Cockshut, A. O. J. *Anthony Trollope: A Critical Study* (London: Collins, 1955).
——. 'Trollope's Liberalism', in Bareham (1980) 161–81.

Coleman, B. *Conservatism and the Conservative Party in Nineteenth-Century Britain* (London: Edward Arnold, 1988).
Collins, I. *Jane Austen and the Clergy* (London: Hambledon Press, 1993).
Craig, G. A. 'Victims and Spokesmen: The Image of Society in the Novel', in P. Appleman et al. (1959) 229–46.
Crowther, M. A. *Church Embattled* (Newton Abbot: David & Charles, 1970).
Davidoff, L. and Hall, C. *Family Fortunes: Men and Women of the English Middle Class, 1780–1850* (Chicago: University of Chicago Press, 1987).
Denning, Lord. *The Influence of Religion on Law* (London: Lawyers' Christian Fellowship, 1989).
Dewey, C. *The Passing of Barchester* (London: Hambledon Press, 1991).
Durey, J. 'In the Spirit of Truth: Anthony Trollope's Ecclesiastical Ancestors and Relatives', *Family History*, XVII, no. 143 (1995) 259–94.
——. 'Church and Family', *Genealogists' Magazine*, XXV no. 11 (1997) 441–50.
Edwards, P. D. 'Trollope to Gladstone: An Unpublished Letter', *Notes and Queries*, May (1968) 184–5.
——. *Anthony Trollope: His Art and Scope* (London: Oxford University Press, 1977).
Escott, T. H. S. *England: Its People, Polity, and Pursuits* (London: Chapman & Hall, 1890).
——. *Anthony Trollope: His Work, Associates and Literary Originals* (London: John Lane, 1913).
Foster, C. I. *An Errand of Mercy: The Evangelical United Front 1790–1837* (Chapel Hill: University of North Carolina Press, 1960).
Fraser, D. (ed.) *The New Poor Law in the Nineteenth Century* (London: Macmillan, 1976).
Gibson, W. T. 'Disraeli's Church Patronage: 1868–1880', *Anglican Episcopal History* LXI (1992) 197–210.
Gilmour, R. 'The Challenge of Barchester Towers', in Bloom (1983) 141–56.
Gladstone, F. *Charity, Law and Social Justice* (London: Bedford Square Press, 1982).
Glendinning, V. *Trollope* (London: Pimlico, 1993).
Gray, B. K. *A History of English Philanthropy: From the Dissolution of the Monasteries to the Taking of the First Census* ([1905] London: Frank Cass, 1967).
Haig, A. *The Victorian Clergy* (London: Croom Helm, 1984).
Hall, N. J. *Trollope: A Biography* (Oxford: Clarendon Press, 1991).
Halperin, J. *Trollope and Politics: A Study of the Pallisers and Others* (London: Macmillan, 1977).
——. (ed.) *Trollope, Centenary Essays* (London: Macmillan – now Palgrave Macmillan, 1982).
——. 'Trollope's Conservatism', *South Atlantic Quarterly*, LXXXII (1983) 56–78.
Harrison, B. 'Philanthropy and the Victorians', *Victorian Studies*, IX (1966) 353–74.
Hawes, D. 'Was Trollope a Freemason?', *Trollopiana*, no. 47 November (1999) 14–22.
Hawthorne, J. et al. [1928] 'He Glowed, a Conversational Stove', in Terry (1987) 146–52.
Heeney, B. *A Different Kind of Gentleman: Parish Clergy as Professional Men in Early and Mid-Victorian England* (Ohio: Shoe String Press, 1976).
Hennessy, J. P. *Anthony Trollope* (London: Jonathan Cape, 1971).
Herbert, C. 'Barchester Towers and the Charms of Imperfection', in Bloom (1987) 157–63.

Hill, M. *The Religious Order: A Study of Virtuoso Religion and its Legitimation in the Nineteenth-Century Church of England* (London: Heinemann, 1973).
Hoch-Smith, J. and Spring, A. (eds) *Women in Ritual and Symbolic Roles* (New York and London: Plenum Press, 1978).
Hodgson, P. C. *Theology in the Fiction of George Eliot* (London: SCM Press, 2001).
Holcombe, L. *Victorian Ladies at Work: Middle-Class Women in England and Wales 1850–1914* (Newton Abbot: David & Charles, 1973).
Hole, R. *Pulpits, Politics and Public Order in England 1760–1832* (Cambridge: Cambridge University Press, 1989).
Humphreys, R. *Sin, Organised Charity and the Poor Law in Victorian England* (Basingstoke: Macmillan – now Palgrave Macmillan, 1995).
Hylson-Smith, K. *Evangelicals in the Church of England 1734–1984* (Edinburgh: T. & T. Clark, 1988).
——. *High Churchmanship in the Church of England: From the Sixteenth Century to the Twentieth Century* (Edinburgh: T. & T. Clark, 1993).
Jaggard, E. 'A Meddlesome Man: The Reverend Thomas Peter Gurney of St Allen, 1763–1848', *Social Science Forum*, IV, no. 2 (1988) 17–27.
Jay, E. *The Evangelical and Oxford Movements* (Cambridge: Cambridge University Press, 1983).
——. *Margaret Oliphant: A Fiction to Herself* (Oxford: Oxford University Press, 1995).
Jillson, F. F. 'The "Professional" Clergyman in Some Novels by Anthony Trollope'. *Hartford Studies in Literature*, I (1969–70) 185–97.
Jones, G. *History of the Law of Charity 1532–1827* (Cambridge: Cambridge University Press, 1969).
Keane, J. 'The Limits of Secularism: Does the Marginalizing of Religion Impose a New Intolerance?', *Times Literary Supplement*, no. 4945, 9 January (1998) 12–13.
Kenney, D. J. 'Anthony Trollope's Theology', *American Notes and Queries*, IX (1970–1) 51–4.
Ker, I. *John Henry Newman: A Biography* (Oxford: Oxford University Press, 1990).
Kincaid, J. 'Barchester Towers and the Nature of Conservative Comedy', *English Literary History*, XXXVII (1970) 595–612.
——. *The Novels of Anthony Trollope* (Oxford: Clarendon Press, 1977).
King, J. 'Watch Out, There's A Charity About', *Spectator*, XXVIII, October (2000) 30–1.
Kitson Clark, G. *Churchmen and the Condition of England 1832–1885* (London: Methuen, 1973).
Knight, F. *The Nineteenth-Century Church and English Society* (Cambridge: Cambridge University Press, 1995).
Kucich, J. 'Transgression in Trollope: Dishonesty and the Antibourgeois Elite', *English Literary History*, LVI, no. 3 (1989) 593–628.
Landow, G. *Victorian Types Victorian Shadows* (London: Routledge & Kegan Paul, 1980).
Lansbury, C. *The Reasonable Man: Trollope's Legal Fiction* (Princeton, NJ: Princeton University Press, 1981).
Letwin, S. R. *The Gentleman in Trollope: Individuality and Moral Conduct* (London: Macmillan – now Palgrave Macmillan, 1982).
Lovegrove, D. W. *Established Church, Sectarian People: Itinerancy and the Transfor-*

mation of English Dissent, 1780–1830 (Cambridge: Cambridge University Press, 1988).

McClatchey, D. *Oxfordshire Clergy 1777–1869: A Study of the Established Church and of the Role of Its Clergy in Local Society* (Oxford: Clarendon Press, 1960).

McCord, N. *British History 1815–1906* (Oxford: Oxford University Press, 1991).

——. 'The Poor Law and Philanthropy', in Fraser (1976) 87–110.

Machin, G. I. T. *Politics and the Churches in Great Britain 1832 to 1868* (Oxford: Clarendon Press, 1977).

McMaster, J. *Trollope's Palliser Novels: Theme and Pattern* (New York: Oxford University Press, 1978).

McMaster, R. D. 'Women in *The Way We Live Now*', *English Studies in Canada*, VII (1981) 68–80.

——. *Trollope and the Law* (New York: St. Martin's Press – now Palgrave Macmillan 1986).

Malmgren, G. (ed.) *Religion in the Lives of English Women, 1760–1930* (London: Croom Helm, 1986).

Markwick, M. *Trollope and Women* (London: Trollope Society, 1997).

Marsh, P. T. *The Victorian Church in Decline* (Pittsburgh: Routledge & Kegan Paul, 1969).

Martin, R. B. *Enter Rumour: Four Early Victorian Scandals* (London: Faber & Faber, 1962).

Massingberd, H. 'All Flats, Fogs and Fens', *Spectator*, VI, August (1994) 20–1.

Mathiesen, W. L. *English Church Reform 1815–1840* (London: Longmans, Green & Co., 1923).

Meckier, J. 'The Cant of Reform: Trollope Rewrites Dickens in *The Warden*', *Studies in the Novel*, XV, no. 3 (1983) 202–23.

Mermin, D. *Godiva's Ride: Women of Letters in England 1830–1880* (Bloomington and Indianapolis: Indiana University Press, 1993).

Merrett, R. J. 'Port and Claret: The Politics of Wine in Trollope's Barsetshire Novels', *Mozaic*, XXIV (1991) 107–25.

Mullen, R. *Anthony Trollope: A Victorian and his World* (Clwyd: Doyle & Associates, 1990).

Mullen, R. with Munson, J. (eds) *The Penguin Companion to Trollope* (London: Penguin, 1996).

Nardin, J. *He Knew She Was Right: The Independent Woman in the Novels of Anthony Trollope* (Carbondale: Southern Illinois University Press, 1989).

——. 'The Social Critic in Anthony Trollope's Novels', *Studies in English Literature*, V, no. 30 (1990) 679–96.

——. *Trollope and Victorian Moral Philosophy* (Athens: Ohio University Press, 1996).

Neville-Sington, P. *Fanny Trollope: The Life and Adventures of a Clever Woman* (London: Viking Press, 1998).

Newsome, D. *The Parting of Friends: A Study of the Wilberforces and Henry Newsome* (London: John Murray, 1966).

Nockles, P. B. *The Oxford Movement in Context: Anglican High Churchmanship 1760–1857* (Cambridge: Cambridge University Press, 1994).

Norman, E. R. *Church and Society in England 1770–1970: A Historical Study* (Oxford: Clarendon Press, 1976).

Olney, R. J. *Lincolnshire Politics 1832–1885* (London: Oxford University Press, 1973).

Owen, A. *The Darkened Room: Women, Power and Spiritualism in Late Nineteenth-Century England* (London: Virago Press, 1989).
Owen, D. *English Philanthropy 1660–1960* (Cambridge, MA: Belknap Press, 1964).
Parry, J. *The Rise and Fall of Liberal Government in Victorian Britain* (New Haven, CT: Yale University Press, 1993).
Perkin, J. *Women and Marriage in Nineteenth-Century England* (London: Routledge, 1989).
Petersen, J. *Family, Love, and Work in the Lives of Victorian Gentlewomen* (Bloomington and Indianapolis: Indiana University Press, 1989).
Polhemus, R. *The Changing World of Anthony Trollope* (London: Cambridge University Press, 1968).
Pollard, A. *Trollope's Political Novels: An Inaugural Lecture* (Hull: University of Hull Press, 1968).
——. *Anthony Trollope* (London: Routledge & Kegan Paul, 1978).
——. 'Trollope and the Evangelicals', *Nineteenth-Century Literature*, XXXVII, no. 3 (1982) 329–39.
——. 'Trollope's Idea of the Gentleman', in Halperin, (1982) 86–94.
Prince, D. 'The Truth about the Loss of Royalties', *Spectator*, XXVII, July (1996) 9–10.
Prochaska, F. K. *Women and Philanthropy in Nineteenth-Century England* (Oxford: Clarendon Press, 1980).
Ransom, T. *Fanny Trollope: A Remarkable Life* (Stroud: Alan Sutton, 1995).
Rathburn, R. and Steinman, M. Jr (eds) *From Jane Austen to Joseph Conrad: Essays Collected in Memory of James T. Hillhouse* (Minneapolis: University of Minneapolis Press, 1958).
Reardon, B. M. G. *Religious Thought in the Victorian Age* (London: Longman, 1995).
Robbins, F. E. 'Chronology and History in Trollope's Barset and Parliamentary Novels', *Nineteenth-Century Fiction*, March (1951) 303–17.
Roberts, D. *Victorian Origins of the British Welfare State* (New York: Archon Books, 1969).
——. *Paternalism in Early Victorian England* (London: Croom Helm, 1979).
Roberts, M. J. D. 'Private Patronage and the Church of England 1800–1900', *Journal of Ecclesiastical History*, XII, no. 2 (1981) 199–223.
Rosman, D. *Evangelicals and Culture* (London: Croom Helm, 1984).
Rubinstein, W. D. 'The End of "Old Corruption" in Britain 1780–1860', *Past and Present*, no. 101 (1983) 55–86.
Sheils, W. J. and Wood, D. (eds) *Women in the Church* (Oxford: Basil Blackwell, 1990).
Sigsworth, E. M. (ed.) *In Search of Victorian Values: Aspects of Nineteenth-Century Thought and Society* (Manchester: Manchester University Press, 1988).
Simpkinson, C. H. *The Life and Work of Bishop Thorold* (London: Isbister & Co., 1896).
Skilton, D. *Anthony Trollope and his Contemporaries: A Study in the Theory and Conventions of Mid-Victorian Fiction* (New York: St. Martin's Press, 1972).
Southgate, D. *The Passing of the Whigs 1832–1886* (London: Macmillan, 1962).
Summers, A. 'Pride and Prejudice: Ladies and Nurses in the Crimean War', *History Workshop: Journal of Socialist and Feminist Historians*, no. 16 (1983) 33–55.
Terry, R. C. (ed.) *Oxford Reader's Companion to Trollope* (Oxford: Oxford University Press, 1999).

Thormahlen, M. *The Brontës and Religion* (Cambridge: Cambridge University Press, 1999).
Tingay, L. O. 'Trollope and the Beverley Election', *Nineteenth-Century Fiction*, V (1950–1) 23–37.
Tompson, R. *The Charity Commission and the Age of Reform* (London: Routledge & Kegan Paul, 1979).
Tracy, R. *Trollope's Later Novels* (Berkeley: University of California Press, 1978).
Valenze, D. M. *Prophetic Sons and Daughters: Female Preaching and Popular Religion in Industrial England* (Princeton, NJ: Princeton University Press, 1985).
Vincent, J. R. *The Formation of the British Liberal Party 1857–1868* (Sussex: Harvester Press, 1976).
Virgin, P. *The Church in an Age of Negligence: Ecclesiastical Structure and Problems of Church Reform 1700–1840* (Cambridge: James Clarke, 1989).
——. *Sydney Smith* (London: HarperCollins, 1994).
Warren, W. T. *St Cross Hospital: near Winchester: Its History and Buildings* (Winchester: Warren & Sons, 1899).
Welsby, P. A. 'Anthony Trollope and the Church of England', *Church Quarterly Review*, CLXIII (1962) 210–20.
Willey, B. 'Darwin and Clerical Orthodoxy', in Appleman et al. (1959) 51–62.
Williams, T. J. and Campbell, A. W. *The Park Village Sisterhood* (London: SPCK, 1965).
Wright, A. *Anthony Trollope: Dream and Art* (Chicago: University of Chicago Press, 1983).
Yates, N. *The Oxford Movement and Anglican Ritualism* (London: Historical Association, 1983).

Unpublished works

Ambler, R. W. 'Social Change and Religious Experience: Aspects of Rural Society in South Lincolnshire with Specific Reference to Primitive Methodism, 1815–1875', Unpublished PhD Thesis, University of Hull (1984).

Index

Abraham, 179
absenteeism, 67–8
academies, 142
adultery, 40, 104, 146–7, 149
advowsons, 70, 72
Africa, 61, 75
Alford, Dean Henry (1820–71; Dean of Canterbury, 1857), 44, 129, 169
Allington, 56
alms, 47–8
Alpine Club, 135
Anglican sisterhoods, see convents
anti-Semitism, 38, 102
Antwerp Cathedral, 69
apostasy, 176
apostolic succession, 78
archbishops, 35, 79, 93, 103, 126, 169
archdeacons, 6–7, 86, 93–4, 111–12, 119, 124, 134, 138–9, 168
Arminian policies, 15
Arnold, Thomas (1795–1842), 12, 143
Athanasian creed, 31
atheism, 147
Athenaeum Club, 135
auricular confession, 33
Austen, Jane (1775–1817), 9
Australia, 39, 148

Baden, 23
Balkans, 136
Balliol College, 136
baptismal regeneration, 78
Barrington, Lord William (1717–93), 71
Bath, 4th Marquess of (John Alexander Thynne) (1831–96), 71
Beaufort, Duke of, 71
Becket, Thomas à (1118?–70), 169
bedesmen, 3, 47, 60, 75, 85, 98, 166
begging, 45–6, 80–1

benefices, 53–4, 69–70
Bethnal Green, 33
Beverley, 110, 140–1, 144
Beverley election, 135, 140–1, 144, 161, 163
Beverley Minster, 140
Bible, 23, 28–9, 66, 167, 177
biblical allusions, 176, 178
bigamy, 39–40, 48, 51
birthright, 43–6, 84–8, 91–2, 96, 99, 101–2, 106
Birtwhistle, the Rev. Canon, 140–1
bishops, 2, 4, 6–7, 14–15, 19, 21, 24, 27–8, 31, 33, 35, 37–40, 44, 49, 54, 57–9, 70, 72, 79, 82, 90, 93–4, 97, 102–4, 108, 111–15, 126–7, 134–5, 138–9, 146, 148–9, 154, 156, 163–4, 167–9, 172, 180
Bland, Florence (1855–1908), 65, 118
Bland, Isabella, 65
Bledington, 70
Bloemfontein, 124
Blomfield, Charles James (1786–1857; Bishop of London, 1828–56), 26, 57
Boughton, Sir W. Rause, 71
Bourne Grammar School, see Free Grammar School of King Charles
Bowles, the Rev. William Lisle (1762–1850), 43
Bradfield, see St Andrew's School
Bremer, Frederika (1801–65), 109
Bristol, Dean of, 135
broad church, 12–13, 17, 19, 24, 28–32, 59, 79, 85, 93, 146, 172
Brougham, Lord Henry (1778–1868), 135
Bruges, 153
burials, 149–53
Burials Act of 1880, 152
Burke, Edmund (1729–97), 60

Index

Butler, William John, 122
Byron, Lord George Gordon (1788–1824), 149

Calvinism, 15, 159
Cambridge, 18, 56, 58, 89–90, 94, 137, 143
Cambridge Act of 1856, 143
Campbeltown, 179
canons, 43, 85
Canterbury, Archbishop of, 26–8, 33, 57, 71, 115, 152, 170
Canterbury Convocation, 147
Carlyle, Thomas (1795–1881), 77
Carrington, Henry, 114
cathedral close, 30, 147
Catholic University, 162
Cauvin, Joseph, 87
celibacy, 15, 121, 124
Central American Church, 139
Chancery, 75
chaplains, 22, 39, 41, 104, 113
charity, *see* philanthropy
Charity Commissioners, 73, 82
charity schools, 144
Charles I (1600–49), 15
Cheapside, 73
Cheltenham, 85, 113
child custody, 146–7
Christ's Hospital, 73
Christianity, 23, 35–6, 41, 52, 179, 182
church abuse, 4, 55, 60–1, 67, 72–4, 166
church candles, 16, 19, 36
Church Commission, The, 19
Church Congress Debate on Marriage and Divorce of 1880, 148
church doctrine, 4–5, 47, 51, 147
church-rates, abolition of, 102, 143, 163
church patronage, 5–7, 15, 27, 42–83
church reform, 4, 7, 13, 44, 55, 167
Church-state relations, 9, 130–74
Cicero (*c.* 106–42 BC), 171; *De Divinatione; De Fato; De Naturâ Deorum*, 179
Civil Service, 43, 136–7, 180
clerical daughters, 118–20

clerical gentlemen, 24, 83–106
clerical wives, 111–16
clergy, 1–3, 5–9, 11, 14, 21–3, 33, 35, 37–43, 45–6, 49, 51, 54, 57–8, 68, 70, 72, 82, 84–5, 87–90, 94, 96–8, 105, 107–9, 111, 113, 117–18, 125, 127, 129, 138–40, 147, 150, 165, 168, 172–3, 175, 178, 181
Close, the Rev. Francis (1797–1882; Dean of Carlisle, 1856), 85, 113
clubs, 135
cohabitation, 139–40, 104, 145
Colenso, Bishop John William (1814–83; Bishop of Natal, 1853), 29–31, 170; *The Pentateuch and Book of Joshua Critically Examined*, 29, 170
Coleridge, Samuel Taylor (1772–1834), 122
collegiate patronage, 56–7
Collins, Irene, 9
colonies, 171
Community of St Margaret, 122
confession, 18
congregation, 23, 25, 51, 113
Conservatives, 132–4, 138, 140–2, 145, 161, 164–5, 168, 170–2
convents, 92–3, 107, 109, 115, 120–4, 127–9
conversion, 17
Convocation, 168–9
Conybeare, W. J. (1815–57), 95
Cook, Mr, 23
corn laws, 102, 163
corn laws, repeal of, 177
Cornwall, 15, 27, 100, 140
Cosmopolitan Club, 135
Costa Rica, 139
County Clare, 157
Court of Arches, 27
Cranworth, Lord Chancellor Bertram (1790–1868), 146
cremation, 150–1
Cremation Society, 150
Crewe, 24
Crimean War, 118
Crowmarsh Gifford, 70–1
Cuba, 179

220 Index

Cunningham, the Rev. John William (1780–1861), 149–50
curates, 22, 27, 35, 43, 53, 68, 78, 95, 97

Danish Church, 179
Dartmouth, Lord, Second Earl (1731–1801), 71
Darwin, Charles (1809–82) and *On the Origin of Species*, 41, 169–70, 176, 178
deacons, 23, 69
deaconesses, 123–5
deans, 22, 37, 39, 44, 58–9, 68–9, 72, 78, 86, 93–4, 97, 102–4, 114, 120, 124, 134, 136, 149
Dean and Chapter Act, 79
de Blois, Henri (12th C), 60
Denison, George Anthony (1805–96; Archdeacon of Wells, 1851), 15
Denning, Lord Alfred T. (1899–1999), 173–4
Derby, Lord (14th Earl) (1799–1868), 164
Devonport sisterhood, 122
Devonshire, 34, 53, 122
Dickens, Charles (1812–70), 75, 77, 84, 129; *Bleak House*, 75, 129; *Martin Chuzzlewit*, 75
dioceses, 4, 14, 78, 169
Disestablishment of the Church of England, 29, 61, 131, 163, 165–74
Disestablishment of the Irish Church, 131, 161–5, 167, 172
disposal of the dead, *see* burial
Disraeli, Benjamin (1804–81), 17, 59, 78–9, 126, 133, 137, 172
dissent, 23, 27, 31, 41, 54, 58, 88, 102, 107, 112, 128, 133, 151–2, 165, 168
Dissenters' Chapel Act of 1844, 165
district visiting, 66–7
divorce, 144–9, 152
Divorce and Matrimonial Causes Act of 1857, 145–7, 149
Dodsworth, the Rev. William (1798–1861), 123
dogma, 41, 56, 171, 181

Dorcas societies, 22, 63–4, 128
Dorchester, 33, 68
Dorset, 135
Dulwich, 74
Durham, Bishop of, 138

East Anglia, 53
East Grinstead, 122
Ecclesiastical Commissioners, 50, 95, 114, 167–9
ecclesiastical connections, 3, 134–6
ecclesiastical patronage, 52–9
Ecclesiastical Titles Act, 156
Edgeworth, Maria (1767–1849) and *Patronage*, 114
education, 22, 142–4, 152–3, 101
Egerton, the Rev. John Coker (d. 1888), 104
Egypt, 139
eleemosynary abuse, 79
Eliot, George (1819–80), 9, 21, 84, 97, 148, 177–8; *Middlemarch*, 97; *Scenes of Clerical Life*, 21
endowments, 162–5
Episcopalian, 18
Erastianism, 14, 29, 148
Essays and Reviews (by F. D. Maurice, Rowland William, C. W. Goodwin and Benjamin Jowett), 29, 169
Established Church, 7, 26, 28, 36, 38, 56, 59, 113, 115, 152, 156, 161, 166–7, 179
Establishment, 152
Eucharist, 19, 33
Europe, 23, 158–9
euthanasia, 151, 178
Evangelical, 4–5, 12–13, 16, 19, 20–8, 32–5, 38–40, 59, 62–3, 66–7, 71–2, 78, 85, 89–91, 93, 107–8, 111–12, 127–8, 133, 135, 138, 140, 149, 156, 166
evangelical sects, 165
Evangelical sororities, 123–5
Exeter, 30, 147, 170
Exeter Hall, 62–3

Faber, F. W. (1824–63), 18, 33
factions, church, 11–41, 78–9

Factory Bill of 1843, 165
fallen women, 48–9
Faroes, 179
Farrar, Frederick William (1831–1903), 136
female patrons, 126–7
Feuerbach, Ludwig (1804–72) and *The Essence of Christianity*, 178
Folkestone, 19
Folkestone, Viscount, 117
Forster, W. E. (1819–86), and Forster's Education Act of 1870, 144
France, 123
Free Grammar School of King Charles, 74
Freeling, Sir Francis (1764–1836), 43, 84
Freemasons, 135
Froude, R. Hurrell (1803–36), 18

Gaelic, 179
Garrick Club, 135
Gaskell, Elizabeth (1810–65), 23, 58, 60–1, 151–2, 156; 'A Parson's Holiday', 23; *Cousin Phillis*, 23; *North and South*, 23, 58; *Ruth*, 151–2; *Sylvia's Lovers*, 60; *Wives and Daughters*, 156
gentlemen clergymen, 6, 83–107
George III (1738–1820), 94
George IV (1762–1830), 94
Gladstone, William Ewart (1809–98), 26, 49, 59, 78, 120, 133, 136–7, 147, 163–5, 169–70
glebes, 56, 70
Goodwin, C. W. (1817–78), 169–70, *see also Essays and Reviews*
Gorham case, 27, 78
Gorham, George Cornelius (1787–1857), 27
Goschen, G. J. (1831–1907), 143
Graham, Sir James, 4th Duke and 7th Marquess (1799–1874), 164
Great Exhibition, 111
Greek, 21, 58, 89, 93, 97, 120, 180
Gurney, the Rev. Peter, 140
Guatemala, 139
Guilford, Earl of (Francis North) (1773–1861), 74, 166

Haberdashers' Company, 73
Hackney Phalanx, 13
Hadley Churchyard, 150
Hamilton, Walter Kerr (1808–60; Bishop of Salisbury, 1854), 12, 15, 29, 32–4, 79, 146, 170
Hampshire, 54
Harrow, 2, 13–14, 76, 119, 136, 143–4, 149
Harting, Vicar of, 66
Hartington, Lord Spencer Compton Cavendish, 169
Hawker, the Rev., 20
Hebrew, 21, 89, 97, 117
Helstone, 23
Herbert, Sydney (1810–61), 119
Hereford, Bishop of, 71
Hereford, Cathedral of, 4
high Anglicanism, *see* high church
high-and-dry churchmen, 4–5, 12, 14–15, 25, 93, 136, 138
high church, 13–20, 25–9, 31–5, 38–40, 59, 66, 78, 93, 108, 121, 123, 135–6, 146, 161, 170
high church clergy, 16, 20–1, 93, 102, 124, 139, 173
high church sisterhoods, *see* convents
Hindustan, 89
Hodgson, Peter, 9
Holy Land, 139
Home Rule, 164
House of Hanover, 102
House of Commons, The, 17, 163
House of Lords, The, 163, 173
Houghton, Lord Richard Monckton Milnes (1809–85), 135
Howley, William (1766–1848; Archbishop of Canterbury, 1828), 57
hunting, 22, 33, 132
Huntingdon, Lady (1707–91), 71
hymns, 17, 26

Iceland, 144
incense, 19
institutional philanthropy, 60–4
intoning, 14, 17, 19
Ireland, 25, 51, 111, 153–5, 157, 160–5, 167

222 Index

Iremonger, the Rev. Frederick, 81
Irish Church, 16, 45, 80, 102, 131, 161–6
Irish Republican Army, 163
Islington, 89

Jameson, Anna (1794–1860), 109
Jervis, the Rev. W. G., 94–5, 97, 125
Jesuits, 16
Jews, 133, 157
Journals, Newspapers and Magazines
Edinburgh Review, 135
Fortnightly Review, 135–6, 171
John Bull, 73
Pall Mall Gazette, 23–4, 44, 50, 62, 92
Punch, 122
Quarterly Review, The, 20, 44, 62–3, 74, 76, 137, 140, 168
Saint Pauls Magazine, 135, 161–2
Saturday Review, The, 24, 127
Spectator, The, 81–2
Times, The, 75
Jowett, the Rev. Benjamin (1817–93), 136–7, 170, see also Essays and Reviews

Keane, John, 9
Keble, John (1792–1866), 14, 17–18, 25, 33
King, Bishop Edward (1829–1910; Principal of Cuddesdon, 1863–73; Bishop of Lincoln, 1885), 134
King, Bishop Walker (Bishop of Rochester, 1809–27), 134
King, Walker (Archdeacon of Rochester, 1827–59), 134
Kings' College, Cambridge, 56

Labuan Islands, 61
Latin, 76, 89
Latin America, 139
Latitudinarian, 136
Latitudinarianism, 28, 31
Laud, Archbishop William (1573–1645; Archbishop of Canterbury, 1633), 15
lay patrons, 53–6, 126, 140

lay patronesses, 85
Leasingham, 72
Lee, Samuel (1783–1852), 89
Leeds, 110, 148
Leeds Mechanics' Institute, 110
Lewes, George Henry (1817–78), 148, 171
Liberals, 132–3, 135–8, 140–1, 143–5, 147, 156, 161, 164, 166, 168, 170–2
Liberalism, 132
Liberationists, 172
Liberation Society, The, 20, 54, 152, 167, 172–3
Liddington, 70
Liddon, Henry Parry (1829–90), 12, 14–15, 17, 26, 29, 32, 35–7, 79, 135–6, 170
Lincolnshire, 14, 53, 72, 74, 134
Literary Fund Dinner, 136
Little Marcle, 70
Littlemore, 15
liturgy, 26, 121, 152
Liverpool Institute, 143–4
London, 24, 39, 49–50, 57, 62, 73, 136, 142, 169–70
London, Bishop of, 138, 170
London, University of, 142
Longley, Charles (1794–1868, Headmaster of Harrow, 1829, Archbishop of York, 1860; of Canterbury, 1862), 13, 143
Longman, William (1813–77), 86
low church, see Evangelical
Lowe, Robert (1811–92), 134, 173; *Duty*, 173
Lyndhurst, John Singleton Copley, Lord Chancellor (1772–1863), 157

Macbeth, 105
Macleane, Douglas, 95, 97, 116
Macleod, Norman (1812–72), 24
malversation, 4, 61
Mammon, 25, 168
Manning, Henry (1808–92; Roman Catholic Archbishop of Westminster, 1865), 14, 26–7, 135
Maritzburg, Bishop of, 30

Marlborough, 78
Marston, 82
Mathaean Exception, 146
Maurice, F. D. (1805–72), *see also*
 Essays and Reviews, 169–70
Maynooth Grant, 161–5
Meetkerke, Cecilia, 153
Meetkerke family, 2, 153
Melbourne, Lord William Lamb
 (1779–1848), 59
Merewether, Charles George, 134
Merit, 43–6
Methodism, 18, 36, 56, 112
Miall, Edward (1809–81), 54, 152
Millais, Sir John Everett (1829–96, 150)
Milner, Isaac (1750–1820; Dean of
 Carlisle, 1791), 89
minor canons, 85, 95, 134
missions, 61–3
Monk, James Henry (1784–1856;
 Bishop of Gloucester and Bristol),
 142
Mora, 57
Morley, John (Viscount Morley of
 Blackburn) (1838–1923), 176
Morwenstow, 20
Moscow, Suffragan Bishop of, 37
mothers of clerical kin, 116–18
Mount of Olives, 177–8

Natal, 29–31
Neale, John Mason (1818–66), 19, 122–3
nepotism, 67, 70–1
Neuchâtel, 23
Newman, John Henry (1801–90),
 14–18, 26, 84, 86, 115, 135, 156,
 161
New Poor Law, 73
newspapers, 4, 16, 32, 49, 74–5,
 134–5
New Testament, 177
New York, 18
Nightingale, Florence (1820–1910), 118
Noel, Thomas (1799–1861), 81
Nonconformists, 23, 26, 133, 143,
 149, 152, 163, 165–7, 171–2

non-residence, 70, 79
Northcote-Trevelyan Report, 136–7
Northumberland, 61
Norwich, Bishop of, 118
Nottingham, 13, 70
nunnery, *see* convents

O'Connell, Daniel (1775–1847), 62, 157
O'Hanlon, William, 62
Old Testament, 31, 176–7, 179
Oliphant, Margaret (1828–97), 61,
 88, 126, 128, 151, 156; *A
 Son of the Soil*, 88; *Phoebe
 Junior*, 61, 88, 151; *The
 Curate in Charge*, 126; *The
 Doctor's Family*, 128; *The Perpetual
 Curate*, 128, 156; *The Rector*, 126,
 128
Oriel College, Oxford, 17
Oxenden, Mr, 113
Oxford, 2, 16–18, 22, 53–4, 56, 68,
 88–9, 94, 111, 136–7, 143, 159,
 177
Oxford Movement, 14, 17, 25, 121–2,
 135–6, 146, 169
Oxford University Act of 1854, 143

Paddington, 49
Palestine, 68, 177
Palmerston, Lord Henry John Temple
 (1784–1865), 28, 133, 138, 145,
 147, 168
Papal Aggression, 15, 17, 111, 115,
 129, 155–6
Papal Bull of 1850, 15, 25, 156
papists, 31
Papua New Guinea, 24, 61
parish, 7, 43–4, 127
Parish Councils Act of 1894, 173
Parker, Matthew (1505–75;
 Archbishop of Canterbury, 1559),
 28
Parliament, 145, 147, 152, 157, 165,
 169
Parr, Harriet and *The Life and Death of
 Jeanne d'Arc*, 179
parsons, 37, 68, 89, 92, 109, 116–8,
 145

Peel, Sir Robert Peel (1788–1850), 133, 157, 161, 165
Pennefather, Catherine (1818–93), 123
Pennefather, William (1816–73), 123
perpetual curates, 2, 6, 44, 95, 98, 103, 140
pessimism, 12, 32–42, 46, 50, 67, 79, 82, 180
Peterborough, Bishop of, 163
philanthropy, 5–6, 42–83, 87, 119, 125, 154
Philpotts, Henry (1778–1869; Bishop of Exeter, 1831), 26–7, 146, 170
Pietermaritzburg, 31
pluralities, 27, 57, 67–70, 72
politics, 2, 4, 7, 9, 111, 130–74
Poole, 135
popery, 15–6, 28, 155
Post Office, 43, 84, 135
potato famine of Ireland, 51, 154–5
preaching, 79, 112–13
prebendal stall, 57, 69, 79
prebendaries, 54, 68–9, 71, 81, 134
prebends, 69, 79, 101, 124
prelates, 113–14
Presbyterians, 24, 31, 162
priests, 69, 76, 91, 109, 154, 158–60, 162, 164
private philanthropy, 64–7
Privy Council, 30
Probate Act of 1857, 147
Protestantism, 15, 20, 26, 115, 153, 159
Protestants, 33, 51, 108–9, 128, 154–5, 157, 160, 162–4
public school education, 92, 144
Public Worship Regulation Act of 1874, 17, 19, 31, 137
Purchas, the Rev. John (1823–72), 20
Pusey, Edward Bouverie (1800–82), 14, 26, 29, 35, 41, 115, 117, 122–3, 135
Pusey, Lucy (1829–1844), 122
Puseyite, 16, 27
Pycroft, James (1813–95), 114

Quakers, 41, 106
Quebec, 158

radicalism, 40–1
Real Presence, 15, 33
rectors, 1, 17, 35, 43, 45, 58, 66, 69–71, 99, 101, 116, 125
Reformation, 47, 53, 78, 94, 109, 122
Reform Bill of 1832, 156, 163, 166
Reform Bill of 1867, 102, 163, 168
Regent's Park, 122
Regium Donum, 161–5
religion, 3, 6, 8–9, 11, 108, 111, 121, 131, 133, 144, 156–7, 160, 163, 167, 171–2, 179
Reykjavik, 180
Ridsdale, 191
Ripon, 20
ritual, 13, 26
ritualism, 4–5, 17–20, 25, 34–6, 41, 111, 156
Robinson, Cecilia, 123
Robinson, Elizabeth, 123
Rochester, 13, 19, 72, 74, 123, 134, 169
Rochester Cathedral Grammar School, 134
Roman Catholic Emancipation Act of 1829, 102, 155–7, 163
Roman Catholicism, 15, 17–18, 26–8, 31, 33–34, 51, 80, 109, 115, 119, 123, 128–9, 131, 133, 139, 153–64, 179, 181
Romantic Lake Poets, 122
Rome, 15–18, 24, 68, 111, 142, 154, 156, 158
Royal Commission on Marriage Law of 1850, 146
Royal, Princess, Victoria (1841–), 143
Russell, Lord William (1820–1907), 156
Russia, 37

Sabbatarianism, 24, 33
St Andrew's School, Bradfield, 135
St Allen, 140
St Cross Hospital, 47, 60–1, 74, 134, 151, 166
St Francis of Assisi, 80
St Giles'-in-the-Fields, 72
St James' Hall, 136
St John's, Leeds, 148

Index 225

St John's College, Oxford, 56
St Just, 27
St Kilda, 179
St Mary-le-Bow, 73
St Pancras, 72
St Paul, 147, 173–4
St Paul's, 72
St Saviour's, 122
Salisbury, 12, 15, 33–4, 49
Salisbury Cathedral, 4, 79, 179
Samaritan, 89
San Remo, 22
Sarawak, 61
schism, 4–5, 11–13, 28–9, 32–42, 127
Scotland, 24, 38, 88, 164
sectarian interests, 51
secular education, 142–4
secularism, 3, 8–9, 23, 36–7, 63, 131, 137, 143, 149, 164, 167, 171, 173, 181
Selborne, Lord Roundell Palmer, Lord Chancellor (1812–95), 172
self-help, 81
sermons, 5–6, 21, 24–6, 62–3, 127, 130, 176, 178, 180
Sewell, Mrs Anna (1820–78) *and The Rose of Cheriton*, 180
Sewells, the, 33
Seymour, Henry Derby, 135
Shaftesbury, Anthony Ashley Cooper, 7th Earl of Shaftesbury (1801–85), 23, 28, 112, 133
Sidmouth, Lord Henry Addington (1757–1844), 167
Simeon, Charles (1759–1836), 21, 25, 72
Simeon Trust, The, 21, 72
simony, 54–5, 67
sinecure, 14, 69, 71, 79, 168
single women, 109, 120–9
sisters, conventual, *see* convents
slavery, 25, 179
Smiles, Samuel (1812–1904) and *Self-Help*, 178
Smith, Sydney (1771–1845), 32, 57–8, 108, 114, 135
Smythe, Lord (1780–1855), 71
social reform, 47, 142–53

Society for Promoting the Employment of Women, 112
Solomon Islands, 61
South Africa, 29–30
Southey, Robert (1774–1843), 122
spiritualism, 112
Stack, John Herbert, 161–2
Stanley, Dean Arthur (1813–81), 172
Stanley, Lord Edward Henry (1826–93), 164
Stanley, Mary, 118–9; *Hospitals and Sisterhoods*, 118
Star and Garter Club, 135
state education, 172
Stephen's Green, 162
Sterling Club, 135
Stow-in-the-Wold, 70
Strauss, David Friedrich (1808–74) and *Das Leben Jesu*, 177
suffragan bishops, 13, 169
Sumner, Charles Richard (1790–1874; Bishop of Llandaff, 1826; and of Winchester, 1827–69), 27, 71, 90
Summer, John Bird (1780–1862; Archbishop of Canterbury, 1848), 27, 146, 171
Sunday school, 7, 63, 71
Syria, 177

Tait, Archibald Campbell (1811–82; Archbishop of Canterbury, 1868), 19, 28–9, 31, 41, 79, 143, 146, 152, 164, 170, 172
'Taking the Veil', 123
Tasmania, 73
Taylor, Jeremy (1613–67; Bishop of Down & Connor), 176
Temple, Canon Henry, 148
Temple, Dr Frederick (1821–1902; Bishop of Exeter, 1869; Archbishop of Canterbury, 1897), 170
Temple, William (1881–1944; Archbishop of York, 1929; and of Canterbury, 1942), 173
Ten Commandments, The, 24
Thackeray, William Makepeace (1811–63), 84
theological colleges, 89–90, 94

226 Index

theology, 30
Thirty-Nine Articles, 58, 143
Thompson, Sir Henry, 150
Thomson, William (1819–90;
   Archbishop of York, 1862), 135
Thorold family, 72, 134
Thorold, Anthony Wilson (1825–95;
   Bishop of Rochester 1877; of
   Winchester, 1891), 13, 21, 72, 82,
   123, 133–4, 169
Thorold, the Rev. Henry Croyland
   (1921–1999), 81–2
Thorold, Sir John (1816–1866), 72
Thurlby, 74
Tilley, Cecilia, *see* Trollope
Tilley, Edith (b. 1846), 65
tithes, 69
Tomline, Sir George Pretyman
   (1750–1827), 27
Tooth, Rev. Arthur (d. 1931), 19
Tories, 117, 133, 155, 168
town incumbent, 95
tracts, 14, 16, 20, 180
Tractarians, 14–21, 25–8, 122
Trimmer, Sarah (1741–1810), 63
Trinity, 171
Trolop, John (d. 1611), 153
Trollope, Anthony (1815–82), *passim*
Novels
  American Senator, The, 55, 70, 98
  Ayala's Angel, 68, 98
  Barchester Towers, 4, 11, 15, 21, 24,
     27–8, 32, 59, 63–4, 67, 77–8,
     85–6, 90, 105, 111, 113–14, 138,
     142–3, 162, 166–7, 171
  Belton Estate, The, 24, 30, 145–6,
     150
  Bertrams, The, 18, 33, 125–6, 150,
     177–8
  Castle Richmond, 16, 51, 80, 143,
     154–5, 162–3
  Claverings, The, 35, 81, 99, 102,
     115–16
  Cousin Henry, 176
  Doctor Thorne, 17–18, 24, 64, 68,
     87, 93
  Dr Wortle's School, 40, 48, 74,
     104–5, 148
  Duke's Children, The, 141

Eustace Diamonds, The, 37–8, 102–3
Eye for an Eye, An, 60
Fixed Period, The, 133, 151, 158,
   178
Framley Parsonage, 24–5, 31, 33, 45,
   61, 69, 78, 87, 96, 111, 117, 119,
   127, 168
Golden Lion of Granpère, The, 158–9
He Knew He Was Right, 19, 30, 50,
   95, 98, 100–101, 114–15, 124,
   146–8
Is He Popenjoy?, 22, 25, 38, 40, 103,
   113, 120, 157–8
John Caldigate, 39
Kellys and the O'Kellys, The, 16, 45,
   154, 161
Kept in the Dark, 95, 148–9
Lady Anna, 66
Landleaguers, The, 160, 164
Last Chronicle of Barset, The, 4, 21,
   36, 43–5, 67–8, 77, 88, 96–8, 103,
   114–15, 119, 139, 168
La Vendée, 123, 154
Linda Tressel, 158–9
Macdermots of Ballycloran, The, 75,
   154, 160, 162
Marion Fay, 40, 79, 105–6
Miss Mackenzie, 19, 34, 49–50, 61,
   67, 90, 128–9
Nina Balatka, 38
Old Man's Love, An, 22
Orley Farm, 92, 122, 176
Phineas Finn, 164
Phineas Redux, 157, 165, 171–2
Prime Minister, The, 157
Rachel Ray, 22–5, 34, 63, 89–90,
   127–8, 168
Ralph the Heir, 65, 71, 141, 163–4,
   175
Small House at Allington, The, 56,
   88, 119
Three Clerks, The, 16, 20, 24, 27, 46,
   137, 145
Vicar of Bullhampton, The, 36–7, 48,
   56, 71, 101–2, 129, 152, 172
Warden, The, 4, 26, 46–8, 58, 60,
   73–6, 79, 85, 98, 105, 112, 128,
   134, 155, 166
Way We Live Now, The, 8, 38, 159

Trollope, Anthony (1815–82) – continued
Short Stories
'Alice Dugdale', 117
'Christmas Day at Kirkby Cottage', 53
'Lady of Launay, The', 53
'Not If I Know It', 178
'Relics of General Chassé, The', 69
'Ride Across Palestine, A', 178
'Two Heroines of Plumplington, The', 31, 105
Non-fiction
Autobiography, An, 1–2, 7–8, 83
Clergymen of the Church of England, 29–31, 35, 43–4, 57–8, 71, 73, 93, 96, 100, 125, 169
Life of Cicero, 171
New Zealander, The, 155–6
Travel Books
Australia and New Zealand, 158
How the 'Mastiffs' Went to Iceland, 144, 179
North America, 18, 75, 158, 167, 179
South Africa, 31, 61, 124
West Indies and the Spanish Main, 139, 179, 181
Articles
'About Hunting', 22
'Archdeacon, The', 168
'Civil Service as a Profession, The', 80
'Fourth Commandmant, The', 24
'Higher Education of Women', 109–10, 121
'Irish Beneficed Clergyman, The', 164
'Irish Church Bill in the Lords, The', 163
'Irish Church Debate, The', 161
'Merivale's History of the Romans', 110
'New Cabinet, and What It Will Do for Us, The', 163
'Novel-Reading', 180
'Politics as a Daily Study for Common People', 110
'Public Schools', 76, 91
'Sisterhood Question, The', 92–3, 122, 128–9
'Zulu in London, The', 67
'What Does Ireland Want?', 163
Trollope, the Rev. Arthur (1799–1848), 72–3
Trollope, Beatrice (Bice) (1853–81), 65
Trollope, Cecilia (1816–49), 65, 121; *Chollerton*, 121
Trollope, Edward (1817–93; Bishop Suffragan of Nottingham, 1877), 13, 21, 70, 72, 81, 169
Trollope, Emily (1818–36), 150
Trollope, Frances (1779–1863), 20, 73, 111, 125, 149–50, 170; *Domestic Manners of the Americans*, 55, 150; *Jessie Phillips*, 73; *Michael Armstrong, the Factory Boy*, 73; *Vicar of Wrexhill*, 20
Trollope, Fred (1847–1910), 148
Trollope, George (b. 1802), 72
Trollope, Jane (1729–1827), 70
Trollope, Henry Merivale (1846–1926), 110
Trollope, the Rev. John (senior) (1729–94), 71
Trollope, the Rev. John (junior) (b. 1800), 70
Trollope, the Rev. John Joseph (1817–93), 71
Trollope, Rose (1820–1917), 111–12, 170
Trollope, Sir John (1800–74), 14, 72, 134
Trollope, Sir Thomas (1691–1784; 4th Bart), 72
Trollope, Thomas Adolphus (1810–92), 65
Trollope, Thomas Anthony (1774–1835), 2, 111, 131, 170; *Encyclopaedia Ecclesiastica*, 131
Trollope, the Rev. Thomas Daniel (1760–1828), 70
Trollope, William (d. 1636), 74
Trollope, the Rev. William (1798–1863), 72
Turks, 136
Tuscany, 111

Unitarian, 23, 165, 170
United States of America, 75, 144, 148, 160
University, 102, 109, 142–3
university education, 1, 89, 143
University of London, 142
University Test Act of 1871, 143
university tests, 143
Upper Slaughter, 70
Utilitarianism, 14

Vavasour, the Rev., 70
via media, 13, 16–7, 19, 28, 31
vicars, 20, 37, 43, 49, 56, 68, 73, 95, 130, 148
Victoria, Queen (1819–1901), 23, 59, 65, 78–9, 115, 126, 143, 150
Virtue, James (1829–92), 135

Wales, 62, 96
Washington, 167
Welby, Alicia, 72
Welby family, 72
Welby, W. E., 72
Welby, Walter William, 72
Wellington, Lord Arthur Wellesley (1769–1852), 157
Wells, Dean of, 123
Wesleyan Methodists, 34, 90, 141
West Indies, 139
Whigs, 59, 132–3, 135, 142
widowhood, 5, 86, 125–9
Wigston Magna, 73
Wilberforce, the Rev. Henry (1807–73), 27, 71

Wilberforce, Samuel (1805–73; Bishop of Winchester, 1869), 23, 26, 71, 137, 146, 148
Wilberforce, William (1759–1833), 25, 71, 163
William IV (1765–1837), 57
Williams, Rowland (1817–70), 17, 169, *see also Essays and Reviews*
Winchester, 13, 27, 60, 71–2, 90, 134, 151, 166
Winchester Cathedral, 4, 43, 81, 143
Winchester College, 2, 13, 54, 76, 91, 134, 144
Windsor, 59
Wiseman, Cardinal Nicholas (1802–65), 16
Witts, the Rev. Francis, 70, 85, 106, 116
Wordsworth, Dr Charles (1806–92; Bishop of St Andrews, 1852), 58, 172
Wordsworth, William (1770–1850), 122
Worth, 57
Wykeham, William (1324–1404), 91–2

Yonge, Charlotte (1823–1901), and *The Monthly Packet*, 122
York, Archbishop of, 26, 135

zeal, 28, 67, 166
zealot, 40, 160